New Directions in African Literature 25

Editor: Ernest N. Emenyonu
Department of Africana Studies,
University of Michigan-Flint
303 East Kearsley Street, Flint, MI 48502, USA

Assistant Editor: Patricia T. Emenyonu
Department of English
University of Michigan-Flint

Associate Editors: Francis Imbuga
Literature Department, Kenyatta University,
PO Box 43844, Nairobi, Kenya

Emmanuel Ngara
Office of the Deputy Vice-Chancellor,
University of Natal,
Private Bag X10, Dalbridge 4014, South Africa

Charles E. Nnolim
Department of English, School of Humanities
University of Port Harcourt, Rivers State, Nigeria

Kwawisi Tekpetey
Department of Humanities,
Central State University,
PO Box 1004, Wilberforce, OH 45384, USA

Iniobong I. Uko
Department of English, Univeristy of Uyo,
Uyo, Akwa Ibom State, Nigeria

Ato Quayson
Pembroke College, Cambridge CB2 1RF, UK

Nana Wilson-Tagoe
SOAS, Thornhaugh Street, London WC1H 0XG

Reviews Editor: James Gibbs
8 Victoria Square, Bristol BS8 4ET, UK
james.gibbs@uwe.ac.uk

New Editor

After 35 years, **Eldred Durosimi Jones** has retired from the editorship of *African Literature Today*.
The announcement that **Ernest N. Emenyonu** has taken on the editorship has been widely welcomed:
'*A very good omen for African literature*' – Wole Soyinka
'*It is a most appropriate and logical development, and a very happy event for African literature.*' – Chinua Achebe

African Literature Today

1-14 were published from London by Heinemann Educational Books and from New York by Africana Publishing Company

Editor: Eldred Durosimi Jones
  1, 2, 3, and 4 Omnibus Edition
  5 The Novel in Africa
  6 Poetry in Africa
  7 Focus on Criticism
  8 Drama in Africa
  9 Africa, America & the Caribbean
  10 Retrospect & Prospect
  11 Myth & History

Editor: Eldred Durosimi Jones
Associate Editor: Eustace Palmer
Assistant Editor: Marjorie Jones
  12 New Writing, New Approaches
  13 Recent Trends in the Novel
  14 Insiders & Outsiders

The new series is published by
James Currey Publishers and Africa World Press
*ALT 15 Women in African Literature Today
*ALT 16 Oral & Written Poetry in African Literature Today
 ALT 17 The Question of Language in African Literature Today
*ALT 18 Orature in African Literature Today
*ALT 19 Critical Theory & African Literature Today
*ALT 20 New Trends & Generations in African Literature
*ALT 21 Childhood in African Literature
*ALT 22 Exile & African Literature
*ALT 23 South & Southern African Literature
*ALT 24 New Women's Writing in African Literature

*Copies of back issues marked with an asterisk may be purchased from your bookseller or direct from James Currey Ltd. Place a standing order with your supplier for future issues.

Forthcoming Titles

Contributions are invited for the following forthcoming titles:

ALT 26 War in African Literature
ALT 27 New Novels in African Literature

Guidelines for Submission of Articles

The Editor invites submission of articles or proposals for articles on the announced themes of forthcoming issues:

Ernest N. Emenyonu, *African Literature Today*
Department of Africana Studies, University of Michigan-Flint
303 East Kearsley Street, Flint MI48502, USA
email: eernest@umflint.edu
Fax: 001 810 766 6719

Submissions will be acknowledged promptly and decisions communicated within six months of the receipt of the paper. Your name and institutional affiliation (with full mailing address and email) should appear on a separate sheet, plus a brief biographical profile of not more than six lines. The editor cannot undertake to return material submitted and contributors are advised to keep a copy of all material sent. Please note that all articles outside the announced themes cannot be considered or acknowledged and that articles should not be submitted via email. Articles should be submitted in the English language.

Length: articles should not exceed 5,000 words

Format: two hard copies plus disk of all articles should be submitted, double-spaced, on one side only of A4 paper, with pages numbered consecutively. Disks may be formatted for PC or AppleMac but please label all files and disks clearly, and save files as Word for Windows or Word for Macintosh.

Style: UK or US spellings, but be consistent. Direct quotations should retain the spelling used in the original source. Check the accuracy of your citations and always give the source, date, and page number in the text and a full reference in the Works Cited at the end of the article. Italicise titles of books or plays. Use single inverted commas throughout except for quotes within quotes which are double. Avoid subtitles or subsection headings within the text.

References: to follow series style (Surname date: page number) in brackets in text. All references/works cited should be listed in full at the end of each article, in the following style:
Surname, name/initial. *title of work*. place, publisher, date
Surname, name/initial. 'title of article'. In surname, name/initial (ed.)
title of work. place of publication, publisher, date
or Surname, name/initial, 'title of article', *Journal*, vol. no.: page no.

Copyright: it is the responsibility of contributors to clear permissions where appropriate

Reviewers should provide full bibliographic details, including the extent, ISBN and price, and submit to the reviews editor
James Gibbs, 8 Victoria Square, Bristol BS8 4ET
james.gibbs@uwe.ac.uk

New Directions in African Literature 25

A Review

Editor: Ernest N. Emenyonu
Assistant Editor: Patricia T. Emenyonu

Associate Editors: Francis Imbuga
Emmanuel Ngara
Charles E. Nnolim
Kwawisi Tekpetey
Iniobong I. Uko
Ato Quayson
Nana Wilson-Tagoe

Reviews Editor: James Gibbs

JAMES CURREY
OXFORD

AFRICA WORLD PRESS
TRENTON, N.J.

HEINEMANN EDUCATIONAL BOOKS (Nigeria) PLC
IBADAN

James Currey
an imprint of Boydell and Brewer Ltd,
PO Box 9, Woodbridge, Suffolk IP12 3DF, UK
and 668 Mount Hope Avenue, Rochester NY 14620-2731, USA
www.jamescurrey.com
www.boydell and brewer.com

Africa World Press, Inc.
PO Box 1892
Trenton NJ 08607
www.africanworld.com

Heineman Educational Books (Nigeria) Plc
1 Ighodaro Rd, Jericho
P.M.B. 5205, Ibadan

© James Currey Ltd 2006
First published 2006

A catalogue record is available from the British Library

ISBN 978–0–85255–570–5

Typeset in 9/11 pt Melior by Long House Publishing Services, Cumbria, UK
Transferred to digital printing

Contents

Notes on Contributors   x

EDITORIAL ARTICLE
New Directions in African Literature:
Building on the Legacies of the 20th Century   xi
   Ernest N. Emenyonu

ARTICLES

African Literature in the 21st Century:
Challenges for Writers & Critics
Charles E. Nnolim   1

Bursting at the Seams:
New Dimensions for African Literature in the 21st Century
Thomas A. Hale   10

New Trends in the Sierra Leonean Novel:
Tradition & Change in Novels by Alasan Mansaray & J. Sorie Conteh
Eustace Palmer   22

Transcultural Identity in African Narratives of Childhood
Richard K. Priebe   41

The Marks Left on the Surface:
Zoë Wicomb's *David's Story*
Kenneth W. Harrow   53

Mothering Daughters & the Other Side of the Story
in Amma Darko, Ama Ata Aidoo & Nozipo Maraire
Monica Bungaro   67

Transcending the Margins: New Directions in Women's Writing
Iniobong I. Uko   82

Re-thinking Nation & Narrative in a Global Era:
Recent African Writing
Nana Wilson-Tagoe   94

A Last Shot at the 20th-Century Canon
Bernth Lindfors 109

BOOK REVIEWS 120

New Fiction from West Africa
Titi Adepitan: Grace Ukala, *The Broken Bond*; Lekan Are,
The Challenge of the Barons; Dwaboyea E.S. Kandakai,
T*he Village Son* 120

Issues in Recent African Writing
Titi Adepitan: F.M. Archibong, *Boko*; Laury Lawrence Ocen,
The Alien Woman; Mary Abago, *Sour Honey*; Kaleni Hiyalwa,
Meekulu's Children; S. N. Ndunguru, *Divine Providence* 124

Scholarship in African Universities
Harry Garuba: Okot p'Bitek, *The Defence of Lawino*;
Felicia Okah Moh, *Ben Okri*; K.E. Yankson, *The Rot of the
Land and the Birth of Beautyful Ones* 128

Esterino Adami: Alessandro Di Maio, *Tutuola at the University* 132

Pauline Dodgson-Katiyo: Robert Muponde and
Mandivavarira Maodzwa-Taruvinga, eds, *Sign and Taboo* 134

Peter Hawkins: David Murphy, *Sembene* 135

The Igbo Novel
Craig McLuckie: Herbert Igboanusi, *Igbo English in the
Nigerian Novel* 137

Drama and Poetry by Wole Soyinka
Helon Habila: Wole Soyinka, *King Baabu*; Wole Soyinka,
Samarkand and other Markets I have Known 138

Ghanaian Poetry & Fiction
A.N. Mensah: Kofi Anyidoho, *PraiseSong for the Land*;
Ayi Kwei Armah, *KMT: In the House of Life* 143

Awo Mana Asiedu: Ama Ata Aidoo, *The Girl Who Can and
Other Stories* 147

Olabisi Gwamna: Samuel Duh, *One More Time* 149

Nigerian Fiction
Craig McLuckie: Kate I Nwankwo, *Fatal Greed*; Sunday Afolayan,
Beyond the Silent Grave; Stella Martins, *Our Moment in Time*;
Agwuncha Arthur Nwankwo, *Season of Hurricane and
Reckoning at Storm End*; Emeka Aniagolu, *Black Mustard Seed* 151

Short notices – James Gibbs, Reviews Editor
Kari Dako, *The Baobabs of Tete and Other Stories*
Kevin Wetmore Jr, *The Athenian Sun in an African Sky*
Toyin Falola and Barbara Harlow, eds, *Palavers of
African Literature and African Writers and Their Readers*   156

Journals
Humanities Review Journal, ed. Foluke M. Ogunleye
*Matatu/No Condition is Permanent: Nigerian Writing and the
Struggle for Democracy*, ed. Holger Ehling and Claus-Peter
Holste-von Mutius   159

Three Playwrights Crossing Borders
Ade-Yemi Ajibade, *Fingers Only and A Man Named Mokai*;
Parcel Post and Behind the Mountain
Pierre Meunier, *The Little Kings*; *The Coffee Party*; *Farin Dutse*
Femi Osofisan, *Recent Outings*; *Insidious Treasures*; *Literature
and the Pressure of Freedom*   161

Nasidi, Taiwo and Ebewo: Three Nigerian Critics
Yakubu A. Nasidi, *Beyond the Experience of Limits: Theory,
Criticism and Power in African Literature*
Oladele Taiwo, *Social Experience in African Literature*
Patrick Ebewo, *Barbs: A Study of Satire in the Plays of
Wole Soyinka*   163

Electronic Publishing
Binyavanga Wanaina, 'Discovering Home'   166

Index   169

Notes on Contributors

Monica Bungaro teaches African Literature and Culture, Critical Theory, and Gender Studies at the University of Birmingham, England. Her articles have appeared in leading journals on African Literature

Thomas A. Hale, author of *Griots and Griottes (1998)*, is Professor of African, French, and Comparative Literature at Pennsylvania State University, Pennsylvania.

Kenneth W. Harrow, a renowned scholar and critic of African Literature, is Professor of English at Michigan State University, East Lansing, Michigan.

Bernth Lindfors, a renowned scholar and critic of African Literature, is in the Department of English, University of Texas, Austin. He has published books and journals extensively in the field of African Literature.

Charles E. Nnolim, former Dean of the School of Arts and Humanities, University of Port Harcourt, Nigeria, is a renowned scholar and critic of African Literature. He is currently in the Department of English at the University of Port Harcourt.

Eustace Palmer, former Chair of the English Department, and Dean, Faculty of Arts and Dean of Graduate Studies, Fourah Bay College, Sierra Leone, is currently Professor of English and Coordinator of African Studies at Georgia College and State University. He is the author of *An Introduction to the African Novel* and *The Growth of African Literature*. He has served as Associate Editor of *African Literature Today*.

Richard K. Priebe is Professor of English at Virginia Commonwealth University, Richmond, Virginia.

Iniobong I. Uko is in the English Department, University of Uyo, Nigeria. She has published in leading journals in African Literature. Her book, *Gender and Identity in the Works of Osonye Tess Onwueme* has recently been published by Africa World Press.

Nana Wilson-Tagoe is at the School of Oriental and African Studies, London where she teaches African Literature. She has published extensively in the field.

Editorial Article
New Directions in African Literature: Building on the Legacies of the Twentieth Century

Ernest N. Emenyonu

With the passing of the 20th century and the inception of a new millennium, it became necessary in various facets of human endeavour, to take a backward glance and ask some piercing questions. Did the events of the past century prepare us for the new millennium? Will the things that we did right motivate us to greater heights? Will the errors in judgement serve as lessons to deter us from future mistakes? Like the inception of a new year, millions of people must have made 'new century resolutions' to guide their actions in the new century. These questions and thoughts preoccupied the minds of good governments, good leaders, good company executives, philosophers, politicians, scientists and not the least, artists, writers and scholars.

How so in African literature? African literature served in the 20th century, especially the second half, as a forum for addressing and redressing issues of education and mis-education in and about Africa; a forum for dismantling myths and distortions about Africa by the outside world; a forum for the assertion of cultural affirmations and re-affirmations; a forum for linguistic experimentations. African writers exposed and exploded old misconceptions and prejudices. They questioned racist theories of black inferiority and attacked the denigration of Africa and Africans by people whose knowledge of both were abysmally limited. African writers through their works undertook a mission of the restoration of the African identity and dignity. They set themselves the task of guiding their communities to understand where 'the rain began to beat them' so that they would be able to know how to dry their bodies, to paraphrase Chinua Achebe. Achebe has often been ascribed the honour of giving form, flesh and teeth to modern African literary tradition. In the second half of the 20th century, he defined African writing – its origins, its mission and its direction. His memorable proclamation comes to mind:

> The fundamental theme in African writing is that African peoples did not hear of culture for the first time from Europeans, their societies were not mindless but frequently had a philosophy of great depth and value and beauty; they had poetry, and above all, they had dignity. It is this dignity that many African

peoples all but lost in the colonial period, and it is this dignity that they must now regain. The worst thing that can happen to any people is the loss of their dignity and self-respect. The writer's duty is to help them regain it by showing them in human terms what happened to them, what they lost. There is a saying in Ibo that a man who can't tell where the rain began to beat him cannot know where he dried his body. The writer can tell the people where the rain began to beat them. The writer's duty is to explore in depth the human condition. In Africa he cannot perform this task unless he has a proper sense on history. (157)

African Literature Today has since inception been involved in raising questions of validity in African literature – What is African literature? What does it take to be its critic? Who do African writers write for? These questions have been raised and debated in the early issues of the journal several decades ago. Now, nearly half a century since those questions were asked, debated and discussed, *ALT*, at the beginning of the 21st century, is raising for debate and discussion follow-up questions about legacies and new directions in African literature. What are the accomplishments of African literature and African writers in the 20th century? What are their legacies? What foundations are there for the writers of the 21st century to build on? What were the critics', teachers', and readers' evaluations of African literature of the 20th century? What should be the concerns of African literature in the 21st century? What challenges does African literature pose for writers, critics, teachers, publishers and the book industry in the 21st century? What are the implications of these challenges for pedagogy in this technological era?

These are the major issues which *ALT 25 New Directions in African Literature* is projecting for close attention, debate, discussion and dialogue. The nine articles in this issue address the various facets of the central issue, 'African Literature: What Vision for the 21st century?' Some articles have approached it from a point of view of reviewing the trends of the past and charting a course for the future.

Charles Nnolim ends his discussion by expanding the frontiers of the inquiry – 'Where is African creative writing headed in the 21st century? What is the dream of African writers in this century?' Then he offers a vision: 'If the dream of the African writer in the last century was to recapture our lost humanity and project the African personality, the African writer in this century is challenged to envision a new Africa which has achieved parity (politically, technologically, economically and militarily) with Europe and America. And he has to widen his canvas as Nuruddin Farah is trying to do and as Ali Mazrui did so successfully in *The Trial of Christopher Okigbo*.'

Thomas Hale, Eustace Palmer, Richard Priebe and Kenneth Harrow follow up with illustrations of widened canvases, widened techniques and new resources in African writing. Thomas Hale categorically states: 'The question that faces us in the 21st century is whether or not studies of African literature can cast off these Euro-blinders [the tendency for scholars and their students to focus on those genres that are most akin to the concept of literature in Europe], and adopt a longer diachronic view of the field, a wider generic range that includes both written and oral forms, and a more global perspective on the African writer.' In his article, he offers 'evidence that will encourage scholars and students in the 21st century to reframe African literature in a larger context based on these dimensions.' Eustace Palmer, Richard Priebe and Kenneth Harrow provide case studies of 'the wider generic range' and ingenious experimentations.

Monica Bungaro and Iniobong I. Uko examine more closely the dimensions of female creativity on the advocated broader canvas. Bungaro contends that 'Family relationships in African postcolonial societies manifest a growing level of tension, conflict and stress as a result of new opportunities, new interests and new dilemmas created by increasing gender and class stratification across Africa, but especially across generations of Africans.' Her article examines 'the tension between generations and between opposing systems', as played out in the conflict between mothers and daughters. Bungaro is of the view that 'One of the new directions African women's writing is taking today is in fact visible in a more blunt attack on traditional foundations of society in its myths and beliefs about maternal love and mother-daughter relationships.' Her paper explores this theory in detail. In her paper, Uko identifies the coming of age of African literature in the 20th century with 'the true and pragmatic feminisation of the literary vision as a way of correcting absurd female images in African literature and culture.' In her study of African female writers (cutting across genres), she 'traces what obtains in select writings by African women in their goal of devising new templates for the signification and appreciation of contemporary African women, without necessarily evolving an ideological jacket or creed.'

Nana Wilson-Tagoe examines African literary creativity 'that continues to link nation, culture and narrative yet centres on traumas of national collapse ...' within the context of growing global trends. 'How do postcolonial Africans write their contradictory positions in this new phase of globalization?' Focusing on 'three recent African novels that deal with global themes', Wilson-Tagoe 'examines the relations between current theories of globalization and the global themes explored in contemporary African literature.'

Bernth Lindfors, in his 'A Last Shot at the 20th century Canon', offers a scheme which 'measured the literary stature of the writers from Anglophone Africa both comparatively and diachronically' up to the end of the 20th century.

This issue of *ALT* seeks to raise challenging questions, views and visions whose main purpose is to open up a dialogue that will move African literature forward in the 21st century. It seeks to invite comments and inquiries into the appropriate directions for African literature in the new millennium – directions which challenge writers, readers, teachers and publishers of African literature to invest their best initiatives in harnessing the 20th century legacies of African writers and African literature towards a consolidated base for the 21st century. We invite responses.

WORK CITED

Achebe, Chinua, 'The Role of a Writer in a New Nation,' *Nigeria Magazine*, 81, 1964.

African Literature in the 21st Century: Challenges for Writers & Critics

Charles E. Nnolim

From its beginnings written African literature in the 19th and 20th centuries from Phyllis Wheatley and Gustav Vassa, down to Achebe and Ngugi wa Thiong'o, was an unhappy one. It was lachrymal. It was a weeping literature, a literature of lamentation, following Africa's unhappy experience with slavery and colonialism. It was Hippolyte Taine who suggested in his 'Introduction to the History of English Literature' that we could recover from the monuments of literature a knowledge of the manner in which men thought and felt a particular epoch in their history. The sociologist Taine had remarked that the distinguishing mark between the early literatures of Great Britain and those of France was that the former was the literature of a defeated people while the latter was the literature of a conquering people (501).

Africans, having lost pride through slavery and colonialism, created a modern literature from the ashes of these past experiences. It became a literature with a strong sense of loss: loss of our dignity; loss of our culture and tradition; loss of our religion, loss of our land; loss of our very humanity. Is it any wonder that the titles of our most celebrated literary works highlighted these losses? Have we forgotten Achebe's *Things Fall Apart*; Ngugi wa Thiongo's *Weep Not, Child*; Alan Paton's *Cry the Beloved Country*? And protest literature over apartheid further irrigated Africa's tears because of man's inhumanity, to a people dubbed the wretched of the earth.

This study will, therefore, be janus-faced. It will cast a backward glance at African literature and criticism in the 20th century and, in the process, look forward to the challenges of the 21st century. While conceding that modern African literature (its written version) arose weeping in reaction to slavery and the colonial experience, one must, of necessity, draw attention to Africa's pre-history, to a time when its oral literature stood alongside the best celebrated epics of Europe. The *Ozidi Saga*, the *Mwindo Epic*, the *Sundiata epic* and so on, stood alongside the epics of Greece and Rome, and other European epics which also had their roots in oral tradition: the Sanskrit (Indian) epic, *Mahabharata*; the Spanish *El*

Cid; the German *Niebelungenslied*; the Greek *Iliad* and *Odyssey*; the Roman *Aeneid*; the French *Chanson de Roland*, and the English *Beowulf*. Each of the above epics, African, Asian and European sang of a noble people in noble pursuits.

Modern African literature (its written version) arose after the psychic trauma of slavery and colonialism had made her literature one with a running sore, a stigmata that forced her writers to dissipate their energies in a dogged fight to re-establish the African personality. African literature in the 20th century thus operated on a narrow canvas, a point that will be pursued later in this study.

The lachrymal nature of modern African literature made it inevitable for that literature to start by blaming the white man for everything wrong with us, castigating him for exploiting our resources and debasing our humanity. We also blamed the white man for not granting us, at least, flag independence to allow us to develop ourselves. And when the white man threw in the towel, our eyes were opened to the rapacity, greed, myopia and the corrupt tendencies of our indigenous politicians.

Before the white man left, and to pay him in his own coin for the haemorrhage he inflicted on our collective psyche, the literature of Negritude was born. The philosophy of Negritude became finally enthroned in the motto of the University of Nigeria: 'to restore the dignity of man'. There may be no space here to recount the obvious, or to repeat all the platitudes surrounding the Negritude movement whose trajectory became overarching from the Harlem Renaissance through the Rastafarian movement in Jamaica to indigenism in Haiti. But after regaining our equilibrium through the Negritude movement, and after unsurefooted attempts by Ayi Kwei Armah at psychic reconstruction in *The Healers* and *Two Thousand Seasons*, African literature in the 20th century seemed to have reached a point of exhaustion.

As we know, literature is judged always in relation to its social function; the better the function is fulfilled, the better the literature. A spiritual vacuum seems to have crept in toward the end of the 20th century, among African writers; an ashen paralysis that has not spared our most celebrated writers of that epoch. 'Art is of little significance in the midst of suffering'. It seems that the devastations of the economic order, the instabilities of governments in most African countries south of the Sahara, the frequent disruptions of the democratic order through military rule, and the ravages of disease, especially, the HIV/Aids pandemic, have taken their toll in the area of literary production.

First, the publishing houses suffered a demise. Time was when publishing houses like Heinemann, Evans Brothers, Oxford University Press, Spectrum Books, Longman, and African Universities Press, offered advance royalties to budding writers to complete their work. In the dying days of the 20th century, the publishing houses turned around to demand large sums of money from budding writers in order to have their works published. Soon, they were joined by new 'publishing' establishments in Nigeria: Kraft Books, ABIC, Malthouse, which insisted on publishing a writer's work on a cash and carry arrangement: and before a new writer could catch his breath, countless but non-descript desktop computer 'publishers' or rather, printers who had purchased ISBN numbers joined the field with no facilities for marketing or distribution of their product. These newcomers to the printing business saw no need to evaluate a manuscript or even offer advice before proceeding to print what the author told them was a novel, a play or a book of poems. With countless self-published books in the field, it became almost impossible to separate the chaff from the grain.

In Nigeria the only hope for discrimination among new books and new authors may lie in the efforts of the poorly funded Association of Nigerian Authors (ANA) through its annual awards. But the major problem with the ANA is its award of prizes for unpublished manuscripts and its lack of promotion of books it considers worthy of attention. The ANA, therefore, needs to source funds to establish a publishing house in order to publish, promote, and market its award-winning authors. *Things Fall Apart*, for example, may have remained an obscure but excellent novel, had Heinemann not undertaken to publish and promote it worldwide.

Since Chinua Achebe, Ngugi wa Thiong'o, Dennis Brutus, Ayi Kwei Armah, Wole Soyinka, Alex La Guma, Peter Abrahams, Buchi Emecheta, Meja Mwangi and Cyprian Ekwensi have definitely passed their prime, carrying with them the youthful vibrancy of the 1960s and 1970s, African literature at the turn of the century has experienced a disquieting lull except for the residual voices of Ben Okri, Nuruddin Farah and Niyi Osundare.

At the onset of the 21st century, something has definitely happened in the lives of old and new writers that have deprived us of the ebullience and revolutionary spirit of the 1960s and 1970s. As Andre Malraux declared at the Congress of Soviet Writers in 1931: 'Art is not an act of submission; it is a victory. The victory of what? Of emotions and the spirit of expressing them.'

If, as Malraux asserts in the above declaration, a work of art is seen as a 'conquest, a struggle between the artist and his world, an accusation against forces that hold humanity in servitude' in order to make men 'conscious of the hidden greatness and dignity in themselves', a new image of the African personality needs to be fashioned, to reposition Africa for the take-off of the 21st century. We need a new spiritual reorientation, a new creative hope to give artistic impetus to a new world order. Our writers, in this new epoch of globalism dominated by a technologically oriented new world order must create a new Africa, a new spirit of optimism, an Africa full of promises, able to feed its teeming populations, with a healthy and vibrant people not dependent on Europe and America for sustenance.

I have already hinted at the smallness of the canvas of the African writer in the last century. The reason for that smallness of artistic canvas was, as discussed earlier, the defensive nature of our literatures and our preoccupation with re-establishing the African personality, glancing backwards to a glorious past, in the process of which looking forward imaginatively eluded us. Our writers should now look forward to the 21st century as one with positive challenges. The 21st century offers the African writer opportunities to carve out a new humanism devoid of the complexes of the 20th century that made him so defensive as a second-class citizen of the world.

The African writer in the 21st century should forget the complexes of the past and be more imaginatively aggressive and expansive, invading other continents and even the skies as new settings, striving to have a global outlook in his creative output, mounting a new international phase and not limiting his canvas to the African soil. He should break away from the *retour aux sources* fixation that informed the Negritude aesthetic of the last century.

Let me explain. The European writer of the 19th and 20th centuries set his sights beyond Europe. Rider Haggard's King *Solomon's Mines*, Orwell's *Burmese Days*, E.M. Forster's *A Passage to India*, Conrad's *Heart of Darkness*, Edgar Wallace's *Sanders of the River* – these displayed the wide canvas of the European writer. Henry James, the American novelist, developed what critics called his 'international theme' in *Daisy Miller*, *The Ambassadors*, *The Portrait of a Lady*, depicting the gaucheries of naïve Americans, among sophisticated Europeans. The European writer widened his literary canvas in writing science fiction. Jules Verne, the French fiction writer invaded the skies in the 1860s with *From the Earth to the Moon* predicting a journey to the moon from a rocket launched from Cape Canaveral. One hundred years later, man landed on the moon in a rocket launched from the same Cape Canaveral in the US. He further invaded the seas under the earth with *Twenty Thousand Leagues under the Sea*. The American science fiction writer Alvin Toffler wrote *Future Shock* with his futuristic insistence that we should be educating for change, that we should be preparing people for the future while warning that unless man quickly learns to control the rate of change in his personal affairs, we are doomed to a massive adaptational breakdown.

It becomes clear when one draws attention to the narrow canvas of the African writer in the 20th century, busy as he was weeping over the losses inflicted on him by past colonial masters, preoccupied with blaming the African political or military leaders for leading us into political and economical quagmire, that the time has come for a more forward looking vision.

The 21st century beckons Africans to embrace new challenges in this epoch of globalization. If African literature in the 20th century suffered from imaginative timidity, it has no reason to be so confined in the 21st century. Our literature should no longer be contented to be fixated on our cultural moorings. Europe invaded Africa and the world with their civilization, religion, and technology and all of us have since then been transfixed. What prevents the African writer in the 21st century from re-inventing Europe and from there developing an international theme in our literatures. The Europeans wrote about Africa after a mere trip (Conrad), or domiciling there for a few years (Elspeth Huxley), why can't Africans write about Europe or America? We have travelled to Europe and America, worked there, studied there, married their sons and daughters, and lived there. Are we so unperceptive not to observe, so blind not to see, so analphabetic not to write about them or about us in their midst?

The idea of science fiction even at its most elementary levels has eluded African writers. African writers must face the future by developing an international theme, by engaging in futuristic literature, by looking forward to the fulfillment of the 'African dream'. The African dream was partially achieved in the 20th century ... the rehabilitation of our humanity through the negritude aesthetic. We should look forward and project a forward-looking utopia for Africa, not the backward-looking utopia of the 20th century that merely healed our psychic wounds. A forward-looking utopia for African writers should project a truly independent Africa politically stable, able to feed her starving peoples, standing side by side with Europe and the west, possessing enough coercive force to earn her respect in the international arena, and become the last refuge for the oppressed all over the world. This is the challenge of the 21st century for African writers.

The wind follows the sun, we read in geography books, just as critical trends follow trends in creative writing. Criticism of African literature in the last century rose in vigorous response to spirited and passionate creative output by our most celebrated writers... Chinua Achebe, Wole Soyinka, Ngugi wa Thiong'o, Ayi Kwei Armah, Christopher Okigbo, Dennis Brutus, Flora Nwapa, Buchi Emecheta, Mariama Bâ, Cyprian Ekwensi, Peter Abrahams and Alex La Guma. Their central theme, which began with the woes of culture-contact with Europe, captured in its sweep problems arising from post-independence, moving on to feminism, socialist concerns and then the various wars in Africa. Inevitably our most respected critics rose to the challenges arising from the concerns of the writers. Ernest Emenyonu engaged Bernth Lindfors on who is the most qualified to be the critic of African literature. The present writer aroused Achebe's ire on the source of one of his novels. Soyinka and the troika (Chinweizu et al.) locked horns over what the former called 'Neo-Tarzanism' in African Literature.

Chinweizu, Jemie and Madubuike's *Toward the Decolonisation of African Literature* (1980) made waves in the critical annals of African literature. Debate over the proper language of expression still lingers among our critics, and establishment of what constitutes the accepted aesthetic of African literature is unresolved. Women soon joined the fray. Chikwenye Ogunyemi vigorously aided by Omolara Ogundipe-Leslie and Helen Chukwuma in promotion of the feminist cause, attacked male critics tagging them with the indelicate sobriquet 'phallic critics'. From here oppositional criticism by radical voices engaged in discursive relations between classes in their theoretical constructs and politicised the cultural basis on which our autochthony was anchored. Although they enjoyed the appellation 'radical', their Marxist socialist fulminations hardly led to new rationalities in the African literary domain. The failure of the Marxist/Socialist ideologues to move African literature forward was resounding. After all, the ultimate aim of the Marxist/Socialist school was utopian: to reorder society so that the dictatorship of the proletariat would take root on African soil. This informs the fact that they started criticism as class warfare, highlighting the skirmishes of the downtrodden against the powers that be.

Now, the 21st century seems to have taken the African writer and critic by surprise. Pioneer writers like Achebe and his contemporaries have fallen silent or are now playing into what soccer enthusiasts refer to as 'injury time'. Ben Okri, Nuruddin Farah, Niyi Osundare and a few others are holding the field, but the enthusiasm, the vibrancy of the 1960s and 1970s are definitely lacking. That leaves the critic with little to do. Who is the new writer on the literary scene today whose message is large enough to elicit spontaneous response from the critics because the critic feels unchallenged by the depth of the writer's insights?

This is not to forget that critics whom I refer to as 'children of de Saussure' are alive and active. They are keen students of structuralism, post-structuralism, modernism, post-modernism, deconstruction and post-colonialism.[1] With the exception of post-colonialism, the regular diet of critical discourse of these children of de Saussure has always in its menu highfalutin terms like *ecriture, archi-ectriture, aporia, semiology* and *semiotics*. For these scholars, writing should be seen as *ecriture* and the literary text as one species of social institution where, in the process of *lecture* (reading) which must be 'creative', at which point according to post-structuralists the reader has reached the state of *recuperation*. A text must be *lisible* (readable) and if it is not (according to Roland Barthes in S/Z) it becomes *illisible* (unreadable) denying the reader the *plaisir* or *jouissance* (orgasmic ecstasy) that Roland Barthes harps upon in *The Pleasure of the Text*).

To be able to follow and popularize the terms mentioned above, the student must have read vital works in the area: Derrida's Of *Grammatology*, and *Writing and Difference* (on deconstruction); Jean Piaget's *Structuralism*; Jonathan Culler's *Structuralist Poetics*; Roland Barthes' *Elements of Semiology*; Claude Levi-Strauss's *Structural Anthropology* (all on structuralism). The more adventurous among these critics may complete their readings with Jacques Lacan: *The Language of the Self*;

Michel Foucault: *The Archaeology of the Self*; Gerard Genette: *Narrative Discourse*. And to belong, one has to be familiar with Julia Kristeva's theory of *intertextuality*.[2]

The point at issue is that since the critic is a mediator between art and its audience and is there to arouse some enthusiasm for the work while pointing out the worth or value of the work, is he still at one with his audience when he is lost in these exercises? Isn't the primary social function of the critic to make a text easier to understand for those who find it hard; to be a midwife between a difficult text and a non-understanding reader?

With all humility one might ask how these dry exercises in structuralist discourses are conducive to solving (at least imaginatively) the problems besetting Africans at the turn of the century. How does deconstruction as a critical engagement address life-denying issues confronting Africans at the beginning of this century... poverty, unstable governments, the HIV/AIDS pandemic? How does deconstruction create, in Matthew Arnold's dictum, 'a current of true and fresh ideas' and propagate 'the best that is known and thought in the world?'

The preoccupations of the 'children of de Saussure' lead to a critical cul-de-sac because one sees them as gradually moving away from the primary questions posed by criticism: What is art? What is its use? Why is it studied? Is it good or bad art? Of what value/worth is art to man? Deconstruction or dismantling of structures may be where Europeans have arrived after four thousand years of their art history. But African written literature and its arrival on the world scene are barely sixty years old. Don't we need to walk before we run, to build before we dismantle? Moreover, deconstruction, and its allied studies seem to deflect and distract the critic from his primary, even elemental functions: to be of some use to the reader by helping him understand the work: to propagate 'the best that is known and thought' in existing works of art; to legislate taste and insist on decorum; to act as a guide to writers through suggestion, advice, demonstration; to explicate, analyse, interpret and in the process arouse enthusiasm for the work by showing that it has or lays definite claims to ultimate values... the good, the true, the beautiful? Finally, it is the function of the critic to discriminate among competing works of art and to defend the work of art against those who doubt its validity.

A new trend in the criticism of African literature which is not likely to lead to a critical cul-de-sac is post-colonialism with its tripartite implications of 'New English Literatures', 'third world literature', and 'commonwealth literature'. Post-colonialism further encompasses within its circuitry of discourse the following:

a. Works by and about the post-colonial adventure, the whites who find themselves in an alien environment and write about it in their own

8 *African Literature in the 21st Century*

   language as we find in Australia, New Zealand, and Canada. They are also found in other settler colonies in India, and Africa (Zimbabwe, Kenya, and South Africa).

b. Work about the Caribbean experience where the post-colonial subjects have experienced dislocations through slavery or indentured labour, finding themselves in an alien environment where they struggle with a new language and a totally new experience.

c. Works by and about the colonial subject as we see in Africa and India where colonial subjects are forced by the intrepid imperialist adventurer, to remain in their own environments with no loss of inheritance but is forced to express this experience in the colonial master's tongue. The tensions between the colonised and the coloniser involved in literature of post-colonialism provide a minefield of unexplored discourse.

In sum, it is the position of this study that African literature and its criticism have suffered a decline at the turn of the century. The causes of this decline are manifold. The downturn in our economic order and the demise of the publishing houses that impeded the availability, distribution as well as the marketing of new literary texts. It is imperative, therefore, that a change of vision and a new attitude of the mind should govern and direct our creative efforts in this century. As Ebong asserts, Africa

> is ripe for a revolution. It is not the promiscuous, violent, bloody revolution of permissive wantonness to life and property, nor is it the cultural revivalism of black humanity asserting itself in protest against the indifference of the west. The revolution for contemporary Africa presupposes the reorganization and the restructuring of the African mind and psyche. (71)

If great writers do not emerge in the 21st century shall we ever again have great critics with the kind of insight that produced *The Writings of Wole Soyinka* (Eldred Jones); *Christopher Okigbo: Creative Rhetoric* (Sunday Anozie); *The Novels of Ayi Kwei Armah* (Robert Fraser); *Cyprian Ekwensi* (Ernest Emenyonu); *The Poetry of Okot p'Bitek* (George A. Heron); *Peter Abrahams* (Michael Wade); and *The Novels and Plays of Ngugi wa Thiong'o* (Douglas Killam). And were great writers to emerge by some miracle in the early days of the century, where would one find the supporting encouragement from publishing houses like Evans Brothers and Heinemann that promoted both the creative output and its attendant criticism of the last century? With self-published works suffering the disability of non-distribution and non-availability, would one be tagged a doomsayer if one predicted that the immediate future of African literature and its criticism are bleak.

Finally, if as we have tried to establish, the creative sun is followed inevitably by the critical wind, what new writers on the African creative horizon are there to excite the critical responses of a new Izevbaye, a new Irele, a new Lindfors, a new Emenyonu? So, *quo vadimus*? Where is

African creative writing headed in the 21st century? What is the dream of African writers in this century? If the dream of the African writer in the last century was to recapture our lost humanity and re-establish the African personality, the African writer in this century is challenged to envision a new Africa, which has achieved parity (politically, technologically, economically and militarily) with Europe and America. And he has to widen his canvas as Nuruddin Farah is trying to do and as Ali Mazrui so successfully did in *The Trial of Christopher Okigbo*.

NOTES

1. See entries on 'Deconstruction' and 'Structuralist Criticism' in M.H. Abrams, *A Glossary of Literary Terms*, 4th ed. New York: Holt, Rinehart and Winston, 1981.
2. A good work on post-colonial literatures is *The Empire Writes Back: Theory and Practice of Post-Colonial Literatures* by Bill Ashcroft, Helen Tiffin and Gareth Griffith. London: Routledge, 1989.

WORKS CITED

Arnold, Matthew, 'The Function of Criticism at the Present Time', in *The Oxford Anthology of English Literature, Vol. 11*, Frank Kermode and John Hollander. New York: OUP, 1973: 1009.

Chinweizu, Jemie, Onwuchekwa and Madubuike, Ihechukwu, *Towards the Decolonisation of African Literature*. Enugu: Fourth Dimension, 1980.

Ebong, Inih Akpan. 'Towards the Revolutionary Consciousness: The writer in contemporary Africa'. In Ernest Emenyonu (ed.), *Literature and Society: Selected Essays on African Literature*. Oguta: Zim Pan-African Literature Publishers, 1986: 71–83.

Taine, Hyppolyte, 'From Introduction to the History of English Literature'. In W. J. Bate (ed.) *Criticism: The Major Texts*. New York: Harcourt, Brace and World Inc., 1952: 501–7.

> Bursting at the Seams:
> New Dimensions for African Literature
> in the 21st Century

Thomas A. Hale

It is hardly surprising that as African literature emerged on the global literary scene during the last half century, there was a tendency for scholars and their students to focus on those genres that are most akin to the concept of literature in Europe: novels, poetry, and drama written in European languages. The works of African writers conveyed a sense to outsiders, especially non-Africans, of what it was like to live and work in villages, towns or cities on the continent, especially the sub-Saharan part of it. But this Eurocentric approach to African literature has unfortunately narrowed our perspective on the field with respect to history, genre, and place. The question that faces us in the 21st century is whether or not studies of African literature can cast off these Euro-blinders and adopt a longer diachronic view of the field, a wider generic range that includes both written and oral forms, and a more global perspective on the African writer. The purpose here is to offer evidence that will encourage scholars and students in the 21st century to reframe African literature in a broader context based on these dimensions.

From synchrony to diachrony

Two decades ago, the c.v. of a new tutor in a literature unit at my university listed 'African literature since 1960' as a sub-specialty. As the only African literature professor here at the time, a situation that is the case in most institutions, I was delighted to see that someone in a sister unit had brought knowledge of the subject to our large but somewhat isolated campus. I was chagrined to discover, however, that this expertise did not go back farther than 1960. Did this mean that Africans wrote nothing of significance before that date, or was it simply a modest admission that the scholar had not explored farther back than the year of independence for most African countries? I have no way of knowing which was the case, but the listing of a sub-specialty of such limited depth may have given the impression to those on the hiring committee that the field really didn't amount to much before 1960 – in other words, it was entirely post-colonial. A recent conversation with a prospective graduate student reflected the same view. When I mentioned African literature, she responded, 'you mean post-colonial'.

A look at the programme at any meeting of the African Literature Association confirms the prevalence of this synchronic view. We are fascinated by the latest wave in African literature, and I will be the first to admit that I share that interest – so much so that at the request of graduate students studying African literature here, they and I team-taught a seminar on African women writers two years ago. We did not list any women writers before 1960 simply because there were none whose texts were easily available and who interested us from before that date.

In this decidedly 'post-colonial' environment, of what value, then, can literary archaeology be if the new wave of writers is so much more interesting? The most obvious answer is the need to clear unwelcome stereotypes from the introductory terrain in our courses. While our students are plunging into the first text on the syllabus, we must deal with one of the most deeply rooted of these poisonous weeds – the belief that there was no writing in Africa prior to the arrival of Europeans.

To erase this stereotype, we need, then, to shift from a synchronous approach to a much more diachronic perspective that traces the history of writing in Africa back 5,000 years. During that journey, we will find not simply evidence of writing, but also examples of narrative that would qualify as literature by any standard.

But to reach that goal, we also need to take a continental approach to Africa. Most of us have tended to focus on writing from sub-Saharan societies, though we have always welcomed to our meetings colleagues who work on North African literature. There has remained, however, a gulf that stems from a separation operating on many levels. Diplomatic services typically house North African concerns in the office of Middle Eastern Affairs. For example, the US government announced in February 2004 plans to propose to the G8 group of major industrialised nations as well as to the summit meeting of NATO states a vast proposal to reform the countries of the 'Greater Middle East'. The map of the proposal includes six countries and one territory in North Africa: Mauritania, Western Sahara, Morocco, Algeria, Tunisia, Libya, and Egypt, as well as more than a dozen other states as far east as Pakistan. The problem of dividing up the continent carries over to the world of researchers. Although the Middle East Studies Association has held one annual meeting in conjunction with the African Studies Association, in general scholars working on North African topics tend to view the world through 'Middle Eastern' rather than African lenses. Finally, museum curators have for generations framed Egypt in the Mediterranean rather than the African context. This reality was illustrated by the experience of a well-known scholar in African Studies based at an institution in New York City who once attempted in the late 1960s to establish a list of all the courses on Africa available within city limits. When he contacted the Metropolitan Museum of Art to ask if that institution provided any short courses, seminars, or other forms of instruction on Africa, the answer was no, but the museum did offer some sessions on Egypt.

Since then, scholars, curators, and others interested in Africa have begun to extend bridges across the great split between North Africa and sub-Saharan Africa. For example, since the late 1970s, the museums of Paris, London, New York, Philadelphia, Baltimore and Washington have all mounted temporary or permanent exhibitions of artifacts from Nubia, the region south of Egypt that once launched armies northward to create the 25th dynasty during the period from 750 to 650 BCE. These displays that tell viewers about peoples who are more closely linked to sub-Saharan than Northern Africa were created from materials that in many cases had been lying in storage for generations. They emphasise both the specificity of the dark-skinned peoples from Nubia as well as the links they maintained with their lighter-skinned neighbours to the North. The importance of reframing Nubia in a wider context appears in catalogues and volumes by the curators that have come out of these exhibitions. David O'Connor's *Ancient Nubia: Egypt's Rival in Africa* (1993) and John H. Taylor's *Egypt and Nubia* (1991) are two examples.

A significant source of this new interest in the links between Egypt and other peoples in Africa is the vigorous debate that has surrounded the publication of books by Cheikh Anta Diop, Molefi Kete Asante, Clinton Crawford, and Martin Bernal, among others. Although these writers have not convinced everyone of their diverse theories about the links between sub-Saharan African peoples and those in Egypt, they have succeeded in throwing a rhetorical bridge across the divide that separates the two parts of the continent in the minds of many researchers. The task now is to cross that bridge in order to see what is on the other side.

It can be a two-way path, as I have discovered on the personal level while taking courses on Egyptian hieroglyphics with Donald Redford at Penn State since 2001. Redford is widely viewed as North America's leading scholar in Egyptian epigraphy, the discipline of deciphering inscriptions on walls, rocks and other surfaces. His latest book, *From Slave to Pharaoh: The Black Experience of Ancient Egypt* (2004), offers a new perspective that is more firmly rooted in the archaeology and writing of the period than any work to appear to date on the subject. While he continually opens my eyes to features of Egyptian culture that match what I know occurs in parts of sub-Saharan Africa, at the same time I am able to convey information that helps him to make connections or explain cultural activities in Egypt that were heretofore mysterious.

From this experience, I am convinced that if we are to view African literature in a diachronic and continental context, then we must begin with Egyptian literature. By this I do not mean simply *The Book of the Dead*

(Budge, 1895, 1967), but poetry and stories composed by Egyptians thousands of years ago, material that is basic for anyone learning Middle or Late Egyptian. Miriam Lichtheim's three volumes, *Ancient Egyptian Literature* (1975), R. B. Parkinson's *The Tale of Sinuhe and other Ancient Egyptian Poems, 1940-1640 BC* (1999), *The Literature of Ancient Egypt: An Anthology of Stories, Instructions, and Poetry*, edited by William Kelly Simpson (1972), John L. Foster's *Ancient Egyptian Literature: An Anthology* (2001) as well as his *Echoes of Egyptian Voices: An Anthology of Ancient Egyptian Poetry* (1992), and *Land of Enchanters: Egyptian Short Stories from the Earliest Times to the Present Day*, edited by Bernard Lewis and Stanley Burstein ([1948], 2001) all offer an extraordinary variety of texts that convey a rich imagination as well as a sense of Egypt's unusual position at the intersection of the Mediterranean and African worlds.

In spite of the diversity of ancient Egyptian literature, it is often argued that there is no real link with writing in other parts of Africa. In fact, writing in Egypt spread southward and took different forms, some of which are still waiting to be deciphered. The focus on Egypt provides both a starting point for African literature and a bridge to writing in African languages in neighbouring parts of Saharan and sub-Saharan Africa.

For example, the first Nubian conqueror of Egypt, King Piankhy, drove his army all the way north to the Nile Delta in a successful effort to lay the foundations for Egypt's 25th dynasty around 750 BCE. He documented his campaign by having a scribe write down the narrative of his conquest in Middle Egyptian hieroglyphics on a six foot high granite stela that was discovered in 1862 in Gebel Barkal, southern Egypt. The account, composed in the 2lst year of his reign in Egypt, around 730 BCE, describes his efforts to defeat an invader from Libya named Tefnakhte (Grimal, 1981).

By 200 BC, the Meroites of Nubia were beginning to write in their own language, using a script adapted from Egyptian hieroglyphs. Some of the inscriptions have been translated, but the language remains only partially readable, in spite of the continuing efforts of a small group of researchers around the world (Taylor, 1991: 50–1).

By the 4th century CE, Ethiopians in Axum were writing the lives of saints in Ge'ez, and a few centuries later began to translate works from Greek. Ishak, governor of Axum and administrator of its cathedral of Mary-Zion, is often credited with authorship of the *Kebra Negast*, the 14th century history of the Solomonic heritage of their rulers (Ferenc, 1985: 263–4). The text is readily available today in a translation by Miguel F. Brooks (1995).

To the west of Egypt, in Libya, Niger, Mali, and Algeria, next to drawings of giraffes, cattle, and other animals, one finds inscriptions in an ancient form of Tifinar, a Libyco-Berber language. Tifinar survives today among the Tuareg in the Sahara. Long viewed as the province of women, who used it for correspondence, it has been given a new role in poetry written by Tuareg poets and in research by scholars. For example, in *Ennän Kel Awal: Les gens de la parole disent*, Alhassan ag Solimane and Saskia Walentowitz offer the reader a fascinating collection of 197 proverbs, each presented in four versions: Tifinar, a transcription of the signs, a word-for-word translation, and a literary translation. Unfortunately, we are still not able to decipher the ancient form of Tifinar on rocks scattered along the trade routes of the Sahara. These inscriptions date to around 3000 BCE (Lhote, 1979). There is some evidence to suggest links between this writing and other forms from farther east in the Fezzan region of southern Libya, but we must await the results of further research. Although no one has found a Rosetta stone for early Tifinar, our inability to decipher these inscriptions does not diminish their importance as examples of early writing in Africa.

The thread between writing in Egypt and its neighbours, then, is clear to the south and uncertain to the west, but there is much evidence to suggest that the kingdoms of the pharaohs were in contact with peoples throughout the surrounding regions for reasons of commerce and diplomacy.

With the arrival of Arabic in North, East and West Africa during the last millennium, new forms of inscriptions appear as early as the 11th century on gravestones in eastern Mali (Moraes Farias, 2004). Lengthy narratives emerge from the Timbuktu region in the 16th and 17th centuries that are both historical and literary because they contain legends about the early populations of the region as well as chronicles of events in the Mali and Songhay empires. For example, in the *Tarîkh el-Fettâch*, a narrator relates a story told to him by the father of one of his contemporaries, who received the story from his grandfather, that Tendirma, a city 90 kilometres upriver from Timbuktu, was once populated by Jews: 'There were seven princes descending from the king of the Jews, each leading twelve thousand horsemen and numerous foot soldiers' (Kâti [1913–14] 1981, 120). Although there are some archaeological hints that these 'beni-Israel' once lived there, what the narrative conveys is more legendary than historical when compared to the precision of dates and names that constitute the bulk of the Timbuktu chronicles.

Writing in African languages expands in the last half of the millennium with the creation of literatures in Hausa and Fulani in West Africa and in Swahili in East Africa, all using Arabic script. Much of it starts as religious poetry and then branches out into longer narratives. A major example by a woman that has appeared in print recently is *One Woman's Jihad*, poetry by Nana Asma'u, a Hausa woman who lived in Sokoto, Nigeria, from 1793 to 1864 (Mack and Boyd, 2000). Her counterpart from East Africa is Mwana Kupona, who wrote what is now called 'Utendi wa Mwana Kupona', a 102-stanza poem in 1858–1860 (Allen, 1971). Anne

Biersteker has provided an excellent analysis of the text as well as references to the different editions of the work in her chapter titled 'Language, Poetry, and Power: A Reconsideration of "Utendi wa Mwana Kupona"' (1991). Jan Knappert's *Four Centuries of Swahili Verse* (1979) offers a long view of poetry in the language from its earliest known written roots to the present. Other volumes that provide an overview from different perspectives on the pre-colonial, colonial, and national eras include *Literatures in African Languages* by Andrzejewski, Pilaszewicz, and Tyloch (1985), *African Language Literatures* by Gérard (1981), and *Littératures et écritures en langues africaines* by Nkashama (1992).

The point, then, is that Africans have been writing all kinds of texts for 5,000 years. Although we still have much to learn about writing in general and literature in particular during this long period, it is essential to convey to students from the outset some sense of the diversity and chronology for both historical reasons as well as to erase the pervasive belief that Europe was the only source of writing in Africa. To reach this goal, we need to view the continent in its entirety.

The cohabitation of oral and written forms of verbal art

The second dimension of African literature that will become increasingly important is verbal art recorded from oral sources. One reason that this branch of African literature has not played a very prominent role in studies in the field is that scholars, critics, and instructors have not had access through translation to the extraordinarily rich and varied corpora that flourish all over the continent. Since 1960, to represent the oral tradition we have usually relied on a handful of texts, primarily the prose version of *Soundjata*, an epic that was recorded by Niane in 1958. But this convenient focus on one genre presented in a reader-friendly format that is closer in form to the novel than to the epic has tended to divert our attention from the diversity of material recorded, transcribed, and translated from oral sources. By diversity, I mean in both genre and gender.

For example, the oral epic has long been viewed as a masculine genre, both in content and in production. African epics are traditionally about male heroes and are narrated by male griots. This view is now being challenged as women come forward to sing or recount epic-like narratives such as the 'subversive' 'Epic of Good Brides and Young Women', a 1,050 line poetic narrative by Safi Hassane that was recorded in Niger in 1995 by Aissata Sidikou (*Recreating Words, Reshaping Worlds: The Verbal Art of Women from Niger, Mali, and Senegal*, pp. 207–47). Whether this is an exception or part of a wider trend remains to be seen. But like the Nubian or Tifinar texts that are partially or entirely undecipherable, the lack of examples of long poetic narratives from women does not mean that the narratives do not exist in their minds. Changes in gender roles and in the education of women are leading to a new set of performance dynamics that are eliciting an extraordinary range of verbal art by women.

The most striking examples are coming from women's songs. A team of 20 researchers is now presenting evidence of an incredibly vigorous form of verbal art by women in the Sahel region of West Africa. Women in this region do not often have a public voice, but the content of their songs reveals that they have much to say, and some of it can be quite shocking to male listeners.

This is a project rooted in both my own research on female griots, or griottes, and that of Aissata Sidikou on women singers from Niger, Mali, and Senegal. By combining our experience and by recruiting other scholars who have been conducting research on the traditions of a variety of peoples in the region (Moor, Wolof, Lebou, Serer, Bamana, Mandinka, Fulani, Songhay, Hausa, Jula, etc.), we have been able to assemble a corpus of over 1,000 songs. Some of them were recorded recently in West Africa, while others were taped several decades ago. Still others were written down nearly a century ago by colonial administrators and travellers.

By comparing the songs across cultures, we are able to identify a variety of themes and forms. Marriage, for example, generates the greatest thematic diversity, with songs about love, courtship, departure from home, lamentations, adultery, advice, Spring-Autumn relationships, performers, guests, sex, polygamy, sterility, abuse, rejection and divorce. These songs fall into a variety of ethnic-specific genres, but the themes cut across the entire region. Above all, they reveal that women enjoy a special freedom to speak out publicly about their relationships with men and with others in society such as relatives and co-wives.

The songs represent a powerful form of female expression that cannot be excluded from our notion of what constitutes African literature today. We hope to make them available to scholars by producing an anthology, a set of conference papers from the meeting in May 2003 of the research team members, and a synthesis of current research on women's songs.

The song collection will help to change one other feature of contemporary African literary criticism: the tendency to view the field from an evolutionary perspective. Specialists in the word have long contended that the evolution of societies depends on the shift from orality to literacy. This was a view espoused for a long time by one of the leading researchers into oral traditions, Jack Goody. That view has unfortunately tended to influence scholars in African literature who see the late arrival of women on the literary scene as a form of evolution from the oral to the written. As d'Almeida, Nnaemeka, Cazenave, and others have so ably demonstrated, women were indeed excluded from the literary scene in large part because Western-style education during the colonial and early national periods was provided mainly to boys, with girls dropping out early as the result of marriage or the perceived need to devote family resources to those offspring who could succeed in a male-oriented world. By eventually acquiring literacy in spite of these limitations, women writers broke the bond of silence that surrounded them.

But from the wider perspective of verbal art, the category that includes both oral and written forms, women have always had a voice. The problem is that the voice was in song, and in languages not understood by those from other parts of Africa or from outside of Africa.

A more comprehensive way, then, of framing the verbal art of women is to say that the two, oral and written, co-exist today. Those women who have benefitted from Western-style education are now using written media to convey their narratives to wider audiences. Some other women, however, continue to express themselves as professional singers. Such an approach reflects Brian Street's view (*Literacy in Theory and Practice*, 1984) about the relationship between orality and literacy: the medium, oral or written, is not what counts; it is the language in which a message or an artform is composed that is of greatest importance.

This is best illustrated in a Sahelian capital such as Niamey where people may greet each other and pray in Arabic, converse in Songhay-Zarma or Hausa, and conduct business at the office in French. Arabic is both written and oral; Songhay-Zarma and Hausa are mainly oral, but there are a few publications in Songhay-Zarma, and a much longer tradition of writing in Hausa; French, the colonial language, can serve for both oral and written purposes. What is most important is what these languages convey: Arabic reflects a major religious tradition imported centuries ago, Songhay-Zarma and Hausa each carry a cultural heritage that is even older; French reflects the impact – and the constraints – of French colonial and post-colonial policies on the government, peoples, and cultural traditions of Niger. Orality and literacy are, then, secondary concerns here when we consider what lies behind each language.

In the domain of song, the written and the oral come together in popular song, a field now dominated by women in some countries such as Mali. There, singers, some of whom have a Western-style education can reach national, regional, and international audiences with songs that combine, for example, Bamana and French. These songs reflect both what they have heard from others as well as what they have read. For example, in Niger, Fati Djado Sekou has experienced twelve years of Western-style education, and has read *Soundjata: l'épopée mandingue*. But she has also heard oral epics narrated by her father, and she combines today her interest in the past, drawn from different sources, to launch a performance career that blends past and present (Sidikou, 2001).

Songs by women, however, are part of a much larger and more complex picture of performances by both men and women that take a regional and multi-ethnic approach. For example, Aaron Rosenberg has been studying the rise of the regional song in East Africa. He has discovered that this genre crosses gender, ethnic, and national boundaries. It is a highly dynamic verbal form that is being used for social criticism and for education ('Language, Form and Theme in the Songs of Remmy Ongala', 2000).

As we widen our generic perspective, expand our ability to read African languages, and facilitate the publication of more texts in both the original and in translation, we will be able in the future to appreciate better the contribution of epics, songs, poems, and other forms to the growing canon of African literature.

The expanding literary diaspora

A third area of African literature that will grow in the 21st century is writing in European languages outside of the continent. African writers have been writing from positions outside of Africa from the early part of the 20th century. Camara Laye's autobiographical narrative about his childhood, *L'Enfant noir*, was written in Paris at mid-century. Cheikh Hamidou Kane's philosophical *récit L'Aventure ambiguë*, conveys the alienation he felt as a student in Paris during the same colonial era. But this early generation of writers was not permanently based outside of Africa. Since the 1980s, a new generation has left the continent for good and now writes in what might be called a permanent African literary diaspora. Buchi Emecheta, Calixthe Beyala, Chinua Achebe and Ngugi wa Thiong'o are just a few of these expatriate authors. Odile Cazenave's new book, *Afrique sur Seine: une nouvelle génération de romanciers africains à Paris* (2003), provides a wider perspective on these writers. Although they may often be viewed as nomads or exiles, in a sense one may say that they are also part of the wider wave of immigrants who are colonising metropolitan countries with their presence and their literature. One can argue that the writers are invigorating, reshaping, and renewing the literatures of Europe and North America as they extend the range of African literature today. It is not clear, however, to what extent these writers will fall into a no-writers-land that is neither African nor European. One wonders if they will be co-opted into a new literary context, or simply become pioneers in a new global village of world literature.

For example, the new writers seem to be welcome in France but they also discomfort the country with their visible presence that reminds people there of the growing minority population. France embraces the new literature they represent to the extent that it can be perceived as extending the influence – what the French call *rayonnement* – of the French language. This includes sending francophone African writers on tours of anglophone countries. But this more visible African presence also contributes to a concern among growing numbers of French who are wondering at what point France will begin to lose its own cultural identity. The debate over headscarves in France and the new law to ban all forms of religious identification in schools appears as a serious effort to stem the rising tide of African – in this case North African – influence on French society.

Looking several generations down the road, is it possible that African literature will continue to flourish in such a way that it begins to overshadow French literature, just as Latin American literature has taken the lead in innovation from Spanish literature? The histories, conditions, peoples, and cultures in this comparison do not match up neatly. But we certainly can anticipate a continued increase in the number of writers and works coming out of Africa and an increased African presence in Europe and North America.

Our notion of diaspora, however, should not be confined to writers in Europe and the New World. As Faulkingham and Goheen point out in the introduction to a special African Diaspora issue of *African Studies Review* (vol. 43, no 1, 2000), there is no single African Diaspora, but instead 'multiple, overlapping, and sometimes disharmonious relationships all seeking to define the meaning of the continent. All take as a given that in its broadest sense the definition of Africa is not confined to the continent. Nor is it bounded by its geography, either historically or today. There is no one historical moment we can say constitutes *the* African Diaspora (i).' African verbal art can be found not only in Europe, North America and South America, but also in the Middle East and around the shores of the Indian Ocean (Alpers, 2000).

The three areas cited above, history, genre, and diaspora, are not the only dimensions of African literature that are expanding in the 21st century. Other scholars will cite a variety of trends that I have not mentioned. For example, Lydie Moudileno, in *Littératures africaines francophones des années 1980 et 1990* (2003), points to detective fiction, romance novels, and children's literature as three genres that have shown much growth in the last two decades and that are likely to spread even more widely.

African literature, then, is bursting at the seams at the beginning of the 21st century. We are re-examining its deepest written roots in Africa and broadening our view of the genres of African literature. Writers as well as performers from Africa are spreading their verbal art around the world in a variety of forms – books, concerts, and recordings. In contrast to what is so often called Afro-pessimism, I find myself looking at the future of African literature from a distinctly optimistic angle. The 21st century will be the century of African literature.

WORKS CITED

Allen, J. W. T. (ed.), *Tendi: Six Examples of a Classical Verse Form with Translation and Notes*. New York: Africana, 1971.
Alpers, Edward A. 'Recollecting Africa: Diasporic Memory in the Indian Ocean World'. *African*

Studies Review (43:1), April 2000: 83–99.
Andrzejewski, B. W., Stanislaw Pilaszewicz, and Witold Tyloch. *Literatures in African Languages: Theoretical Issues and Sample Surveys*. Cambridge: Cambridge University Press, 1985.
Asante, Molefi Kete. *Kemet, Afrocentricity, and Knowledge*. Trenton: Africa World Press, 1990.
Bernal, Martin. *Black Athena: The Afro-Asiatic Roots of Classical Civilization*. New Brunswick: Rutgers University Press, Vol. 1, *The Fabrication of Ancient Greece, 1785–1985*. 1987. Vol. 2, *The Archaeological and Documentary Evidence*, 1991.
Biersteker, Anne. 'Language, Poetry, and Power: A Reconsideration of "Utendi wa Mwana Kupona".' In Kenneth W. Harrow (ed.) *Faces of Islam in African Literature*. Portsmouth: Heinemann, 1991.
Brooks, Miguel. *Kebra Negast (The Glory of Kings)*. Trenton: Red Sea Press, 1995.
Budge, W. A. Wallis. *The Egyptian Book of the Dead* [1895]. New York: Dover, 1967.
Cazenave, Odile. *Rebellious Women: The New Generation of Female African Novelists*. Boulder: Rienner, 2000.
——. *Afrique sur Seine: une nouvelle génération de romanciers africains à Paris*. Paris: Harmattan, 2003.
Crawford, Clinton. *Recasting Ancient Egypt in the African Context*. Trenton, NJ: Africa World Press, 1996.
d'Almeida, Irène Assiba. *Francophone African Women Writers: Destroying the Emptiness of Silence*. Gainesville: University Press of Florida, 1994.
Diop, Cheikh Anta. *The African Origins of Civilizations: Myth or Reality*. Trans. M. Cook. Westport: Hill, 1974.
Faulkingham, Ralph, and Mitzi Goheen. 'From the Editors'. *African Studies Review* (43.1), April 2000: i–ii.
Ferenc, Aleksander. 'Writing and Literature in Classical Ethiopian (Giiz)' in Andrewzejewski, Pilaszewicz, and Tyloch, 1985, pp. 255–300.
Foster, John L. *Echoes of Egyptian Voices: An Anthology of Ancient Egyptian Poetry*. Norman: University of Oklahoma Press, 1992.
——. *Ancient Egyptian Literature: An Anthology*. Austin: University of Texas Press, 2001.
Gérard, Albert. *African Language Literatures: An Introduction to the Literary History of Sub-Saharan Africa*. Burnt Mill: Longman, 1981.
Goody, Jack. *The Interface Between the Written and the Oral*. Cambridge: Cambridge University Press, 1987.
Grimal, N.-C. *La Stèle triomphale de Pi(ankh)y au Musée du Caire*. Cairo: French Institute of Oriental Archaeology, 1981.
Kane, Cheikh Hamidou. *L'Aventure ambiguë*. Paris: Juillard, 1961.
Kâti, Mahmoûd. *Tarîkh el-Fettâch, ou chronique du chercheur pour servir à l'histoire des villes, des armées et des principaux personnages du Tekrour*. Trans. Octave Houdas and Maurice Delafosse. Paris: Maisonneuve [1913–14], 1981.
Knappert, Jan. *Four Centuries of Swahili Verse: A Literary History and Anthology*. London: Heinemann, 1979.
Laye, Camara. *L'Enfant noir*. Paris: Plon, 1953.
Lewis, Bernard and Stanley Burstein. *Land of Enchanters: Egyptian Short Stories from the Earliest Times to the Present Day*. London: Harvill [1948]; Princeton: Markus Wiener, 2001.
Lhote, Henri. *Les Gravures de l'oued Mammanet*. Dakar: Nouvelles Editions Africaines, 1979.
Lichtheim, Miriam. *Ancient Egyptian Literature*. 3 vols. Berkeley: University of California Press, 1975.
Mack, Beverly, and Jean Boyd. *One Woman's Jihad: Nana Asma'u, Scholar and Scribe*. Bloomington: Indiana University Press, 2000.
Moraes Farias, Paulo de. *Arabic Medieval Inscriptions from the Republic of Mali: Epigraphy, Chronicles and Songhay-Tuareg History*. London and Oxford: Oxford University Press/British Academy, Fontes Historiae Africanae, New Series: Sources of African History, 2004.
Moudileno, Lydie. *Littératures africaines francophones des années 1980 et 1990*. Dakar: Conseil pour le développement de la recherche en sciences sociales en Afrique, 2003.

Niane, Djibril Tamsir. *Soundjata ou l'épopée mandingue*. Paris: Présence Africaine, 1960. English edition: *Sundiata: An Epic of Old Mali*, trans. G. D. Pickett. London: Longman, 1965.

Nkashama, Pius Ngandu. *Littératures et écritures en langues africaines*. Paris: Harmattan, 1992.

Nnaemeka, Obioma, 'From Orality to Writing: African Women Writers and the (Re)inscription of Womanhood'. *Research in African Literatures* (25:4) 1994: 137–57.

O'Connor, David., *Ancient Nubia: Egypt's Rival in Africa*. Philadelphia: The University of Pennsylvania Museum of Archeology and Anthropology, 1993.

Parkinson, R. B. *The Tale of Sinuhe and Other Ancient Egyptian Poems, 1940–1640 BC*. Oxford: Oxford University Press, 1999.

Redford, Donald. *From Slave to Pharaoh: The Black Experience of Ancient Egypt*. Baltimore, Johns Hopkins UP, 2004.

Rosenberg, Aaron, 'Language, Form and Theme in the Songs of Remmy Ongala', paper presented at the African Literature Association annual meeting, Nashville, 2000.

Sidikou, Aissata. *Recreating Words, Reshaping Worlds. The Verbal Art of Women from Niger, Mali, and Senegal*. Trenton, NJ: Africa World Press, 2001.

Simpson, William Kelly. *The Literature of Ancient Egypt: An Anthology of Stories, Instructions, and Poetry*. New Haven: Yale University Press, 1972.

Solimane, Alhassan ag, and Saskia Walentowitz. *Ennän Kel Awal: Les gens de la parole disent*. [n.p]: Kephalonia, 1996.

Street, Brian V. *Literacy in Theory and Practice*. Cambridge: Cambridge University Press, 1984.

Taylor, John H. *Egypt and Nubia*. Cambridge: Harvard UP, 1991.

New Trends in the Sierra Leonean Novel: Tradition & Change in Novels by Alasan Mansaray and J. Sorie Conteh

Eustace Palmer

The present writer once expressed the view that the Sierra Leonean novel would reach a very significant stage in its development when Sierra Leoneans from the interior (as opposed to Freetown and the Western Area) begin to write and to utilise their rich traditional heritage in their works as Achebe and other African writers have done. There is every indication that this is happening now. A discernible trend in the emerging Sierra Leonean novel is precisely this preoccupation with the presentation of traditional society. Of all the earlier Sierra Leonean novelists, only Sarif Easmon could be said to have given the issue much concern, and his portrait of traditional Mende society was open to objections from several angles, not the least of which was that it could not be said to be a presentation from the inside. Recent novels by Alasan Mansaray, Tibbie Kposowa and J. Sorie Conteh are now setting the record straight and presenting the experiences of their characters against the background of a vibrant traditional heritage, showing how that heritage sustains the characters or that they turn their backs on it or try to subvert it at their peril. This paper will be a study of Alasan Mansaray's *A Haunting Heritage* and J. Sorie Conteh's *The Diamonds*. It will explore, among other issues, the authors' preoccupation with tradition versus the new. In Mansaray's case, the new consists of the protagonist's experiences in the United States, while in Conteh's case change consists of attitudes induced by the new diamond and wealth-grabbing culture.

Alasan Mansaray's *A Haunting Heritage* is that celebration of aspects of Sierra Leonean indigenous culture which some people might have looked for in vain in the Sierra Leonean literature hitherto published. Alasan Mansaray belongs to the Mandinka, an ancient and notable West African people now found in several West African countries whose remarkable history goes way back to medieval days and famous empires like Mali and Songhai and whose kings include almost legendary figures such as Mansa Musa and Sundiata. The novel revolves around the experiences of a young graduate and civil servant, Yaya LaTale, who discovers to his dismay that he has been selected by his dying grandmother,

Fatu, to succeed her as one of the two traditional bone-healers in the entire country. Apparently, bone-healing is a mystic art entrusted to a select few. Each practitioner practices the art in the traditional milieu until his or her death. Shortly before this event, however, the identity of the successor, who has actually been selected by the spirits of the ancestors, is communicated to the selected individual and to him or her alone, by the dying predecessor. The person selected has no choice but to accept, for refusal would incur the wrath of the ancestors and would lead to certain madness and possible death.

One can therefore understand the predicament of this young and promising graduate who, after obtaining an honours degree from his country's only university and an important position in the civil service, seems set for a brilliant career and comfortable life in modern Sierra Leone, identified in the novel as Manika Kunda. His selection at the early age of twenty-five, as the successor to the traditional bone-healer, means that he must abandon all this and retire to a remote part of the country (the village of Taenyadu) without adequate transportation, electricity, or running water and all the other appurtenances of modern life, an environment within which his painfully acquired Western education would probably be quite meaningless. And he seems to have no choice. Yaya seems trapped by the demands of an exacting traditional culture which he, in spite of his Western education, has always respected, but which now seems determined to shatter all his plans.

One cannot resist the temptation to compare Yaya's predicament with that of Egbo in Soyinka's *The Interpreters*. Both are young intellectuals who have been exposed to both African and Western culture, the traditional and the modern, and who are now called upon, not to reconcile the two or to simply interpret one to the other, but to choose one and abandon the other. Egbo is called upon to abandon his colourless though lucrative modern job in the Nigerian Foreign service and become his grandfather's successor as traditional ruler of his people within the traditional milieu. It is a position which would enable him to be of real service to his people. Similarly, as traditional bone-healer, Yaya would be saving lives and being of service not only to his tribe, but to the entire nation. But Egbo, at least, has a choice; indeed, he chooses in the end to throw his lot with the modern and abandon the traditional. Yaya has no such choice. His destiny has been mapped out for him by the ancestors, and we sense a hopeless feeling of entrapment and a desperate but unavailing desire to escape:

> We're now going to seal your new carved bond with the ancestors who passed down this gift to us. And then I'll leave you in the hands of their spirits for companions....
>
> *Not quite yet, Grandma Fatu*! he tried to get up, to run and free himself, but he felt glued and had no control over his body, even as his mind kept telling him: '*Run, run, run, Yaya!*'

> He realized it was hopeless. He tried to speak but his mouth was heavy. There were tremors in his temple, yet he couldn't utter a word. Yaya wished to scream: 'No, Grandma, no! Please let me go! I don't need this gift or any bond! I love my ancestors and that's enough Now, can't you see, this is not for me? I already have a career in the civil service and I live differently in Sobala. Please, it's a big family. Give it to Wusu, your son, or anybody, but ...
> Grandma Fatu had gotten up. She came to stand over him, casting a shadow over his body like a cage. (161)

In his despair, Yaya consults Kondorfili Bonsor, the only other traditional bone-healer in the country, in the hope that the latter would understand his predicament and be in a position to advise him. However, he does not know that Kondorfili is an evil man, secretly envious of Grandma Fatu's success and reputation and longing to be the only bone-healer in the country and the only possessor of the secret. He is therefore enraged that this sacred gift has been passed on to this modern upstart Yaya, who does not deserve it and does not want it anyway. He therefore wrongly and maliciously advises Yaya that he could avoid the consequences of the gift by fleeing the country for the United States and staying away for twenty-six moons or two years after his grandmother's death. The will of the ancestors, according to Kondorfili, cannot cross the great ocean, and after twenty-six moons have elapsed they will be forced to give the gift to another member of the family and leave Yaya alone. The innocent Yaya does not know that the wrath of the ancestors can pursue him even beyond the great ocean and bring him to a disastrous end. This would suit Kondorfili's evil plans, leaving him the only possessor of the secret of bone-healing in the entire country. The unsuspecting Yaya, who, like a number of other young Manika Kundians in particular and Africans in general, has often thought of the possibility of going to the United States to further his education and escape the economic, political, and social malaise at home, hurriedly makes his plans and leaves for the Western world.

The stage is therefore set for one of the novel's main preoccupations, the presentation of the clash between the old and the new, or the traditional and the modern. On another level, this concern could be regarded as a study of the clash of two opposing cultures, the Sierra Leonean and the Western/American. In a sense, the art of bone-healing could be regarded as being symbolic of the traditional; therefore, in fleeing to the United States and rejecting the call to be a traditional bone-healer, Yaya might seem to be turning his back on all that is best in African traditional life and culture. This is certainly how the ancestors see it; to them he seems to be an African apostate or renegade, though, paradoxically, he is much prouder of and more responsive to African culture than most of the Manika Kundians he meets in the United States. He is not the typical westernised or detribalised African. This pride in African culture even includes his attitude towards the practice of bone-healing, even though he would rather not be a bone-healer himself.

The art of bone-healing is certainly invested in the novel with great mystique as it is in actual Sierra Leonean life. As in the novel, the art is passed down from generation to generation to selected individuals. Real-life bone-healers perform near miracles of healing, often curing individuals who could only have looked forward to amputation if they had gone to the Western style hospitals. These bone-healers give the impression that their power is derived from some supernatural source. When a patient is brought along, the healer will ask for, among other things, a white chicken. After saying incantations in which it would seem as if the assistance of the ancestors or gods is being invoked, the healer will break the chicken's leg and set it free, before proceeding to the physical aspects of the curative process. All this would seem to invest the procedure with a mystical aura because it would seem as if the assistance of supernatural powers is being invoked and that the healer derives his or her powers from that source. There are those, however, who claim that the procedure is perfectly scientific and shows the advances that African science has made. They claim, for instance, that when the healer breaks the chicken's leg and sets the chicken free, it is not to suggest or invoke any supernatural intervention (as it is in the novel), but merely to gauge, scientifically, the passage of time and the progress of the curative process, for she assumes that bone is bone and that the chicken's broken bone will heal at about the same rate as the broken human bone.

In the novel itself there is no doubt of the supernatural mystique with which the art is invested. The secret is a gift from the ancestors who carefully select the recipient, and that recipient is not permitted to reject it. The recipient is trained through mystical dreams, and the chicken's leg is broken in order to discover from the ancestors whether the healer should proceed with the cure in question. If the chicken, on being released, walks away normally immediately after its leg is broken, then it's a cure the healer can proceed with; if it does not, then the patient's broken bone was not caused by natural means, but by witchcraft, and the healer cannot proceed. The entire bone-healing process involves several factors such as sacrifice (the sacrifice of the chicken as well as of the selected healer who must sacrifice everything else), the noble art of healing and mending what has been broken, the power and assistance of the ancestors and of the supernatural, service to the community as a whole, and African knowledge at its best. This is why it represents the best in African life and culture at a time when much in African life is being derided and why it becomes symbolic of the traditional.

We see the celebration of the beauty and validity of that tradition and culture not just in the scenes which are set in traditional Africa, but in some of those set in the United States. Some of them are deliberately intended as set pieces. This is true, for instance, of the naming ceremony of the kakay baby. It is presented as a significant rite of passage and invested with a grandeur which understandably makes Yaya proud to be an African and a Manika Kundian, and which gives tremendous meaning to the lives of all those participating. Throughout his stay in the United States Yaya is proud of his culture and views with dismay the ridiculous efforts of those, like his friend Basi, who seem bent on doing everything to distance themselves from that culture and pretend to be Americans, and, in the process, doom themselves to extinction.

All this suggests that although the celebration of African culture and tradition is an important concern in this novel, another major preoccupation is the experiences of Africans in the United States and their relationships with African Americans. Indeed, this novel's greatest claim to attention is, perhaps, that it is one of the few written by an African to present an extensive study of the experiences of the increasing number of Africans immigrating to the United States. It seems likely that this will be a significant trend in the development of the African novel in the early part of the 21st century. The experiences of African Americans in Africa have been extensively covered; witness Alice Walker's *The Color Purple* (1982) and *Possessing the Secret of Joy* (1992). It is refreshing to have the picture from the other side. Americans are accustomed to regarding their country as a land of freedom and opportunity beckoning to the dispossessed and the disadvantaged all over the world to go and find refuge there. The traditional wisdom is that if these new immigrants are determined and hardworking there is no limit to what they can achieve. This is the American dream. Little do Americans know that for a good number of immigrants, particularly those who are people of colour, this is far from being the true situation. The brutal and barbaric sodomisation of a Haitian and the senseless killing of a Guinean, both acts perpetrated by law enforcement officers in New York, have probably alerted the American public to the true situation that many immigrants of colour have to endure. It is issues such as these that this novel explores.

The fact is that many Africans arriving in the United States are immediately drawn into the chaotic vortex in which many African Americans find themselves and they begin to share in the prevailing African-American experience of oppression and racial discrimination. Ever since their separation which began in the 16th century with the slave trade, the two peoples have actually had a shared experience consisting of oppression, discrimination and deprivation. In the case of the African Americans, oppression took the form of slavery and all its attendant circumstances, while in the case of the Africans it was the oppressive force of colonialism; in both cases racial discrimination was one of the attendant forces of oppression; in both cases, also, deprivation was a common denominator. In the African-American situation it was an accompanying factor of slavery and is a product of modern inequity. In the African case it is a consequence of corruption and political and economic mismanagement.

The experiences of both peoples are very similar. In the United States itself, however, Africans seem to operate under a kind of double jeopardy.

Not only are they drawn into the vortex of oppression, racial discrimination, and deprivation from which African Americans suffer, they are also the victims of occasional xenophobia. The moment they open their mouths to speak and it is realised that they have 'an accent' they are subjected to additional discrimination.

Many Africans immigrating to the United States look forward to living in a land of freedom and plenty where their lot will be infinitely better than it was in their countries of origin. This is partly due to the reputation that the United States has acquired as a land of freedom and opportunity and partly to the deliberate lies told by fellow African immigrants returning home for the holidays. Unwilling to give the impression of being failures or of barely surviving, they spin fantastic yarns of incredible wealth and splendor, thus creating traps for the unsuspecting and the naive. The hero of the novel, Yaya LaTale, is one such naive African at the start of his American Odyssey. Dazzled by the all-encompassing signs of material progress and technological advancement he sees around him on his arrival, he is full of praise for the American system and, in a sense, could hardly wait to begin to be Americanised. Gradually, however, his eyes are opened to the reality of oppression, racial discrimination, and inequity. Indeed, Yaya's progress is from naivety to knowledge and the gradual removal of his blinkers.

The process of Yaya's education begins almost immediately after his arrival when the car in which he and his four friends are driving is quite unjustifiably stopped by the police, in a blatant display of racial stereotyping, and they are given a ticket for alleged speeding. He learns that some of his friends, in spite of their hard work and enviable qualifications, are still almost at the bottom of the employment ladder. Abu Janneh, who worked hard through school and earned a degree with a major in finance and a three grade point average, is still, at the age of twenty-eight, delivering newspapers to residential areas and pizza to hungry customers, in spite of the fact that he is the proud possessor of a 'Green Card'; Sidi, Yaya's host, who had struggled his way through school, working hard and playing by the rules and eventually graduating summa cum laude with a degree in civil engineering, had first to take a job as a cleaner and then as maintenance man in a hotel, the most junior of a crew 'of basically high school graduates, most of whom bossed him all day' (195). When Yaya takes a walk around the neighbourhood he finds that the mainly white inhabitants cast suspicious glances at him because they feel he must be a thief intending to break into their cars or highjack them. It is ironic that most of these incidents happen in Philadelphia, 'the City of Brotherly Love', home of the Liberty Bell, and the place from which the Declaration of Independence and the Bill of Rights were proclaimed. The reader sympathizes with Yaya as he languishes month after month without any employment or means of support and gradually comes to feel that he was better off in his native land even with all the problems that he had there.

Yaya discovers to his chagrin that there are certain areas in the United States where the people are as deprived as those in many developing countries. He learns, for instance, that the Fifth Ward of Mansfield, North Carolina, where Sidi's wife Pat comes from, is 'even worse than some villages in Third World Africa' and that on visiting the neighborhood one is confronted with 'hopeless poverty and misery' (205). Worst of all, however, is the unspeakable violence resulting from America's gun culture. Yaya had already been given a foretaste in the story of a friend of his who had gone to the United States but had been put back on the next plane and returned to Manika Kunda, because the Peace Corps friend who was supposed to meet him at the airport and be responsible for him had been killed half an hour earlier by a stray bullet in a drive-by shooting. Now the violence is forcefully brought home to Yaya by the constant whining of police and ambulance sirens and the senseless murder of his friend and patron, Basi, in Houston, Texas.

The situation is further compounded by the unrealistic expectations people back home have of Africans who migrate to the United States. To many of these people the United States is a modern El Dorado where the streets are paved with gold that is available for the taking. The combination of the extended family system and these unrealistic expectations places an intolerable burden on the new immigrant. For instance, soon after Yaya's arrival in the United States and while he is still unemployed and penniless, he receives a number of letters from back home. One is from a distant relative whom he had not seen for twenty years and whom he cannot remember, but this man wants him to buy him a wheelchair, send him one thousand dollars as a contribution to the repair of a family home and another one thousand dollars for his own personal expenses, and take responsibility for the further education of his eldest son in the United States. One is from his former girl friend, Abie, who had unceremoniously ditched him in Freetown for a doctor, but who now wishes Yaya to send for her so that they can be married. One is from another former girl friend who makes the same proposal, and the last is from an old friend, Sam, who wants Yaya to lend him money to get him to the United States and pay his college fees.

It might have been expected that because of their history of shared experiences Africans and African Americans would get on very well together in the United States. The reality, however, is quite different. The problem is partly caused by preconceived notions on both sides. Basing their judgement on the movies of American life that are exported to Africa, a number of Africans see African Americans as barbaric gangsters, drug addicts, and dropouts who would shoot and kill one without notice if provoked. Similarly, African Americans, basing their views on Tarzan movies and one-sided news features from CNN, see Africans as kinky-haired, dirty, malnourished individuals constantly engaged in barbaric civil wars. The problem is also partly caused by cultural differences which are themselves the result of four hundred years of separation. Africans value the extended family system which ensures that kinsmen take care of and show hospitality to each other wherever they may be, whereas rugged American individualism dictates that everyone should look out for himself or herself. Also, the African practice of polygamy is likely to be regarded with horror by the African American who, like other Americans, has accepted the one man one wife concept, even though, in reality and practice, the average American male is probably just as polygamous as his African counterpart. In the African social context women are generally subordinate and show deference to their males and there is a strict division of roles. It is generally the African wife who cooks and cleans up after her male, and most African males would consider involvement in such tasks demeaning. The American wife, on the other hand, demands equality and flexibility in the allocation of roles.

All these problems are crystallised in the relations between Yaya's Manika Kundian friend and host Sidi, his African American wife Pat, and Yaya. Pat is one of those African Americans for whom the African heritage and African values are completely meaningless. As far as she is concerned, her husband's resources must be spent entirely on them; none of it must be squandered by being sent to Manika Kunda to help out indigent and lazy relations, even if they are her husband's parents. She regards Yaya's sojourn with them as an unwarranted intrusion into her private space and another example of a lazy African freeloading on his friends. When her husband Sidi innocently and politely converses with his countrywomen at the naming ceremony, she flies into a jealous rage, seeing it as an example of the polygamous African's desire for affairs with multiple women. This most unattractive woman is superbly characterised by Mansaray as a woman without culture, manners, or refinement. She has no qualms whatever about referring to another black person as a 'kinky-haired African nigger' and threatening to turn his 'black ass' over to the immigration authorities. She seems to represent the worst of American life.

However, Mansaray is anxious to underscore the fact that not all African Americans are like Pat. There is the genial and friendly Bill, who has been to Africa and is a friend of Africans, and there is Basi's exemplary wife, Joy. Indeed, one of the hallmarks of this novel is the careful contrast between two sets of African/African American married couples: Sidi and Pat and Basi and Joy. The contrast could not be more marked. The vulgar, xenophobic Pat is obviously the dominant partner in her relationship with Sidi. She shows no respect whatever for Sidi's relations, friends, or culture, and can sit in the living room, nonchalantly manicuring her nails, while her husband is in the kitchen laboriously frying chicken for her to take to the Kakays as her own contribution to the food for the naming ceremony. It is almost as though she feels she has done Sidi a favour by marrying him, and while she talks to him in any way she pleases and even threatens the use of violence, he does everything to ensure that he does not ruffle her feelings. On the other hand, Joy, the highly educated, highly intelligent and civilised university graduate and devoted Christian, defers to and respects her husband. Though Basi is, in some ways, a rotten husband who stays away from home as often as he can and even has extra-marital affairs, Joy performs her marital duties to perfection, taking very good care of her home and her husband and never raising her voice to him. Unlike Pat, Joy has tremendous interest in and respect for African culture, and she does her best to alleviate Yaya's frustrations and to get him to settle down to life in the United States. And yet, one never forms the impression that Joy is soft or passive. Indeed, she is a quiet tower of strength who believes in harmony rather than disruption and is quite capable of rebuking her husband for his snobbery, insensitivity, and indifference towards Yaya and his problems. The two Sierra Leonean husbands are also opposites. Sidi is more pliant and accommodating. He is proud of his indigenous culture and aware of his responsibility to help his cousin Yaya. On the other hand, the snobbish, inflexible, class-conscious Basi wishes to become completely Americanised and shows no concern for his culture. Far from helping Yaya with his problems, he reduces him to the status of a servant, refers to him as a primitive African straight from the bush, and then ignores him.

Mansaray's characterisation in *A Haunting Heritage* is quite commendable. The portrayal of Sidi and Pat is particularly well done. Mansaray is able to penetrate Pat's psyche and display the basis and motivations of her actions and conduct and, by the use of powerful dialogue, he also convincingly portrays the relations between this couple. The portrayal of Basi and Joy is also excellent. Joy's self-sacrificing goodness does come through without any hint of sentimentality. If there are any reservations about the characterisation at all, they would concern the portrayal of the protagonist, Yaya. This is not to imply that the characterisation is not compelling; in many ways it is. Once Mansaray gets Yaya on to American soil his portrayal of him is outstanding. The reader does feel his frustration, restlessness, stress, anxiety, and internal torment as he is relentlessly pursued by his grandmother's spirit and wonders whether the curse would be accomplished or not. However, one does not quite get the same feeling when Yaya is on Sierra Leonean soil. For instance, shortly after being informed about his selection by the ancestors and the threatened curse should he decline, Yaya is supposed to deteriorate quite fast, to the point of losing his job and neglecting his girl friend. However, the reader does not feel this deterioration; we do not sense the damage done to his psyche or his emotions in quite the same way in which we feel it when he relocates to the United States. Similarly, the motivation for Kondorfili Bonsor's evil schemes is not convincingly done. Of course, his advice to Yaya is essential in order to get the latter to leave the country and relocate to America, but the suggestion that Kondorfili does this largely to bring about Yaya's destruction and ensure that he, Kondorfili, will now become the sole possessor of the gift of bone-healing is difficult to accept since he himself sincerely mentions the possibility that the ancestors would name another practitioner of the art if they could not get Yaya.

Towards the end, the novel almost assumes the quality of a thriller as the reader also wonders whether the ancestors will get Yaya in the end. Mansaray's skill in creating tension and suspense at this point is admirable. The dramatic irony contributes to the tension since the reader, having been exposed to the antics of Kondorfili Bonsor and the divination of Cherinor Tejani Jalloh, has crucial information that is denied to the protagonist, Yaya, and knows, therefore, that the latter is in even greater danger than he supposes.

In the end, Yaya does not have to pay the penalty for declining the role the ancestors have imposed on him. The novel therefore ends happily for him and is rescued from a tragic conclusion. However, there are a few problems with this conclusion. In the first place, the problem of an outdated and constricting traditional practice is not solved. The reader has felt the restriction on Yaya's personal freedom very powerfully and his virtual enslavement by the dictates of a tradition with which he was unfamiliar. In the end he is released from it, not because the ancestral spirits conjured up by Cherinor Jalloh see the rightness of his cause, but because in punishing Kondorfili their need for vengeance has been satisfied. Yaya, they say, was misled by Kondorfili into thinking he could run away. But the problem was caused, not by Yaya's running away, but by his rejection of his selection. The ancestors continue to insist on the justification of their selection and on the need for obeying it. One wonders who their next victim would be and whether he or she would have any chance of avoiding a totally unwelcome destiny. Part of Mansaray's problem is his failure to find a linguistic medium which convincingly conveys the aura of supernaturality in this novel. The conjuring of the spirits of the dead ancestors as well as those of the living Yaya and Kondorfili Bonsor and their being brought together in a kind of trial would be acceptable if the author somehow convinces us to suspend our disbelief. This could have been done had the author contrived the appropriate setting and linguistic register. The reader must be convinced that the creatures speaking are really spirits and not human beings using at times a mundane, ordinary style of delivery. The conjuring scene lacks awe, majesty, and grandeur and sounds throughout like an everyday gathering of village elders settling a petty local dispute. The spirits of the ancestors fail to carry conviction. When all is said and done, however, Mansaray's achievement in *A Haunting Heritage* is highly commendable, particularly for a first novel.

J. Sorie Conteh's first novel, *The Diamonds*, explores a subject that has had tremendous fascination for Sierra Leoneans in general and is beginning to take hold of the imagination of writers in particular. Indeed, it seems very likely that the emergence of a 'diamond' literature will be one of the most striking developments in the Sierra Leonean literary scene in the 21st century. Actually, the trail had already been blazed by Prince Dowu Palmer, with the publication in 1982 of his accomplished, but sadly neglected, novel, *The Mockingstones*. Palmer's concern was with relationships and the way in which the country's citizens had allowed foreigners to determine these and everything else associated with the diamond industry. Similarly, J. Sorie Conteh presents the devastating impact of diamonds on the very fabric of the nation.

That Sierra Leoneans should be so obsessed with the impact of diamonds is perfectly understandable. Their discovery in 1929 was supposed to herald the country's transition from a very poor colony of the United Kingdom to a wealthy and prosperous nation with every one of its citizens benefiting from the fabulous gems. However, those were the days of colonialism and the diamond wealth was exploited for the benefit, not of the citizens of Sierra Leone, but of the colonial power. With the advent of independence and the end of empire, however, it was felt that the people would now begin to enjoy the fruits of their God-given resources. This was not to be. The enormous wealth accruing from the diamonds was now going to be enjoyed by a few members of the political elite, their relations, and hosts of foreigners in league with the politicians, while ordinary Sierra Leoneans continued to languish in poverty, and the actual diamond-bearing areas of the country continued to look like the most under-developed and abused areas of the world. What should have been a blessing, therefore, turned out to be a curse, as diamond exploitation and its consequences took a severe toll on every aspect of the nation's life. Unfortunately, this has been very powerfully reinforced recently by the vicious civil war which was really about who should control the nation's diamonds. The barbaric atrocities that were committed in that horrible strife are an indication of the depths to which human beings can sink in order to secure, not so much power, as wealth, in this case, wealth from diamonds. For a fairly lengthy period, the rebels were in control of the diamond producing areas, and the proceeds from their diamond smuggling activities not only enriched their leaders and some foreign powers who also wanted a piece of the action, but also enabled them to buy terrible armaments with which they continued to terrorise and brutalise the nation. No doubt, we will soon see the appearance of novels detailing the atrocities committed in that war and the contribution of diamonds to the process. Indeed, because of their very nature and the way in which they have been used in Sierra Leone, diamonds can become a prism through which writers interested in social comment could view the decadence of the nation.

In the meantime, Conteh has written an accomplished novel presenting the devastating consequences of diamond exploitation on almost every aspect of the nation's life: on personal relationships, on morals, on traditional life and mores, on married life, on agriculture, and on the development of children and youngsters generally. The events of the novel revolve around the fortunes of the protagonist Gibao. At the start he is a young farmer who is perfectly attuned to his traditional environment. He has mastered most of the traditional skills, has lived his life according to the traditional mores, played his traditional roles very competently and is enormously successful. He reminds one of Okonkwo in Achebe's *Things Fall Apart* (1958), who has similarly tried to live his life according to what he considers the traditional mores, has lived up to the traditional aspirations of his people, and has earned their respect. Here is what Gibao's society thinks of his accomplishments:

> He was now a grown man with three wives and six children. He was the most successful and accomplished farmer around his home village called Semabu. He was a hunter, fisherman, palm wine tapper, carver and good dancer. The people admired him and were proud of him. None of his equals nor his elders could defeat him in a wrestling contest. (10)

Does this sound familiar? However, unlike Okonkwo who achieves greatness by trying to be everything that his father was not, Gibao succeeds by measuring up to the demands of his father. By sheer determination, hard work, and adherence to the society's mores, Gibao has reached the pinnacle of success in his traditional milieu. But he is still not another Okonkwo because, unlike Okonkwo, he does not radiate the same force of character and he soon becomes dissatisfied with the traditional life he has lived so successfully and succumbs to the temptations of greed and the seductive power of diamond wealth. His life, which from then on is one of progressive deterioration (although he does not realise it), is an object lesson about the insidious and destructive power of diamonds and about the way in which even the best individuals can become dehumanised and ultimately destroyed by its seductive allure.

Gibao's deterioration and ultimate destruction are foreshadowed by some early symbolic events and scenes in this novel which makes very compelling use of symbols and images. At harvest time Gibao's mother notices that her son has moved from the traditional merriment and is sitting meditatively by himself on what he took to be a big log but is actually a mortar. However, it is a taboo for men to sit on a mortar. The traditional wisdom in this part of Africa is that men who sit on mortars in which women pound food could eventually become impotent. Gibao is subverting the traditional, even if unconsciously, and he will pay the penalty by becoming impotent in the ultimate sense of the word. His very 'unconsciousness' is significant because he seems to be totally unaware of the possible disastrous consequences of what he is about to attempt – traffic in diamonds. We are also informed that at birth Gibao's placenta 'was buried near the kola tree, which then became more than just a tree' (4). We shall soon see the enormous symbolic significance of the kola tree; however, it is necessary to mention now that the burying of his placenta in his village suggests his link to the village and traditional life and in wishing to leave the village he is turning his back on traditional life, on life itself, and on his responsibilities, cutting the umbilical cord as it were, and committing an act which is potentially self-destructive. As his mother says, 'Sewa can destroy you'(12).

Images of light and darkness permeate the novel at this stage. As Jibao continues to sit on the mortar regardless of his mother's warnings we are told that 'it was now very dark, oppressively dark, the moon having set' (9). Then as Gibao leaves his village for the diamond areas he points a small torch he is carrying straight ahead and moves into the darkness. We are told that he 'traveled by torchlight now towards a strange mysterious place...' (34). The passage demonstrates the total inadequacy of the light by which Gibao hopes to see. Far from seeing, he will be morally and spiritually blind and will end up being engulfed by the darkness. However, the most powerful symbol at this stage is that of clothes. Gibao leaves his village in his normal clothes, but once he gets to a stream, the threshold as it were, he changes his entire outfit completely in order to suit himself for the new life in the urban, diamond bearing area:

> He opened his suitcase and changed his khaki shorts for a pair of white trousers.... He took his powder, the latest in Bintu el Sudan, rubbing some on his face and on his neck. The powder blotched parts of his skin while giving him a conspicuous look, as if he had just graduated from a secret society dubbed with a white clay.... He put on a red shirt.... He dressed himself this way in a bold attempt to look like an educated person from Moyamba, rather than like someone from a remote village. Gibao looked at himself in a pocket mirror and smiled. He looked like a caricature, some overdressed doll, like one of the scarecrows he used on the farm. (34–5)

His new dress suggests his complete transformation from someone who was morally sound to one who is ridiculous and morally decadent. Gibao had looked much more dignified in his villager's rags than in his modern clothes, which he deliberately chooses now that greed, materialism, and the desire for diamond wealth have taken complete possession of his personality.

From now onwards, Gibao plunges into the corrupt and immoral diamond mining world of Sewa and he does so with tremendous relish, although there are several portents, like the ghastly deaths of some other miners, warning him of the possibility of disaster and destruction. In order to acquire wealth in the diamond mines, Gibao must be prepared not just to dig but to steal diamonds from his master and sell them illicitly. Gibao will go back on his word and his oath, forget his extended and polygamous family whom he had abandoned in his home village, plunge into immorality and consort with prostitutes and the wives of other men. Indeed, at this stage in the novel, Conteh concentrates not so much on Gibao's avarice and greed, as on his moral and spiritual degeneration. The more wealth he acquires, the more he degenerates.

Although Gibao has become wealthy, and although he had been warned by diviners that he must return home as soon as he had acquired sufficient wealth, he is unsatisfied and wishes to go on acquiring more and more. The insidious power of the diamonds and of greed has eaten into the very fabric of his nature and he is now prepared to play God and manipulate natural and supernatural phenomena to ensure further wealth. Gibao who had believed in the value of life and that 'the finality of death should be treated with soberness, deep concern and regret' (96) is now prepared to engage in human sacrifice in order to ensure material success, without the least thought about the value of the life of the individual he is about to sacrifice. He is so blinded and degenerate by this time that it does not even occur to him that he is about to commit the most terrible crime. He has become completely dehumanised, completely without a conscience and all sense of morality. Eventually, the murder is discovered; he is arrested, tried and executed; and his entire family is dispersed. It is to this that his inordinate desire for wealth has led him.

The events of the novel are played out mostly in Sewa, an area that Conteh would have us believe is the major diamond producing region of Sierra Leone. The author would also have us believe that all the vices abound in this area on an exaggerated scale. It is verily a den of iniquity: murder, quarrelling and fighting, adultery, infidelity, robbery, drunkenness, and prostitution. The sanctions and taboos that helped to knit traditional society and gave it its aura of stability, dignity and respectability are completely absent here, as everything takes second place to the relentless drive for wealth. Individuals, who were dependable husbands and fathers and who, within the extended family system, provided for the not-so-fortunate, plunge into decadence and immorality in Sewa and turn their backs on their traditional responsibilities. It is a dog-eat-dog society in which only the strongest survive. Men who were considered ideal and exemplary in their traditional environment easily become corrupt and decadent in the mining area and might even descend to murder. The scramble for diamonds can also mean the breaking up of the secure family unit as men abandon their wives and other members of their families and head for the diamond areas where they easily become prone to sexual temptation. The moral imperatives of the traditional environment are completely overturned in Sewa, for diamonds and decadence go together. The scramble for diamonds also causes depopulation in the rural areas as everyone – men, women, and children – abandon their homes and converge on Sewa 'like hungry vultures on a carcass' (33). It was generally believed 'that if children deserted their homes one would only have to journey to Sewa to find them. If a wife was missing, she could be found in Sewa' (33). Indeed, Conteh gives the most thorough-going and realistic presentation that has ever been attempted of the inner workings of the diamond industry and the diamond rush in Sierra Leone and its destructive impact on the country.

Most striking of all in the description of Sewa is the extent of sexual decadence and immorality. Prostitution is rife as even the married women become prostitutes in order to obtain the material benefits that their husbands cannot give them. One wife puts it this way: 'You see you men want to be proud of your wives to show them off as beautiful, decent, well-dressed and well cared for but you don't want to provide for them. That is why we also look for boyfriends. Don't you know the saying in Sewa these days that one man cannot fill a suitcase?' (164) Married men, too, consort with prostitutes and have no qualms about making these affairs public. It seems as if it is the accepted norm that every individual, male or female, must be having an illicit relationship of one kind or the other. Given the normal traditional attitudes, it is the behaviour of the married women that is most astonishing. We are told that women in Sewa do not love one man (88). All of Alhaji's eight wives, for instance, have their lovers or unofficial husbands with whom they spend most of their time and to whom they are much more devoted than the husband they clearly do not love. And all this is public knowledge. It seems as if even the cuckolded husband knows about it but is prepared to turn a blind eye as long as there is no scandal: 'Since their marriages to Alhaji, each wife had been unfaithful, but, thank God, there had been no open scandal. A few times Alhaji had suspected them, scolded them, and even threatened them, but mostly he had left them in peace, because the outside world was not aware of the suspicions' (135). Another husband, Gibao himself, can even say to his own wives, 'I know all of you have male friends. But, be careful about my workers…'(195). This is arguably the most astonishing statement made in the entire novel. The husband, in other words, is prepared to permit his wives to take lovers, as long as they don't compromise his authority by having affairs with his workers. We recall that Gibao himself was launched on the road to prosperity by having an affair with one of his own boss's wives.

Inevitably, a novel of this kind will address issues around the condition and status of women, a subject that the African novel was very much concerned with in the last quarter of the 20th century. There is every sign that this preoccupation will continue well into the 21st and that it will be a major concern of the male Sierra Leonean novelists. Where some African writers have been accused in the past of failing to present the totality of the African woman's experience or of ignoring the African woman's point of view, this charge could hardly be laid at Conteh's door. He shows a remarkable capacity for presenting the inner character of the women in the novel and for describing experiences from their point of view. Conteh's presentation is rounded and quite objective and it seems that this might be a continuing trend in the Sierra Leonean novel. Conteh describes the traditional preference for boys as the means of carrying on the line. He also shows the misery of the wife in a polygamous household when, on one of the few nights in the week that it is her 'turn' to be with him, her husband ignores her completely either because he is drunk or because he has his mind on other matters such as diamonds. For many of these men wives are nothing more than objects in their special collections designed to show off their wealth. This is certainly true of Alhaji, an old man who already has seven wives, most of them young, and who is so far from satisfying them that they all have lovers outside the home. However, Alhaji is already negotiating for the eighth wife, and spending money lavishly on her, though there is little chance that he will achieve his aim.

Conteh shows that fathers have proprietary rights over their daughters and the final say as to their choice of husbands. Indeed, the daughter has no say in the matter at all; she simply has to marry a husband chosen for her by her father. We therefore experience the misery of a young and gifted girl like Ntuma who is removed from school at the age of about sixteen and forced to marry an illiterate old man who already has six wives. She thus becomes the latest item in his collection. We feel a tremendous sense of wasted potential, for all the signs suggest that had Ntuma been allowed to finish her education she could have gone on to do great things. Instead she degenerates into an embittered woman who enjoys little empathy with her co-wives and indulges in disastrous extra-marital affairs.

Examples of male egoism, irrationality and harshness abound in the novel. For instance, Ntuma's father, a fanatical orthodox Muslim, always blames the mother for their daughter's sexual indiscretions and proceeds to punish both mother and daughter. We are told that he had sent away one of his wives and her daughter because the latter had become pregnant; both mother and daughter had never been heard of again. When Ntuma's infidelity forces her to leave her husband's house and she goes back to her parent's home to take stock of her situation the father once more blames the mother and rails at both of them:

> 'Now look at your eldest daughter,' he started scolding Hawa. 'You have no blessing with her. That is why Satan can succeed in misdirecting your own daughter. You are all infidels! Let me tell you. The fire of hell will consume you all. And I have warned you all. The fire of hell is ten times greater than the fire on earth. So! You and your daughter should prepare to be consumed by that fire. Believe me. When that time comes and I am called to rescue you, I will disown you. You daughter, leave my house today. I cannot accommodate sinners, and my word in this is final'. (167)

That he has largely contributed to the disaster by forcing his daughter into a loveless marriage does not even occur to him. When it is discovered that Ntuma's sister, the unfortunate Tewoh, has also been sexually precocious, the father badgers both the daughter and the mother until the latter becomes seriously ill. There is a Sierra Leonean proverb, mentioned in the novel, to the effect that there is no bad bush into which to throw a bad child. In other words, no matter how much a child has transgressed he or she must still be kept within the family fold and shown love and compassion. Ntuma's father's principles and conduct run completely counter to this traditional wisdom, for he believes in casting out delinquent children, especially if they are girls.

However, in the treatment of the feminist theme Conteh shows commendable balance of judgement. If the men are harsh, dictatorial, and inconsiderate, the women too can be callous, selfish, and vindictive. If the men are polygamists, the women seem for all practical purposes to be polyandrists. We have already seen that women in the Sewa environment do not believe in having just one man; all of them have multiple lovers and they display the fact openly. Indeed, these 'unfaithful' or polyandrous wives seem to have their own unwritten codes designed to ensure that matters do not get out of hand and take a disastrous turn, as they do with Ntuma's affairs. The senior wife in a polygamous household even seems to give mini lectures to the younger wives on how to conduct their extra-marital affairs successfully. The women are quite capable of open rebellion and of standing up to those of their men who do not realise that in the transformed social and economic situation in Sewa the gender playing-field has been more or less levelled. Thus when the weak Kemoh attempts to upbraid his wives about their sexual infidelities they laugh at him derisively and make no attempt to conceal their scorn. 'He felt sorry himself because of their apparent lack of respect. Age was catching up on him. Years ago none of his wives would dare cough when he spoke. Now they made fun of him' (147). In this new social environment the women are far from being victims. While the men seem emasculated, the women are very much more spirited. No male approaches Ntuma, Fudia, or Yebu in courage, spiritedness, or audacity. Indeed, some of the women act irresponsibly and contribute to the disasters that overtake others. By having an affair with the married man Gibao, by marrying him and encouraging him to be unfair to his other wives, Ntuma makes a major contribution to the other women's misery. She knows she is deliberately upsetting the traditional arrangements, but she disregards this in her own self-interest.

Inevitably, the issue of polygamy is extensively explored in this novel. The conventional wisdom has been that polygamy thrives best in the traditional areas where it has the backing of traditional sanctions, where the men adhere to the rules and fulfil their obligation to be fair to their wives, and where they have the authority to control them. As long as he is content with his lot in the traditional milieu, Gibao is a model polygamous husband. The moment, however, that he begins to dream of diamonds and of wealth is the moment that his rapid deterioration commences. Once he gets to Sewa he becomes a poster boy for marital infidelity both before and after his wives join him. He is neither fair, nor does he possess the strength of character to keep his wives in order. Thus when he buys a new house and opens a shop he places his favourite and most recent wife Ntuma in charge when by right and tradition that position should have gone to a more senior wife. He conspires with Ntuma who is determined to undermine the position of the other wives and thus he accelerates the household's slide into chaos and dysfunction. In his novel Conteh gives one of the most realistic analyses of the situation in a polygamous household that has ever been given. He shows the myriad jealousies and suspicions; the groupings and cliques; the frustrations, cruelties and misery; the contempt for in-laws; and the desire for revenge.

Like Mansaray, Conteh gives a compelling portrait of traditional society. He is particularly skilful at presenting the charm and mystique of the process of divination and he shows that in the traditional milieu the diviner is justly admired and respected. In the debased world of diamond mining, however, even the once revered process of divination has become considerably tainted. The diviner, no less than any other individuals, has become engulfed in the drive for illicit wealth and has lost sight of his traditional function. While the diviners in traditional society revelled in the fact that they appeared poor and lived in very humble circumstances, Pa Finoh, the leading diviner in Sewa, glories in his wealth, drives his own Mercedes Benz and insists on a haughty dignity. He has no qualms about stipulating the murder of an innocent girl and fails to see that this is inconsistent with his role, not only of diviner, but also of Islamic Imam. Pa Finoh's conduct is the ultimate index of society's degradation and corruption in the unrelenting pursuit of diamonds and wealth.

One of the most compelling aspects of Conteh's art is the use of symbols and images. We have already noted the use of images of light and darkness and the symbolic use of clothing. Equally powerful is the symbol of the kola tree. The novel in fact begins with the kola tree and Gibao's conviction that his life has received its sustenance from the roots of that tree. The kola nut, of course, is extremely important in West African life. It is supposed to be nourishing and sustaining. It gives energy and diminishes hunger. It is widely used in rituals of all kinds and is regarded as life-giving and life-sustaining. This is the role the kola tree plays in the novel. It is the force that has sustained Gibao's life in the traditional milieu and is therefore partly responsible for his success. When Gibao sat under the tree he felt he was communing with the ancestors who inhabited the area around the tree. His umbilical cord was buried near the tree. When, therefore, Gibao decided to go away from his traditional milieu he was severing his connection with the umbilical cord and removing himself from the protection of the ancestors and the life-sustaining kola tree. It is significant that at the end he is executed on a gallows made from the kola tree. The kola tree is there at the end as it was at the beginning. It is thus the symbol of continuity. Tyrants, thieves, murderers, and other corrupt human beings will come and go, but the kola tree will live on as the symbol of the life-sustaining and life-giving forces of nature and of tradition.

These two writers have demonstrated in their individual ways that Sierra Leonean fiction has at last come into its own. Their novels are a good indication of the direction in which the Sierra Leonean novel will move in the early 21st century. It will be increasingly written by people who are in close touch with the indigenous tradition and it will combine a powerful presentation of traditional life with brilliant evocation and convincing characterisation.

WORKS CITED

Achebe, Chinua. *Things Fall Apart.* London, Heinemann, 1958.
Conteh, J. Sorie. *The Diamonds.* New York: Lekon New Dimensions Publishing, 1997.
Mansaray, Alasan. *A Haunting Heritage.* Dallas: Sahara Publishing, 1995.
Palmer, Prince Dowu. *The Mockingstones.* Harlow, Essex: Longman, 1982.
Soyinka, Wole. *The Interpreters.* London, Heinemann, 1965.
Walker, Alice. *Possessing the Secret of Joy.* New York: Harcourt Brace Jovanovich, 1992.
——. *The Color Purple.* New York: Harcourt Brace Jovanovich, 1982.

Transcultural Identity in African Narratives of Childhood

Richard K. Priebe

In thinking about our children, real or imagined, we are impelled to think about the future. In writing about children, no less than in having them, we think about possibility. We hope our children will make a better future by learning from our mistakes, and in narrating the lives of children we can show a future we imagine as well as a present and past we wish to improve. This is no less true if the child we create in our narration is based on our own earlier self or is totally fictional. A natural symbol of the future everywhere, the child has particular resonance across Africa as a cultural icon, and it is thus not surprising that over the past fifty years a good number of the best narratives being produced by African writers have focused on children. Sometimes autobiographical, sometimes fictional, and often a mix, these narratives sometimes focus just on the early years of the child and sometimes take us from childhood through adulthood. Elsewhere I have shown that these narratives constitute a new genre I call the African Childhood, though here I wish to examine what this genre might point to about its future in African literature, especially in relation to a very basic and defining element.[1] African Childhoods are always about identity formation and growing up in a multicultural/transcultural world. What critics once discussed as the theme of being 'between two worlds' is more accurately in these narratives the story of two transitions: from child to adult and from monocultural to transcultural world. I intend to examine this point in relation to three relatively recent Childhoods, but will first establish some historical context through brief attention to some earlier Childhoods.

The best-known narrative of African childhood is also one of the first, Camara Laye's *L'enfant noir* (*The Dark Child*, but also published in English as *The African Child*). It is so well known that the text overshadows our thinking on all other Childhoods. The grammatical and rhetorical impact of the English translations of the title, even more than the original French title, inscribes this autobiographical novel in our consciousness as the urtext about the identity of the African child, an identity primarily defined in terms of race and continent and not by specific nationality, ethnicity, or even gender. Coming just a few years later, William Conton's novel, *The African* has a title that has a similar grammatical and rhetorical effect, only generalizing the idea of identity to include all Africans regardless of age.

The African, a novel informed by a very Pan-African vision of identity, came out in 1960, something of a watershed year in terms of the great numbers of African countries that gained or were about to gain their independence. The protagonist, Kisimi Kamara, grows up in a fictional West African British colony, receiving his education there before going off to England for his higher education. So far it is like *L'enfant noir*, but this Childhood extends into the adulthood of the protagonist. He returns and with the help of friends from various ethnic groups, friends met in his secondary school years, unifies the ethnically fractured colony to unity and independence. He and the head of another newly emergent African country share a vision of doing the same for a united Africa. The name of Kisimi's country, Songhai, is of course the same as one of the great medieval empires of the Western Sudan, and is in the same referential mold followed by real post-colonial African states such as Ghana and Mali. The idea of a historical link to a unified nation state is explicit in the text, and the idea of English as being a unifying language is implicitly there in the childhood base of the novel. The idea of linguistic unity is, of course problematic, and Conton rather awkwardly tries to get around it by making Kisimi a linguistic prodigy who picks up languages very quickly.

Conton, who died in 2003, lived a peripatetic life that broadly reflected that of Kisimi. Born in Gambia in 1925, he was educated in Gambia, Guinea, Sierra Leone, and England after which he held various posts in education in Ghana and Sierra Leone. As reflected in *The African*, he held a deep belief in the power of good English and the importance of understanding history as shown in his having written a two-volume study of West African history. Conton's life and work clearly reflect the major concern with generic African identity formation that we find in the Childhood, and rarely, if at all, does the genre show any concern about identity in a national state.[2]

The exception that proves the rule is Nuruddin Farah's *Maps*, the story of a boy's search for his identity within the nation state of Somalia. The title, however, is the give-away; born in a disputed border area between Somalia and Ethiopia, the Ogaden, Askar finds that clear borders of his identity are as difficult to map as the shifting borders of what he wants to think of as his father's land and his mother's land (though he is unsure even of their origins). His self-interrogation leads him to trace ethnic, linguistic and gender connections as he searches for stability in his perceived national identity, finding only that one needs multiple perspectives on, and 'maps' for, one's identity. Ostensibly, Tahar Ben Jelloun's novel, *L'enfant de sable* (*The Sand Child*), is also about a character who from birth is associated with a nation, in this case Morocco. When Ahmed is born his father has an announcement printed in a 'great national newspaper' that his son's 'birth will bring fertility to the land, peace, and prosperity to the country. Long live Ahmed! Long live Morocco!' (19). Ahmed, however, is not really a son, but a daughter. As with *Maps*, the title points to lack of stability in identity, since Ahmed and Morocco are both metaphorically aligned with the shifting nature of sand.

The titles of African Childhoods are instructive in terms of what they say and what they fail to say about place in identity formation. In a moment we'll come back to this, but first let us turn our attention to some general observations about how the child, any child, first maps out his or her place in the world. The primal connection is with the mother. With some mobility we begin to develop a sense of spatial borders – crib, room, house, yard, etc. I remember when I was in my last year in elementary school I would draw concentric rings in my notebook with myself at the center, then the classroom, the school, the town, and onward out to include progressively larger places in the universe. I was not alone in this exercise for my classmates would make similar drawings and we would compete to see who could come up with the greatest number of rings. I remember one classmate cleverly 'winning' through going in two opposite spatial directions with the circles. Within the self there was the stomach, then a cell, and then whatever particles on the molecular and atomic levels my classmate was aware of. I happen to be European American and my 'winning' classmate was African American, but ethnic identity was, I think, incidental to our egocentric exercises. Needless to say it was a déjà vu moment when years later I saw young students in Nigeria playing their own version of this game. We all seek the ordinate points of our existence, and that seeking is ultimately ontological, epistemological, and historical as well as spatially physical. Askar in Farah's *Maps* was engaged in similar exercises, though ostensibly driven by a need to find his ethnic essence.

Wole Soyinka's memoir of his early years is one of the most profound of the explorations of these ordinate points of identity. The title, *Aké, the Years of Childhood*, refers both to the place where his earliest memories of cognitive connection with the world began and to the temporal process of expanding beyond that beginning point. Like the clever classmate of my youth he also works backward as he maps out his concentric circles in writing a prequel to his Childhood, a biography of his father, *Ìsarà, A Voyage Around 'Essay'*. Soyinka himself in his introduction to Ìsarà, a work that had its origins in a moment of discovery of some of his late father's papers two years after he had finished *Aké*, makes the connection between the two works. The first part of the title of the biography, *Ìsarà*, refers, like *Aké*, to a place of origin, only in this case his father's hometown. The 'voyage' of the subtitle is his journey of discovery of his father, identified here by his nickname 'Essay'. The father's name, we have learned in *Aké*, is derived from the initials, S.A., which are further

44 Transcultural Identity

derived from an English/Yoruba bilingual pun. But the name, 'Essay', is also associated with what the father, a teacher, does and is thus a rather complex trope. Ultimately, both books are complex explorations, as in the mode of the essay as form, of Soyinka's essay-like impulse to answer the Montaigne question of *qui suis-je*, and what he finds goes well beyond the boundaries of his Yoruba hometown, or the nation of Nigeria.

In the multitude of African Childhoods one has to search long and hard to find the very rare ones that have titles or even subtitles referring to either specific ethnic or even national identity. Virtually all make reference to a generic quality, a generic process, or a generic state, with the occasional reference to a specific place, often a village or city. Hence, to name just a few, we have *The Narrow Path* by Francis Selormey; *Une vie de boy* (*Boy* or *Houseboy*) by Ferdinand Oyono; *Martha Quest* by Doris Lessing, *L'aîné des orphelins* (*The Oldest Orphan*) by Tierno Monénembo; *Notes from the Hyena's Belly* by Nega Mezlekia; *Tell Freedom* by Peter Abrahams; *Child of Two Worlds* by R. Mugo Gatheru; *De Tilène au plateau: Une enfance Dakaroise* (*A Dakar Childhood*) by Nafissatou Diallo; *Nervous Conditions* by Tsitsi Dangarembga; *The Children of Soweto* by Mbulelo Vizikhungo Mzamane, *The River Between* by Ngũgĩ wa Thiong'o, and the only Childhood title I know with a reference in the title to a nation, *Kaffir Boy: The True Story of a Black Youth's Coming of Age in Apartheid South Africa* by Mark Matabane. All of these works have appeared between the 1950s and the present and all, with varying emphasis, deal with the struggle and process of negotiating and finding a sense of identity in the midst of multiple linguistic, ethnic and cultural possibilities within the protagonist's community and even his or her family.

Here I wish to shift specific focus to three fairly recent Childhoods that I have chosen because they represent the great ethnic and geographical diversity of the genre while showing, often unwittingly, an increasing attention to an emergent transcultural identity in the Childhood. One is by a Nigerian writer who is currently living in England. This very autobiographical novel narrates the experience of a young girl who is sent to England by her warm and loving West African family for her education and shows her search for a stable identity in the midst of all the social and cultural change she experiences. The second is by a South African writer who recently left South Africa to live in Australia and the US. This work is a very novelistic autobiography that tells of a young boy growing up in South Africa in a very troubled family, and his going off to school and searching for a stable identity in the midst of the linguistic and cultural duality he experiences. The third is a novel (in no way autobiographical) by a Congolese writer currently living in the US. This work narrates the lives of two teenagers, one male and one female, who have neither parents nor school and must struggle with matters of basic survival while forging stable identities in the midst of apocalyptic violence.

I've mentioned these three works in rather flat generic terms in order to highlight some basic elements of similarity and difference, one common element being the search for stable identity in the three narratives. Before going into the particulars of the three narratives, I want to make a point about the fragility of cultural identity from my own family experience. My wife's ancestors were Pennsylvania Dutch (speakers of a form of creolized German). My father emigrated from Germany and my mother was third generation American from Pennsylvania. My wife and I have always thought of ourselves as Northerners – even though we have now lived most of our lives in Richmond, Virginia, well below the Mason Dixon line (a line that linguists tell us decides whether you pronounce the 's' in 'greasy' as a 'c' sound or a 'z' sound). Many years ago when our then ten-year-old son came home from a history lesson in elementary school, he inadvertently taught us a lesson about how easily cultural identity changes from generation to generation. Proud of what he had learned that day he told us at dinner, 'I am really happy that we lost the Civil War.' My wife and I stared blankly at each other for we were not part of the losing side of that so-called 'war of northern aggression' and thus his 'we' was not ours.

Shifting to a more inclusive 'our', I make an obvious point: our agricultural grandparents had a cradle to the grave charter that allowed for stable transference of cultural identity from one generation to another – mobility, literacy and education have fractured that charter. The particulars of how that happened in Africa account for the particulars of the African narratives of childhood. I thus want to look less at what constitute new developments in these narratives and more at the elements that tie them together across time and place.

Detail in any narrative, fictional or autobiographical, works only if it is well shaped into significant form. Simi Bedford's *Yoruba Girl Dancing* (1991) often fails in this, but it is an interesting work nonetheless, given what it shows of the narrator/protagonist's troubled search for her ethnic identity. It also succeeds in showing the fiction of truth and the truth of fiction (elements of autobiography versus the novel) that we find in most good Childhoods. Bedford starts her autobiographical novel with scenes involving the large extended family of Remi Foster, the central character. Remi has spent most of her early years in the home of her wealthy grandfather where she was raised by several aunts and relatives. One of the aunts is originally from Warri, and is thus possibly Uhrobo, an ethnic group of the Niger delta. The relative she is closest to, known only as Bigmama, is a white English woman married to the grandfather. Bigmama never had any of her own children but did raise all her husband's. Remi's parents live in Enugu in Eastern Nigeria where her father is a lawyer. Remi is close to her parents, but for practical reasons never made very clear, Remi needs to spend most of her time in Lagos. The title at first seems most curious as it refers to Remi's sense of her identity as Yoruba.

She lives in a Yoruba part of Nigeria, and she speaks Yoruba as one of her languages, but her relatives are not Yoruba, and one infers that her first language was probably English. In the second sentence of the novel we learn that in her house in Lagos they spoke four languages 'and two of them were English' (1). Thus we understand that Standard English and Pidgin English are spoken in addition to Yoruba and Fante, and that Remi's parents prefer to live in an Ibo-speaking part of Nigeria. In effect, Remi lives in, and is connected to, a very creolised world, a very multicultural/transcultural world.

Bedford's narrative broadens and deepens our understanding of the complexity of this creolised world and Remi's somewhat confused sense of identity in it. Yoruba children taunt the young Remi calling her 'oyinbo' (white person) when they hear her speak English even though they can see she is black. We learn that Remi's blood grandmother, the woman with whom the grandfather had several of his children, was Fante and that her grandfather's great great grandfather had been a slave who had left America after the Civil War and settled in Sierra Leone. Oral family history has it that the great grandfather had proof that his ancestors had originally been from near Abeokuta, a Yoruba city in Nigeria. The grandfather, who lived for a while in England, where he studied law, settled with his English wife in The Gambia before moving to Lagos. The family background to her identity is more nomadic than national.

Much of the novel focuses on the shock and adjustment that Remi experiences in going off to England as young teenager to a girls' boarding school. She faces the expected encounters with white racism and some unexpected problems trying to identify with the West Indians she meets. At the edge of adulthood Remi meets some Nigerian students in England and inexplicitly asserts her Yoruba identity, ending the narrative with a rather awkward turn as so much of the work has been a celebration of her transcultural, even transnational roots.

Where Bedford announces specific identity in her title, another author hides it in a generic title, but the sense of alienation in relation to a transcultural reality is much darker and much more clearly apparent in J.M. Coetzee's *Boyhood*. While it is not surprising that *Yoruba Girl Dancing* is told in the first person, it is rather curious that Coetzee's more explicitly autobiographical work is told in the third person. His is a more bare bones psychological narrative on the trauma of growing up with one's identity being wrenched in an emotional tug of war starting with an overly protective mother and an alcoholic father. The book ostensibly chronicles the love and resentment the child has in relation to the mother and the growing disdain he has for his father, but this Freudian family romance is really a side issue. More fully at the centre of this powerful drama is the rejection of an Afrikaans' identity, a strong, even erotic, identification with South African coloureds, and the forced acceptance of an identity as English South African. There is a strong sense of guilt at being born white and great resentment at being born poor, lower class – the shame, as it were, in discovering that you are poor, white trash.

Though he has recently received a lot of general attention as the 2003 Nobel Laureate in Literature, the fourth African writer in less than twenty years to receive this prize, it is important to know that Coetzee writes in English, that he is in fact an accomplished author who writes only in English. From *Boyhood*, however, we learn that his parents are Afrikaans but spoke only English at home and sent their son off to English-speaking schools where, as in other parts of his life he learns, we are told, to live like an imposter. One time he comically and not very successfully tries to pass himself off as Catholic, but most of the book is simply a meditation on his failure to fit in.

Oddly, as with much in this book, the young Coetzee loves the time he spends on his uncle's farm in the high, dry *veld*. In this we see a convention common to many African Childhoods starting with the earliest ones where city and country contrasts dominate the narrative. We see this, for example, both in Laye's *L'enfant noir* and Lessing's *Martha Quest*. In *Boyhood* Coetzee emphasises a very conventional pastoral contrast showing the poor and restrictive suburb where his family lives in opposition to the relative's farm which offers space and freedom. In relation to the farm he even comes close to reflecting affectionately on his father as he remembers moments they had hunting together, however inept his father was as a hunter. But on the farm, no less than at home or in school, he finds himself to be a stranger in a strange land, as language and race both prove to be barriers to his sense of self. He is attracted to the coloured hired help on the farm, but confused by the apparently contradictory rules of proximity and distance he must maintain in relation to them, and shocked by the cruel way the help is treated under cover of a professed paternalism. The resistance of his relatives to speaking to him in Afrikaans further confuses him as he knows the language well. So strictly tied is the narrative to the restricted awareness of the boy that we never get direct commentary or even speculation about why some things are as they are. Narrative choice looks more and more like an artful ruse where presumed objectivity of third person narration hides subjective resistance to full disclosure of the elements that went into shaping young Coetzee's awareness of self. Essentially, the narrative choice is but an inversion of what we find in Bedford's novel, where first person narration with the real names changed is also but an artful ruse in which pretended subjective narration hides resistance to full objective disclosure.

In almost all African Childhoods education is shown as *the* way of transcending the limits of the identity given us by birth. In traditional, non-literate societies our identity is set by our lineage. Education is thus a tool for empowerment regarding individual choice, but the literacy it produces comes with a broader sense of transcultural identity.[3] Education, not surprisingly, is equally important in both *Yoruba Girl Dancing* and in *Boyhood*. Most of Bedford's book focuses on the education Remi receives in England, as much of Coetzee's book focuses on his formal education in South Africa. In the end, *Boyhood* comes together more as a portrait of the artist as a young man as the boy's identity grows out of a necessity, as he announces at the end, to hold stories in his mind and tell them. Exile will follow as we learn in the companion memoir, *Youth*. But this is no retelling of a Joycean European Childhood for this is, as are all Childhoods, a politically charged work, and it is clearly in the protagonist's academic and intellectual success that a positive vision of his adult identity is molded.

Emmanuel Dongala's *Johnny chien méchant*,[4] our third Childhood, shares with Coetzee's work in having an interesting and artful narrative strategy, though it is on the surface quite different from the work of either Bedford or Coetzee. Dongala focuses on two sixteen-year-olds, a boy and a girl, and their parallel but contrasting narratives about their reactions to, and involvement in, a violent and genocidal struggle in central Africa. It is in no way autobiographical as are the Childhoods of Coetzee and Bedford, but in every respect it shares the basic generic qualities of all African narratives of childhood. *Johnny chien méchant* also belongs with a particular group of recent Childhoods that focus on genocidal violence where children are both perpetrators and victims. Tierno Monénembo's *L'aîné des orphelins*, Nega Mezlekia's *Notes from the Hyena's Belly*, and Ahmadou Kourouma's *Allah n'est pas obligé* being some of the other works in this group. *Johnny*, though, is *sui generis* in having two children as central characters.

Childhood, however specifically constructed in a given culture, is a period of protection from adult responsibilities with regard to the creating of life, the protection of life and the taking of life. Formal education thus tends to extend childhood beyond puberty when the child has begun to gain the physical abilities of the adult. It allows time for completion of socialisation and positive identity construction, time surely needed given the complications brought about by literacy and multicultural realities. Johnny, the man-child of Dongala's novel appears almost as a natural born killer, pure id with no social restraints. But Johnny's narrative is darkly comic as we see him and his friends, having been taught by adults how to discount the ethnic Other, adopt and adapt individual and group identities based on names they know from action films, pop culture and pop history. Thus, though engaged in real fighting in the Congo, they see their enemies as another 'tribe' they call the Chechens. They play at adopting identities, but it is deadly play. One thus adopts the name 'Rambo', another the name 'Giap', and yet another is simply called 'Mâle-Lourd'. Johnny runs through several names for himself and his gang. All their names and actions simply reflect young male hormone-driven fantasies run amuck. With their AK-47s in hand they wantonly steal, rape, and kill. Much of the comic irony of this tragic-comedy comes from Johnny's sure sense of himself as an intellectual, superior not only to those he rapes and kills, but also even to his friends. He is part Siegfried and part young Faust, a child intellectually and emotionally incapable of seeing he has made a pact with the devil, and all his lustful gratification will come not simply at the expense of destroying others but himself as well.

Dongala's novel, however, is no simple *Lord of the Flies* story of unsupervised youth. Johnny's story is parallelled with Laokolé's story, the story of a sixteen-year-old who must become mother to her mother and to her brother. To be sure, Laokolé and Johnny are diametrically opposite in their affective responses to the world. They look at the same moon and one sees beauty and hope where the other sees nothing but evil and threats. Most telling, however, is that Laokolé wants to be an intellectual and has all the natural talent for it, seeing both beauty and power even in a well-constructed wall. She also knows she has much to learn, and can even appreciate the knowledge of those who live in traditional societies. Rational and intelligent, she cannot accept essentialist difference based on racially, ethnically, gendered or culturally, perceived difference that fuels Johnny's sense of alienation. Johnny, in contrast, is taught and accepts an artificial construction of ethnic difference and the idea that the Other is always threatening. He can thus easily rationalise killing anyone not of his group as easily as he kills anyone who has something he wants. At the same time he has no trouble rationalising away the fact that his girlfriend is of the same ethnic group as those he would exterminate as vermin. Perception is reality and the two perceptions, two very different realities of Johnny and Laokolé, converge ironically in the end, showing one position to be based on false notions of scientific and humanistic understandings of the world.

Dongala clearly accepts, even embraces, the transcultural reality of Africa where the Childhoods of Coetzee and Bedford recognise that reality but struggle against it. Noteworthy also is the fact that Dongala's achievement comes without his denying the importance of being connected with the specific cultures that are undergoing transformation. Laokolé flees the ashes of destruction carrying on her back her crippled mother (an intriguing image of the past here) and goes into an uncertain future with her younger brother. She is unable to save either, but we see in her actions a symbolic transformation that shows she has the right stuff to face and make her new world. She goes through her own *rite de passage* that includes a reconnection with the traditional world in the rain forest she runs to in order to find protection. She finds that protection and is ritually cleansed by the torrential rains. It is no accident that in the end we see her transformed into a mother, not by a reproductive act, but in her saving an abandoned child who is now her child. There is a marvellous sculpture in the National Museum of Florence that is a concrete correlative to the idea Dongala embraces. Bellini, an Italian Renaissance sculptor, has given us a symbolic representation in marble of Virgil's epic,

The Aeneid. Aeneas fleeing from the ashes of Troy, heading off to found a new culture that will be Roman, carries on his back his father (the heavy, but necessary weight of the past) and holds the hand of his son who pulls both father and grandfather into the future.

Science is part of the transcultural world that Laokolé embraces, a world where equality of potential is not limited by socially constructed identities of race and gender. It is no accident that Laokolé dreams of being a scientist, dreams that are based in her own empirical understanding of the world. Johnny, of course represents another transcultural possibility, but it is only a *cul-de-sac*, a dead-end future of a deadened soul. With Johnny no viable identity formation is possible. He is without parents and without any sense of his own past, and he has survived only by creating himself out of the superficial and destructive images he has gleaned from the media of a global pop culture. Thinking himself an intellectual, he cannot think and has no way to see himself as the pastiche of those images he has become. If, as the socio-biologists tell us, we all have selfish genes that assure the survival of our genes through altruism, his genes are wired for self-destruction, as he has no understanding of how he can be his own father of the man. He can procreate, but he cannot create. His sense of the future is as shallow as his sense of intellect and education. In the end we learn that Johnny will never again even be able to procreate. The poetic justice of his sterility/castration fits into the scientific thrust of what the novel says about a transcultural world and makes the novel into a virtuoso triumph, a tour de force.

These three Childhoods, tales of four children, share other defining qualities of the genre, qualities that are very much interconnected,[5] but they share the key element that has become increasingly prominent in the most recent Childhoods, namely the focus on identity construction and the adjustment to living in a complexly multicultural/ transcultural world. Despite the remarkable generic stability of the African Childhood over the past fifty years, the form has shown, as evidenced by these three works, great and varied possibilities for aesthetically rich and powerful narratives. The genre continues to be written by writers who come from almost every geographical area in Africa, a fact that likely reflects the increasing presence of the transcultural theme and the likelihood that we will see an increasing number of works written in this genre well into our new century. It is, in conclusion, worth emphasising this point and noting that a slight shift in the generic qualities of the African Childhood over the past fifty years may reflect a very big social and cultural shift on the continent that these writers are addressing. The earliest writers of Childhoods were addressing concerns about new bi- or even tri-cultural identities (see for example Laye) against an emergent print culture. The most recent writers of Childhoods appear to be addressing a concern that a shift has taken place, that instead of living in a multicultural world made up of easily identifiable cultures, we are living in a more fluid transcultural and even transnational world. The three primary authors I looked at in this study are all, like many contemporary African writers living in exile from Africa. Their children, if they become writers, are likely to be even more transcultural and transnational than their parents. Fifty years ago Marshall McLuhan gave us new buzz words that have long since become old clichés about the global village and the medium being the message. These new African Childhoods give us a fresh perspective on McLuhan's observations.

NOTES

1 The term Childhood as a literary genre was first advanced by Richard Coe in his study of autobiographical narratives of childhood, *When the Grass Was Taller*. Coe's idea of the genre as being primarily autobiographical and apolitical works rather well for most of the examples he draws on, but his inclusion of African literature is very limited and misleading. See note 5 below for the defining characteristics of the African Childhood.
2 In his book, *Tell Me Africa*, James Olney made a very strong and interesting case in 1973 for the idea that there is an almost allegorical connection between the author's identity and Africa in Conton's novel as well as Laye's *L'enfant noir* and several other African autobiographical narratives.
3 A good example of this is to be found in Buchi Emecheta's *The Joys of Motherhood* where we see the literate children moving away from the expected prescribed roles for them in their parent's traditional world.
4 Given the centrality of childhood in two of Emmanuel Dongala's earlier novels, Le feu des origins (*The Fire of Origins*) and *Les petits garçons naissent aussi des étoiles* (*Little Boys Come from the Stars*), they too are African Childhoods.
5 What distinguishes the African Childhood is a combination of six factors: 1) a focus on education, generally formal classroom education and the acquisition of literacy; 2) identity formation; 3) growing up in a multicultural/transcultural world (between two worlds, the story of two transitions: from child to adult and from monocultural to transcultural world); 4) a clear presence of the political context in which the child is growing up; 5) an unusual power the child has in actuality or potentiality; 6) an allegorical connection between the child and Africa; and 7) exceeding versus succeeding one's parents. Two other elements pertain to many of the narratives. There is often a tension between city and country where country tends to represent the past and the city the future of the protagonist. Additionally, there is often the fact of the protagonist going into exile on reaching maturity and thus effecting a rupture in the allegorical connection with the condition of the land.

WORKS CITED

Abrahams, Peter. *Tell Freedom: Memories of Africa*. New York: Knopf, 1954.
Bedford, Simi. *Yoruba Girl Dancing*. New York: Penguin, 1991.
Ben Jelloun, Tahar. *L'enfant de sable*. Paris: Éditions du Seuil, 1985. (*The Sand Child*. Baltimore, MD: Johns Hopkins University Press, 2000.)
Coe, Richard N. *When the Grass Was Taller: Autobiography and the Experience of Childhood*. New Haven: Yale University Press, 1984.
Coetzee, J. M. *Boyhood*. New York: Penguin, 1997.

———. *Youth*. New York: Penguin, 2003.
Conton, William. *The African*. London: Heinemann, 1960.
Dangarembga, Tsitsi. *Nervous Conditions*. London: The Women's Press, 1988.
Diallo, Nafissatou. *De Tilène au plateau: Une enfance dakaroise*. Dakar: Les Nouvelles Editions Africaines, 1975. (*A Dakar Childhood*. Trans. Dorothy S. Blair. Essex: Longman, 1982.)
Dongala, Emmanuel. *Johnny chien méchant*. Paris: Le Serpent à Plumes, 2002.
———. *Le feu des origins*. Paris: Éditions Albin Michel, 1987. (*The Fire of Origins*. New York: Lawrence Hill Books, 2003.)
———. *Les petits garçons naissent aussi des étoiles*. Paris: Le Serpent à Plumes, 1998. (*Little Boys Come from the Stars*. New York: Farrar, Strauss and Giroux, 2001.)
Emecheta, Buchi. *The Joys of Motherhood*. London: Heinemann, 1979.
Farah, Nuruddin. *Maps*. New York: Pantheon, 1986.
Gatheru, R. Mugo. *Child of Two Worlds*. London: Heinemann, 1966.
Kourouma, Ahmadou. *Allah n'est pas obligé*. Paris: Éditions du Seuil, 2000.
Laye, Camara. *L'enfant noir*. Paris: Librairie Plon, 1953. (*The Black Boys: The Autobiography of an African Boy*. Trans. James Kirkup and Ernest Jones. New York: Farrar, Strauss and Giroux, 1954.)
Lessing, Doris. *Martha Quest*. New York: Viking, 1952.
Matabane, Mark. *Kaffir Boy: The True Story of a Black Youth's Coming of Age in Apartheid South Africa*. New York: Macmillan, 1986.
Mezlekia, Nega. *Notes from the Hyena's Belly*. New York: Picador, 2000.
Monénembo, Tierno. *L'aîné des orphelins*. Paris: Éditions du Seuil, 2000. (*The Oldest Orphan*. Trans. Monique Fleury Nagam. Intro. Adele King. Lincoln: University of Nebraska Press, 2004.)
Mzamane, Mbulelo Vizikhungo. *The Children of Soweto*. Harlow, Essex: Longman, 1982.
Ngũgĩ wa Thiong'o. *The River Between*. London: Heinemann, 1965.
———. *Weep Not, Child*. London: Heinemann, 1964.
Olney, James. *Tell Me Africa: An Approach to African Literature*. Princeton, N.J.: Princeton University Press, 1973.
Oyono, Ferdinand. *Une vie de boy*. Paris: Julliard, 1956. (*Houseboy*. London: Heinemann, 1966.)
Selormey, Francis. *The Narrow Path*. London: Heinemann, 1967.
Soyinka, Wole. *Aké, the Years of Childhood*. London: Rex Collings, 1981.
———. *Ìsarà, A Voyage Around 'Essay'*. New York: Random House, 1989.

The Marks Left on the Surface
Zoë Wicomb's *David's Story*

Kenneth W. Harrow

David's Story places us between two locations: that of the subject, with his doubts, flaws, subjectivity, and language – his story; and that of the movement, the struggle, the national stage of history, with which he intersects. Between the two are those stories of Dulcie, the scribe, David's mother and grandmother, and all the other women whose appearances and narratives revise both his story and the history, not into a series of herstories, but into a deconstruction of History. For this dramatic passage, we need to re-place the site of the body into the narrative, rather than to use it as a springboard for the analysis of the 'real' motives of personal or historical action. That is where torture comes in. In *Discipline and Punish* (1995), Foucault refers to its 'trace' in the modern penal system where the notion of punishment has not been entirely expunged from the penal discipline based on correction and cure. Where else should we look for that trace except on the body, the soles of the feet, the diamond marks etched on the skin? What's more, the trace encompasses more than the immediate political moment, with its threats of betrayal, the dangers of spies having infiltrated the movement, the loss of agents, or the dismantlement of a network. The traces that are carried along into the currents of immediate political action, that ride on the basic assumptions of truth and struggle, are markers of an age and its power/knowledge. Thus, as with the earlier autocracy of David's forefather le Fleur and the passage of the Griquas across the land, so too the importance of the remote backwater Kokstad lies in the trace that is left in the narrative. The history of great criminals of the 18th century in France was recorded on the surface of society in broadsheets, similar to what we would nowadays identify with market or popular literature in Africa. There it was that regicides or murderers might be transformed into legendary folk heroes:

> Black hero or reconciled criminal, defender of the true right or an indomitable force, the criminal of the broadsheets, pamphlets, almanacs and adventure stories brought with him, beneath the apparent morality of the example not to be followed, *a whole memory of struggle and confrontations*. (67, my emphasis)

The 'struggles and confrontations' were revised in the narratives: the villains turned into 'black heroes', and most of all the coercion employed by oppressive ruling powers was refigured in the traces left in the memory of those who retold these stories. What is crucial to grasp here is how this passage from an overt use of torture before the demise of the Ancien Regime to the enlightened penal system of the 19th century marked the ascendancy of the new disciplines of knowledge and power. This is where David's story now should be situated – in the postcolonial period of transition, a transition whose oblique lineaments only now begin to emerge in Wicomb's account.

When we turn to Foucault to explore that transition, we find ourselves faced with the same limitations that inspired Ann Stoler to write *Race and the Education of Desire* (1995), that is, his failure to note the importance of colonialism in the development of his thesis on the development of sexuality as an instrument of power in *The History of Sexuality*, vol. I. Similarly for us, the transition from a regime of torture to one of Reason, as given in *Discipline and Punish*, is too narrowly defined as it is limited to the French hexagon. Foucault writes:

> The reduction in the use of torture was a tendency that was rooted in the great transformation of the years 1760–1840, but did not end there; it can be said that the practice of the public execution haunted our penal system for a long time and still haunts it today. (15)

Foucault goes on to develop the historical sequence that saw the gradual change from a system of publicly displayed punishment whose use of torture was intended to impress the masses with the power of the sovereign, to one in which the totally sequestered and sanitised practice of capital punishment, when still carried out, was thought to have been the response to a humanitarian impulse of reform. In short, in his terms, we passed from punishment to discipline, from the direct expression of public power to the internalisation of systems of control through a panopticon of ubiquitous surveillance. And despite the disclaimer that traces of the former practices still subsist, along with the features of the struggles they were intended to end, the precise dating of the transformation makes clear that the changes in the penal system, the forms of its prisons, its rationalisations, its publicity, were directly linked to the contemporary technologies of power and of the body that extended to all spheres of society and of social thought.

However, nowhere in *Discipline and Punish* do we see the broader picture of punishment as meted out in the 'hinterlands' of Empire. Elsewhere literary and historical accounts abound in the details of this system. We might note the openly brutal, public display of severed hands, or even heads, that appeared not only in Conrad's fictional account of Kurtz's compound, but in the quite real collection stations spread throughout King Leopold's Congo in the last decade of the 19th century and the first of the 20th century, as so well described in Adam Hochschild's *King Leopold's Ghost* (1999), to appreciate how colonial systems of mineral, rubber, and ivory extraction relied upon the earlier forms of punishment. Hochschild estimates that five to eight million lives were lost during the rapacious decades of Leopold's Congo Free State, and similar estimates of brutal rule and punishment, with a proportionate loss of life, were made with regard to the construction of the railway in the French Congo across the river from Leopold's Congo. Forced labour was employed for road gangs throughout Africa during much of the colonial period. Whippings were routinely administered in Cameroon during World War II when Cameroonians failed to meet their quotas in the collection of rubber. Physical exactions, sometimes disguised under the clothing of public works, and frequently associated with large plantation labour practices, were the order of the day during most of the colonial period.

Mbembe (2001) makes the point that the great autocrats who assumed power in the 1960s and 1970s were equally determined to make public displays of their exalted positions by public punishments. When the former prime minister of Cameroon, Paul Mbida, challenged Ahmadou Ahidjo early in 1962, he and his colleagues from the United National Front were imprisoned. Mbida remained in a cachot, not unlike those dark cells lacking light described by Foucault; and the effect was the same: When Mbida emerged years later, he was blind, and the story of his punishment was made known to all Cameroonians.

Similarly, South African brutalities, witnessed in the 18th and 19th century genocides of the Khoisan and of the Khoikhoi, did not simply cease without a trace with the arrival of 'enlightened' British rule. Just as Leopold created a vast publicity campaign around the notion of ending slavery so as to mask the atrocities carried out by his agents, by the 'Force Publique', so too did the British abolitionist rhetoric mask the despoliation of African lands and displacement of the majority of the population by successive white governments throughout the entire period of British colonial and white South African apartheid rule. In fact, we cannot limit the ravages of colonial rule simply to the application of brutal force. John Comaroff (1997) shows how the arrival of British nonconformist missionaries from 1810 to 1840 corresponded to the institutionalisation of three types of colonialism that link us closely to the changes in Europe signaled by Foucault in *Discipline and Punish*. The first is identified as 'state colonialism', and involves the extension of rule over territories inhabited by Africans (179). Here, although concerned with exploration and dominion, the policies were informed by the rhetoric of abolition (notably, abolition of slavery, not the death penalty) and of civilization. The missionary John Moffat stated in 1842, 'It is a wise policy in Government, to render every facility to the advancement of knowledge and civilization among the aborigines' (180). Even without the explicit language of discipline, it is clear that conquest was joined with the Enlightenment project, and specifically with its methods of control. Comaroff writes, 'State colonialism, as I said, was to change over time. It would involve, in due course, the imposition of taxes, the limitation of chiefly authority, and many other (typically legalistic, punitive) *forms of regulation* (180, my emphasis).

Most distant from the explicit language of Enlightenment values was 'settler colonialism', in this instance that associated with the Boers' expropriation of African lands in their Great Trek north in the 1830s, and in their virtual enslavement of the conquered populations. But even there, Afrikaner apologists offered defences that relied on similar understandings of social functions and obligations: They had, so the argument goes, 'conferred free citizenship on people like the Southern Tswana. In return for protection, peace, and the right to live within the settler territories, these people had, like citizens everywhere, to undertake military service and to pay taxes in cash or labor' (Comaroff, 185). Thus a discipline of regulation, not unlike that imposed on the debtors and the poor in 19th century Britain, was associated with rule by force and domination of conquered populations.

Lastly came the 'civilising colonialism' of the missionaries that most closely associated with the specific disciplines delineated by Foucault in *Discipline and Punish*. Although the penitentiary system was not mentioned by Comaroff, others included medicine, education, and the socialisation of space in urbanisation, housing and domesticity. The famous phrase utilised by David Livingstone to denote the goals of their mission was 'civilization, commerce and Christianity' (Comaroff, 183). The impulse that led to the expansion of Enlightenment values was directed, as Conrad would show in *Heart of Darkness*, from the imperial centre: Livingstone was one of many churchmen sent by the London Missionary Society whose ultimate goal was 'to subordinate Africa to the dominance of the European order' (ibid. 182), and to do so by 'replacing native economy and society with an imagined world of free, propertied, and prosperous peasant families' (ibid. 182). Needless to add, this could come about solely through colonial dominion.

Foucault saw the ultimate mechanism of social control in the form of the panopticon. He focused on the penal system, and its transformation from a system of public punishment, to one of unseen, 'humanised', and ultimately interiorised control. But the vision of the colonialists, beginning around the same time as David's ancestors Eduard la Fleur and Adam Kok enter into the story in the early 19th century, was not so different in its ultimate institutionalisation of panopticist goals. The eye of God, which becomes that of the panopticon, is clearly described by Comaroff as functioning in similar ways in the imaginary of the 'civilising' colonialists whose vision was no less all-encompassing: 'It was a world in which God-inspired authority, pervading the reasoning mind and the receptive soul of every person, would reign through ever more enlightened secular rulers' (182). Christianity and civilisation, at war with each other during the *siècle des lumières*, are joined here in the one overarching discipline ignored by Foucault, the colonial discipline. And as the discipline that eventually gave rise to the panopticon was the result of a long period of reform that signalled the ascendancy of the bourgeoisie, so was the colonial project no less driven by class values and the all-encompassing urge to extend their dominion: 'So it was that the triumph of the bourgeoisie at home would be made into an imperial dominion of middle-class liberal virtue' (Comaroff 184).

Ultimately, the three colonialisms – state, settler, civilising – were resolved into regional types: Cape Colony came to be identified with British State values, the central interior with those of the Boer settlers, and 'stations either beyond the frontier or within insulated pockets dotted across the remote countryside' (Comaroff 191) with the civilising missions. They provided the foundation for competing systems of control, all of which ultimately were resolved into the hegemonical rule of apartheid. There, too, the issue of using force openly so as to intimidate a dominated population continued. The public policy of controlling the black population through pass laws was matched by the public displays of punishment, and the undisguised use of penal systems as the instrument of state control in the imprisonment of approximately half the adult male population for pass law violations. The defenestration of leaders of the black opposition like Steve Biko was intended to impress the public and discourage resistance. The death penalty, always at the heart of punishment, was applied unequally along racial lines: whites killing blacks tended to go unpunished, whereas blacks killing whites were highly likely to be executed.

It would be a mistake to see these instances of brutal force as indications of an unchanged, earlier epistemological social order, as though the great disciplinary orders of knowledge of the Enlightenment had not come to operate on African soil. In fact, the passage to 'modernism', as Gikandi has so brilliantly demonstrated in *Maps of Englishness*, was more of a joint effort by Africans and Europeans than the invention of the latter and an importation by the former. But modernism could not be understood without its opposite – what is termed traditionalism, in the African context, and royalty in the Foucauldian model. Foucault writes that

> at the beginning of the nineteenth century, then, the great spectacle of physical punishment disappeared; the tortured body was avoided; the theatrical representation of pain was excluded from punishment. The ago of sobriety in punishment had begun (14).

In post-independence Africa, public executions, too, had largely disappeared, and when occasionally they recurred, their relative infrequency was all the more noted. Thus the exceptional, and visibly violent, executions of common thieves or murderers on the beaches of Lagos in the 1970s, and similar displays in the 1960s in Cameroon, were intended to publicise the suppression of the opposition party as well as to intimidate criminals whose executions by firing squads occurred in the early 1970s in the quartier of Madagascar in Yaoundé.

The altogether unique historical span that marks in *David's Story* the passage from Adam Kok and Eduard le Fleur to David, Dulcie, and Sally, encompasses, on the one hand, a Foucauldian passage from the age of punishment and open violence to the sobriety of totalising systems of Enlightenment disciplines. At the same time, through the organisation and suppression of organised resistance, we can attest to the continuation of violent struggle, and to the marks left as physical traces on the bodies of the protagonists. Those marks are left to be deciphered as the palimpsest of a story that refuses total assimilation into either a narrative of punishment or of discipline. It is in that refusal that Wicomb reads, obliquely, these histories of generations of women as establishing the uncertain basis for David's own account of himself and his past.

Since *David's Story* insists on resisting foreclosure, we can approach it only through a simulation of conventional historical analysis. As such, in one sense, it might seem to be a novel about *the* celebration: apartheid coming to an end; Mandela out of prison. The long term clandestine political operatives and militants coming home, coming out, joining the toy-toying dance in the street. On the other hand, there is the secrecy of David's unexplained relationship with Dulcie, the mysteries over who, if anyone, is torturing her, and who, if anyone, tortured him; why he died; what betrayals in his private life, or his political life, actually took place. And more importantly, not what actually did happen, since what happened occurred between the words, between the letters, in the cracks and signposts left scattered across the textual landscape, but what tension is created by the narrative accounts that cry out to us and demand that we bear witness for the accounting. What is at stake is a terrible accounting: David's honesty, his truth, his work for freedom; the ANC's integrity as a movement; the integrity of protest and resistance movements, in the time of struggle and in the time of coming to power. Ultimately, Wicomb forces us to question our own commitment to struggle, to struggles that can no longer be viewed as simple or even upright, as we had once believed them to be; where complications cannot be erased, even if silenced by torture or assassination. Winnie Mandela has gone on trial again; the Truth and Justice Commission elicited stories that detailed the practice of torture at the ANC's Quatro "rehabilitation" camp in Angola between 1979 and 1989. Pits were excavated and those accused of betrayal were held and tortured. The accounting is not just for the past historical record, not just for distant lands: it is for how one stands today in the face of Guantanamo, again, and again, as the muscled politics of imperialist force repeats the gestures of conquest in the teeth of protests of millions.

The conventional notion of truth would hold that appearances hide an underlying reality: that we see symptoms on a surface, but must read them to understand the hidden, repressed drives which they convey; that appearance is a form of displacement or representation, and that reality lies beneath the surface. Earlier Marxist truisms held that the economic base provides the explanation for the manifestation of what appears visibly in the form of the superstructure; and even Said's model of Orientalism rests upon this manifest-latent bipolarity. In terms of a narrative, 'truth' may be thought to reside in the motives that characters hide, or in the solutions to mysteries about their actions. It is always there, and in *David's Story*, this is thematised as the unspoken agreements charted by the comrades whose very cell meetings are shrouded in surface deceptions intended to hide their actual actions. Thus when David's cellmates meet, they pour themselves drinks, which they never touch, to give the appearance of a social gathering; the reality, the truth, is in their political intentions, not in the liquor that the coloureds are supposed to favour.

So, when David goes to Kokstad in 1991, it is only apparently to take a breather, to do research on le Fleur or the Griquas. We understand that that is his cover, or might be his cover; we also understand that he packs a pistol, that he is approached by someone, ostensibly an operative, who tries to enmesh him in a scheme to smuggle diamonds out of the country, or else who has used that scheme in an attempt to entrap David. We don't have any clear idea who that weird operative, disguised as a voluble old man, might be working for – the UDF, the ANC, or the Apartheid government – or else just diamond smugglers. We do know that David is always looking over his shoulder, directing our gaze along the same direction, thus suggesting that there is always something else, something out of sight, behind the door, to which we really have to attend, while David continues to chat up the girl at the bar or take a drink with the manager:

> The man at the door rests his eyes on David's well-ironed but unbuttoned collar. He puts out a hand to restrain him, then turns round and, as if he had been given the nod by someone – someone who identifies him as guest? – wishes David a very pleasant evening in a manner that suggests the delay was all about conventions of politeness. The breakfast waiter, with no trace of his earlier obsequious manner, hurries by and nods at David, a professional tower of plates on his arm. There is something familiar about the shaven-headed man, something that lies just underneath the red-and-black waiter's uniform, that he cannot put his finger on, that draws him to the man, whose figure he follows with his eyes across the candlelit room. He loses him and the band plays 'Smoke Gets in Your Eyes'. (108-9)

In fact, one could have chosen any passage at random in this novel to get at this sense of the doubled nature of reality, of a hidden level lying beneath the surface. Thus, above, when the man at the door looks at David's collar, he is prompting us to evoke the memory of Sally, David's wife, who ironed that collar, somewhat embittered at the thought that she was preparing her man for a romantic interlude. That it is unbuttoned returns us to David's informality within the context of the evening. The act of restraining him is likewise ambivalent: that he receives a nod from an unseen other, that there is a question about whether David is recognised to be a guest, or else one who is pretending to be one; that the waiter's demeanor and uniform hide another unidentifiable something that 'he cannot put his finger on', and so on, all lead to the tongue-in-cheek title of the song. The mysteries here are all suggestive of a world of operatives, not betrayal. If the surface is obscured by the smoke, the unseen, the uncertain, this does not suggest double-dealing. For that we need to pry into the cracks in the flesh where treason and torture would seem to contain the same kind of letters as truth – that is, letters that get etched in the surface of the body, and in so doing, rewrite the textualities of signification. The disintegrations of the word corresponding to those of the skin. In this, Wicomb would seem to be moving in the same direction as Foucault in *Discipline and Punish* who inverts the binary soul/body, so that it is to the body that we must go to understand what is subsequently formulated as the inner workings of the soul. His goal, he says, is to

> try to discover whether this entry of the soul on to the scene of penal justice, and with it the insertion in legal practice of a whole corpus of 'scientific' knowledge, is not the effect of a transformation of the way in which the body itself is invested by power relations. (24)

In a sense it all begins with terror. Learning to swim, an innocuous and childish paddling, is conflated with transgression and domination in *David's Story*. When Sally was being taught to swim at the training camp in Mozambique, she encountered terror and demands for confession: 'Up, draw up your legs, and out, kick, flap the ankle, hands forward, round, and again. And how poorly she performed, unable to confess her terror' (123). If the context appears innocuous, its innocence is quickly disabused:

> He said, as they made their way gingerly across the burning sand, A fuck, that's what you need, and she saw his bulging shorts and knew that her time had come, as she had known it would come sooner or later, this unspoken part of a girl's training'. (123)

Sally chooses to dispose of her virginity with this unnamed comrade, as she disposes of his sperm by washing herself out vigorously with the sea water, turning abjection into choice. The marks left by this event remain invisible, so that when, in the passage that immediately follows the above, we read of her attempt to teach her daughter Chantal to swim, she is left with no technique with which to impart the instruction:

> ... for she is determined that the child should learn to swim today, no later than today. Chantal slips out of her hands, a sea creature tormenting her, so that, exasperated, she smacks the child, and Ouma, surfacing out of the cool blues and greens of sleep, holds out her arms unsteadily to receive the sobbing little girl. (123)

Terror and torture leave indeterminate marks, indelible, ambiguous marks. Like David's tinnitus:

... the muffled silencers of the gunshots amplified into thunder in his ears. The doctor called it tinnitus and prescribed a week's rest, but a day of doing nothing did the trick. Others have lost limbs, but nothing untoward has happened to Comrade Dadzo. Only there were deep scars on the soles of both his feet, and the dislocation of the bone on the ball of the left foot gave him a slight emphasis on the right when walking. (11–12)

The sign of the torture was transmogrified into something like Alcibiades's lisp, a private defect that came to be emulated in public by the Athenian youth as a mark of distinction. David's 'mannerism [was one] which both men and women with an eye for detail found attractive' (12).

The rapid passage from pain to desire, scars and limping to attractiveness, has the effect of blurring the reality. It passes quickly from the grasp of the symbolic into the indefinable space of *l'objet a* where polymorphous, perverse desires of those 'with an eye for detail' might rest. This we see with the work of stylistic details noted by the narrator, the transcriber – David's amenuensis who comes dangerously close to the figure of Dulcie. She notes how Dulcie's 'hands are beautiful', her fingers 'long and slender' (18). After observing her wash 'the sticky red from her hands' (18) and observing her Lady MacBeth-like obsession with ablution, our gaze follows the imaginary trace of the kisses on each fingertip made by 'a nice man of whom no questions will be asked and who will ask no questions about her left thumb with its neat crisscross-patterned tattoo' (18). Lest the implication of some dark tribal ritual rise to the surface, the narrative eye quickly notes, 'The corner of each diamond is marked by a darker point where lines cross and where the fine instrument lingered, burning into the flesh' (18). Her back as well provides the surface on which are inscribed the geometrical patterns of residual scars that followed the torture, leaving there 'a square ... marked with 4 cent-sized circles forming the corners of a smaller inner square, meticulously staked out with blue ballpoint pen before the insertion of a red-hot poker between the bones' (19). These passages introduce the image of Dulcie to us, Dulcie represented in the imagination of David, transcribed by his nameless scribe. She doesn't speak, doesn't move into plain view. Eventually we learn of her techniques of resistance to torture, of the repeated visitations of her tormentors, without ever knowing who they are, what they would hope to obtain from her, what she might have done to bring them down on her – all information which she refuses to divulge. Her ordeal is presented as though it were in the normal order of things, not unlike those inquisitions that rendered David lame, or that eventually resulted in his death. This is the price paid by operatives in the Movement it would appear; maybe the realistic cost of obtaining freedom, or of entering into the public domains of the political. A world beyond the painterly surfaces of the aesthetic or ethical symbolic order of the comfortable middle-class. A world of intrigue, torture, and death; of 'big men'. When David questioned the treatment accorded mutineers in the

Quatro camp in Angola, it earned him 'days of interrogation and so forth by the big men from security' (195). We don't know when he acquired the scars on the soles of his feet. But the revolution remains abstracted, disembodied, and inviolate for him – perhaps accounting for his death, apparently a suicide that followed charges of collaboration as he was caught in a compromising photograph, seated at a table with a man sent to spy on him in Glasgow.

David does not disintegrate with the threats or the danger. But in his defense of the Movement and its realpolitik, he comes down to a rationalisation for torture and death, one that has marked the rhetoric of the Bush administration since 9/11. In other words, Wicomb has taken on the sacred cow of Revolution at the moment of its ultimate success, and has done so in deploying the tools of a postmodernist sensibility. Not one whose tunings derive from the endless deferrals of signification, but rather from the challenges to the pain and terror that have marked modes of signification bound up in the grand narrative of Revolution – what might also be termed that of modernist progress. This is the modernism of war, in which the ideal embraced by the grand narrative rises above the dirty means required to establish it, and which is dependent on its opponent as in the Hegelian master-slave dialectic. For David, the 'and so forth' treatment he received at Quatro was the consequence of treachery within the Movement that gave rise to paranoia. This reading is truly Foucauldian, as it is the disciplinary stripes that are etched on the body that produce the very form of the insurgent or criminal, that create the criminality In Foucault's well-known formulation,

> The individual is no doubt the fictitious atom of an 'ideological' representation of society; but he is also a reality fabricated by this specific technology of power that I have called 'discipline'. We must cease once and for all to describe the effects of power in negative terms: it 'excludes', 'it 'represses', it 'censors', it 'abstracts', it 'masks', it 'conceals'. In fact, power produces; it produces reality; it produces domains of objects and rituals of truth. The individual and the knowledge that may be gained of him belong to this production. (194)

David frames this notion of production along similar lines:

> It was war, for God's sake. Every movement produces its crackpots, its powermongers who cross over into a corrupted version of the freedom they set out to defend. That does not discredit the Movement itself. If things go off course, that course is also determined by the very system we attack. And it's enemy tactics, he repeats, that produce corruption. (196)

Thus it is al-Qaeda that is responsible for Guantanamo, and if the space for that torture prison is supposed to be set outside the boundaries of civilised, modern, God-fearing American territory, that is the fault of the 'evil-doers' who do not permit us to fight them with clean hands. David evokes this very logic in his dismissal of his scribe's objections:

> Keeping your hands clean is a luxury that no revolutionary can afford; there's corruption in every institution. It's only you arty types who think of such

problems as something special.... Stick to the real world and you'll find the buzz of bluebottles deafening.... People who tend their gardens and polish their sensibilities in the morality of art have no idea about the business of survival out there in the bush with no resources. There things do get distorted and ideals do drift out of sight. You who are too fastidious to use the word *comrade*, what would you know about such things? (196).

The scribe follows the movements of an ant that 'disappears down a crack' (197), listening as David pleads with her to represent the sacred struggle, as he terms it, faithfully: 'it must not be misrepresented' (197). The peregrinations of the ant, carrying a tremendous burden, and disappearing down a crack, indicate the antiphonal response to David's conventional rhetoric. The revolution has had its most eloquent theodicy. David is about to disappear.

The crack is not simply noted haphazardly, incidentally. It informs the narration of David's truth, the terror, torture, and death that are inscribed on the various surfaces of his story. They are not stylistic flourishes, or worst of all, disembodied textuality. They are intrinsic to the narrativisation of Revolution, of history. If they appear in the tree-like scars on the back of an escaped slave woman in Ohio, and if David's beloved bears the signs of South Africa's diamonds, as well as squares and circles, it is because the marks that are left on the surface of the text are the only signs by which we can come to know about 'such things' as the fastidious would feign ignore. The letters run red, reel, crack, and disintegrate – or simply flutter, as in a memory in which the truth makes its appearance. David recollects an incident when he was a child encountering an old black man outside the wall of his family compound. Did he speak with him, exchange a smooth stone for a cowrie shell – a forerunner of the moment when Thomas shows him another smooth stone in an effort to entrap him or enlist him? When the memory of the incident returns a second time, the old man never awakens, never speaks, and no stone or cowrie was exchanged. More than the unreliability of memory is at stake, for David. It is truth, or the certainty that truth can be known, that evades him – or that mocks him.

He discovers a list of names in his hotel in Kokstad, in which both his and Dulcie's names are inscribed. He recognises the names of those who were eliminated, of others 'connected with informers' (114). It is at this moment that the major motifs of the novel come together. It is, as he names it, a hit list. And in so naming, he calls into existence himself and Dulcie as traitors. The truth of the accusation, his own responsibility for Dulcie's name appearing due to her connection with him, the purpose for the list having been left for him, are all left undetermined. The narration depends on him for its coherence, and at the moment when his own responsibility is called into question, the substantiality of the evidence begins to dissolve. The verb Wicomb uses at the moment when David recognises Dulcie's name is 'hailed':

Just as that name uttered in any crowd leapt out of the murmur, breaking the continuum of sound, and, lifted, is carried on a higher crystal pitch, for all the world as if it were spelled aloud. So that for a moment he would stop in midsentence, as if he had been hailed. (114)

Only here it is not the repressive apparatus of the state that is hailing him, not the policeman whose 'hey you' calls out his location in relationship to the institution and its power. It is the Movement in its function as anonymous bearer of the sacred, of truth, that names him as outsider and traitor. The only basis of certainty in this act of hailing lies in his perception of the names, since the list itself could easily be destroyed. But the list, an 'aide-memoire', is also an 'instrument of terror', and as such begins to undermine his very hold on perception. Hailed in terror he can only respond in pain:

> Here the name in writing takes on a different hue, lifts out from the rest of the girlish script and starts to tremble in a flush of red, the fancy strokes disintegrating, the letters separating as the colour grows deeper and deeper until they disappear entirely in a pool of blood. (114)

For Althusser (1971) the act of hailing calls forth the social identity of the one being hailed, it positions the one whose recognition of his or her name, and whose response, constitutes the construction of a subject position. It is an act of misrecognition, since the response to hailing is framed within a context in which the imaginary functions to organise a patterned sense of wholeness, of unity, out of the disparate pieces of experience and perception. An identity is born. But in terror, in being hailed by an instrument of terror, the hold on the symbolic dissolves, and the letters which function as its building blocks, dissipate. 'Can it be', David wonders, 'can it be true that he does not know the truth? Or worse, that it stares him in the face, the truth which he cannot bear? And is truth not what he has been pursuing all these years of trouble and strife and *dalliance with death* – the grand struggle for freedom' (116, my emphasis).

The very words needed to nail down the truth – like 'dalliance with death' – shift as the instability of his private life informs the marks of signification, His dalliance with Dulcie's image follows next; the inclusion of his name on a list of informers, of Dulcie's name beneath his, no matter how uncertainly their appearance is made, inevitably leads from betrayal to betrayal: 'And does this betrayal of his family brand him as traitor through and through, someone on whom his comrades have to keep a watchful eye?' (116). One has to wonder how far Zoë Wicomb can go in calling into question the truth of the struggle. After all, if the great Satan, the trokolos of apartheid, cannot function as the marker for a just resistance, what standards of truth would be left? 'No,' David 'mentally clicks his heels, his honour is unquestionable and the truth lies in black and white, unquestionably, in the struggle for freedom' (116). But it is also in black and white that he finds his name on the list, that he finds himself one of those intended for elimination – 'intended', as in the intended young woman meant for marriage – as slippery a signifier as the marks left on the surface of memory. In an attempt to rewrite the black and white marks, he scratches out Dulcie's name with a blue ballpoint pen. But instead of certainty, he finds his act reinscribed, involuntarily, into the enemy's camp. 'The terror mounts with each stroke of the blue ballpoint. When the name is completely obliterated, he shudders at what he has done. Has he, the intended, been directed into acting, into becoming the agent for others?' (117). And we recall that it is his ancestor, the Griqua chief Andrew (Andries) le Fleur, who celebrates the Native Land Act, who calls for the Griqua and Natives Homelands, who claims the Boers as good neighbours, and so on. His call for a Griqua homeland, for something like a Griqua Free State, is inscribed within the struggle for freedom that provides the black and white basis for truth. When David strikes out Dulcie's name, he loses track of the line between us and them. Having obliterated Dulcie's name, he then writes, 'It is they who obliterated her name,' but in response to the scribe's question, 'David does not answer my questions about who *they* are' (117).

Long before his death, bound up in the uncertainty of a compromising photograph of two black, or coloured, men caught eating together at a white wrought-iron table in Scotland, David seems to have lost track of the truth. The scribe finds the last page of an unfinished section on Saartie Baartman covered in scribbles, doodles, and scratched out copies of Dulcie's name. Dulcie seems to have become the palimpsest of the Revolution's truth – scratched out by the torture and terror, obliterated from the memory of the camps where the big men of security, in the real world apart from the flower gardens and dilettantism of the artsy bourgeoisie, held dominion. 'Truth,' writes the scribe, 'is the word that cannot be written' (136). And so it is changed to TRURT, a Cape Flats – that is, coloured – spelling, where it can return, and turn again in palindromic fashion, to the text. The words then go crazy: 'TRURT, TRURT, TRURT, TRURT – the words speed across the page, driven as a toy car is driven by a child, with lips pouted and spit flying, wheels squealing around the Dulcie obstacles' (136). The textual breakdown becomes complete: 'Your words break down into letters that bounce about the hall, chasing each other until they fall plop through baskets jutting out from the walls, as if they have arrived' (136). And a few lines further on, 'TRURT' again, 'TRURT ... TRURT ... TRURT ... TRURT ... the trurt in black and white ... colouring the truth to say that ... which cannot be said the thing of no name ...' (136). When the scribe returns, with her apostrophe to the 'dear reader', to express her, and the computer's impatience, it is with a sense that we have lost all hold of the text, and can only content ourselves with the metatextual commentary.

David's Story situates us at the heart of two interrelated issues: how we are to think the truth of the struggle, the Movement, that has animated liberation politics from the onset of decolonisation; and how we are to relate colonial discourse analysis and deconstruction with the concreteness and materiality of the struggle. Dulcie's body offers itself as the site for our speculations on these questions since we cannot separate that which is inscribed on it from the truth of the Movement, just as we cannot separate what was exhibited, in life and in death, of Saartie Baartman's body from the truth of western Enlightenment epistemology. The novel ends with the nameless scribe's gestures joining her to those of Dulcie, the one whose name and story were obliterated. Her computer blasted to pieces by a gunshot,

> My screen is in shards.
> The words escape me.
> I do not acknowledge this scrambled thing as mine.
> I will have nothing more to do with it.
> I wash my hands of the whole story (213).

It remains for us to rethink Spivak's call (1988) for a strategic essentialism in light of the questions Wicomb has posed with this refocalisation of the struggle, seen from the start from the viewpoint of the women who inform the Griqua history and *David's Story*, because it is the marks that are left by these women's presence that provide the space to question the certainties of TRURT. And we no longer seek to interpret those marks on the basis of a hermeneutics of depth, but now remain fixated on the surface, the only site available for a fast car to run its course, or for us to track it to the end.

WORKS CITED

Althusser, Louis. *Reading Capital*. New York: Pantheon Books, 1971.
Comaroff, John. 'Images of Empire, Contests of Conscience: Models of Colonial Domination in South Africa.' In Frederick Cooper and Ann Laura Stoler, eds., *Tensions of Empire: Colonial Cultures in a Bourgeois World*, Berkeley, CA: University of California Press, 1997.
Conrad, Joseph. *Heart of Darkness* [1899], in *Youth: and Two Other Stories*. Garden City, NY: Doubleday, 1902.
Foucault, Michel. *Discipline and Punish* [1975]. Trans. Alan Sheridan. New York: Vintage Books, 1995.
———. *The History of Sexuality*, Vol. 1. New York: Vintage Books, 1990.
Gikandi, Simon. *Maps of Englishness*. New York: Columbia University Press, 1996.
Hochschild, Adam. *King Leopold's Ghost*. Boston, New York: Houghton Mifflin, 1999.
Mbembe, Achille. *On the Postcolony*. Berkeley, CA: University of California Press, 2001.
Spivak, Gayatri C. *In Other Worlds: Essays in Cultural Politics*. New York: Routledge, 1988.
Stoler, Ann L. *Race and the Education of Desire: Foucault's History of Sexuality and the Colonial Order of Things*. Durham, NC: Duke University Press, 1995.
Wicomb, Zoë. *David's Story*. New York: The Feminist Press, 2001.

> Mothering Daughters & the Other Side of the Story
> in Amma Darko, Ama Ata Aidoo
> & Nozipo Maraire

Monica Bungaro

The mother–daughter relation

Fiction in one way or another reflects the tensions and preoccupations at work in society. On this assumption, the dynamics of power in African societies is a major preoccupation expressed in African women's writing today. Family relationships in African post-colonial societies manifest a growing level of tension, conflict and stress as a result of new opportunities, new interests and new dilemmas created by increasing gender and class stratification across Africa, but especially across generations of Africans.

This tension between generations and between opposing systems is played out in the conflict between mothers and daughters. One of the new directions African women's writing is taking today is in fact visible in a more blunt attack on the traditional foundations of society in its myths and beliefs about maternal love and mother–daughter relationships.

The question of maternal love, the duties of 'motherhood' and of 'obligatory' maternity, were already explored in the 1980s by Anglophone writers such as Buchi Emecheta and Flora Nwapa. In *The Joys of Motherhood* (1979), Emecheta showed, through Nnu Ego's single-minded devotion to the construction of herself as mother, that motherhood in Africa defines female identity. In the novel the pursuit of motherhood is portrayed as the sovereign means for female identity formation and the woman is valued for her self-abnegation. As John Gillis puts it, giving 'birth ceased to be something that happens to a woman and became the ultimate source of adult female identity' (Gillis 1996: 174). Flora Nwapa's radical heroines, Efuru and Amaka in *Efuru* (1966) and *One is Enough* (1981) respectively, appear more reluctant in accepting society's restrictions and impositions (Davies and Graves, 1986). Yet, though Emecheta and Nwapa's novels portray the mother's role in society, there has been so far a literary and sociological silence hanging over the mother–daughter relation in Africa. For women writers today to consider this relationship is innovative in itself. But for women writers to assume a frank, often frightening, perspective on this relationship is an act of pure courage.

Images of good motherhood and of mother–child bonding have been deployed in remarkably diverse ways for progressive as well as conservative causes. Dispelling the possibility of a politically unified maternity, the novels and short stories examined here indicate the ambiguity and flexibility of the institution itself. Motherhood has always been idealised and commonly represented as a full-time occupation. In most African societies, women are still defined by their ability to procreate and maternity is supposed to occupy a woman's perpetual interest. Foucault's statement that 'Motherhood is a biological–moral responsibility lasting through the entire period of the children's education' (Foucault, 1990: 104) seems particularly relevant to African societies. African women writers today are not only showing that perfect motherhood does not exist in women's novels because it does not exist in real life but are self-consciously rejecting proliferating images that suggest otherwise.

The development of the mother–daughter plot in African literature is a recent event that helps us to understand the wider politics of African post-colonial societies. It appears that ideologies, rooted in Africa, impact on the female and the ensuing conflicts may lead to a questioning of tradition, which is played out in mother and daughter power dynamics. The cultural clash in the relationship across generations of females, which was characteristic of some works of the 1980s, is now dramatised through the mother–daughter relationship, a relationship that is shown to generate malaise and traumas.

Amma Darko (*The Housemaid*, 1998), Ama Ata Aidoo (*The Girl Who Can*, 1992), and Nozipo Maraire (*Zenzele: A Letter for My Daughter*, 1995), explore this relation trying to identify the ambiguity between mothers and daughters. They all highlight in their works, the ways in which ideas of motherhood force renegotiation of power dynamics. Arguably, the dominant norms of African identity are altered, and alternate ideas of femaleness and motherhood are introduced, sometimes in their extreme form. Each of these works calls for a reassessment of the daughter's status and of the image of the traditional bonding between mother and child.

Some main common points emerge from the study of these texts: the daughter in revolt against the mother, the daughter's exploitation by the mother and the daughter's perception of that exploitation, the mother's inability to provide comfort and support to the daughter, the conflict between generations (mother–daughter–grandmother with the mother and grandmother as two diametrically opposite forces), the mother as incapable of possessing the so-called sacred love for her child, and the daughter's need to separate from the mother. However, daughters' dissatisfactions with their mothers and what they represent are presented in different ways in the novels. In Nozipo Maraire's *Zenzele: A Letter for My Daughter* tensions between mother and daughter, though taking the form of a cultural clash, do not appear to feed on anger and resentment. If an overall positive picture of the mother and of the mother–daughter relationship can be drawn from *Zenzele*, Amma Darko's *The Housemaid* depicts the mother as a failure and the daughter as psychologically wounded. Here economic restrictions play a major role in mother–daughter strained relations. In Ama Ata Aidoo's short story *The Girl Who Can*, the mother sides with the daughter against her grandmother's attacks.

In contrast to Western feminist accounts of mother–daughter relations, African daughters' relationships with their mothers are not marked by female rivalry. If in Western novels, 'mothers and daughters compete as sexual rivals for the dubious privilege of being transacted among men' (Greenfield, 2002: 128), in African women's novels, daughters' relationships with their mothers are complicated and distorted by African and colonial constructions of womanhood. Leonore Davidoff and Catherine Hall state that: 'In Victorian England, the equation of women with domesticity came to be one of the fixed points of middle-class status' (Davidoff and Hall, 1987: 275), and motherhood came to be one of the fixed points of domesticity. Victorian ideologies aimed at containing women's power in society along with indigenous forms of idealisation of the mother role in Africa reinforced conventional maternal narratives in African societies. Adrienne Rich has amply demonstrated that the idealisation of maternity gave rise to modern 'motherhood' (Rich, 1977).

African women have historically interrogated patriarchy and their stories are the expression of social dissidence. Stories of mothers and daughters are told in the context of a changing world, with regard to women's rights, and the rebellion of the female characters reflects a wider developing feminist consciousness. The questioning of norms of femininity and maternity are at the centre of African women's agenda. Women writers today are putting their cards on the table as they are re-conceptualising motherhood, pointing out both its regenerative and destructive potential, not just for the mother, but also, for the daughter. Stereotypical images of the mother (and grandmother) figure as carrier of life and eternal nurturer are subverted, and cultural practices are often viewed as abusive. By challenging constructions of motherhood and daughterhood, new areas of generational conflict have opened up in modern society.

Maternal authority is interrogated and sometimes disconcerting scenarios are brought to light. The clash of values, between traditional and modern, has always created tensions. The difference now is that women are courageously portraying the way in which women are equal to men, including in their weakness and greed. In the general struggle for survival and/or success, women are shown to be complicit in neo-colonial forms of exploitation. In this respect, in all the works examined here, the mother–daughter relationship becomes pivotal, as the characters consider their mothers and grandmothers as being complicit with the inherent patriarchal and neo-colonial system. Education (*Zenzele*) and money (*The Housemaid*) are shown to deeply affect relations, and conflicts are most of the time due to a Western over-emphasis on their importance. In this context it is no surprise that there is a decreasing sense of obligation to family. Family, in this case, mothers, can sometimes be the daughter's worst enemy and directly participate in the daughter's destruction.

Revolts against the mother, revolts against society: Amma Darko's The Housemaid

In *The Housemaid*, we find a world composed primarily of women in which men intervene only as passing characters, official or transitory lovers, drunken or weak fathers, and/or oppressors. The main relationship is between mother and daughter, and in two out of three mother–daughter dyads (Bibio and Mami Korkor, Efia and her mother, Tika and Sekyiwa), either the mother or the daughter function as prostitutes (Efia, Tika and Sekyiwa). Common to each of these dyads is the daughter's repulsion toward the mother (though less evident in Efia's case). The relationship is played out in terms of power and domination: the mother portrayed as heartless, cold and calculating (Sekyiwa and Efia's mother and grandmother), authoritarian (Efia's mother and grandmother) or weak and powerless (Mami Korkor).

In each case, the mother is represented as a failure. The choice of this dual context of prostitution and failure underlies Darko's assault on the traditional assumption about the mother as a designated totem figure as defined by Luce Irigaray, 'Our societies presuppose that the mother nurse the child for free, before and after giving birth, and that she remains the nurse of men and society' (Irigaray 1987: 97). In *The Housemaid*, the mother is shown to betray the institutionalised notion of maternal love and devotion.

The relationship between Bibio, an eight-year-old girl and her mother is exemplary in this respect. The first encounter with the mother–daughter interaction occurs early in the novel when Bibio rudely approaches her mother who is late from one of the markets in Accra where she works as a fresh-fish hawker. Bibio is very irritated by her mother's late arrival as she is waiting for some money to buy a bar of soap to wash something her brother and his friend have just found in the rubbish dump. Mami Korkor's delay and the bar of soap are clearly just pretexts for Bibio to start up a fight that seems to be part of their everyday relationship. Darko constructs most of the novel out of the voices of her characters. Bibio's relationship with her mother is, in fact, revealed to the reader through the constant use of dialogue. The following is an example:

> **B:** Your son and his friend, they brought me something from the rubbish dump....
> **M:** They still go scavenging on the rubbish dump? Haven't I told you not to allow them?

B: Mami Korkor, which of the two boys did I bring into the world?
M: 'I don't like your tone, Bibio.'
B: 'Too bad. You should have sent me to school to learn some manners then. But since you rather let me stay home to play mother to you and your friend's sons, where else can I learn my manners but in the streets? And don't forget, Mami Korkor that this very blouse I am wearing also came from the rubbish dump.'
M: (But how could she change things? She had to hawk fish from dawn to dusk to earn just enough to feed herself and her four children. Not a pesewa came from their father).
B: 'Why after making Nereley with him, when you realised how irresponsible he was, did you go ahead to make Akai, me and Nii Boi as well?' (11)

The mother here is featured as a target of aggression. The terms that are utilized in the dialogue denote the presence of two semantic networks, one signalling aggression, and the other signalling judgement. In confronting her mother, Bibio adopts the double role of judge and aggressor. In her mind, Mami Korkor cannot afford to reproach her, as she is the cause of her own and her children's misery. The dialogue is indicative of the 'non-communication' in which mother and daughter become trapped, with the daughter assaulting the mother and the mother unable to deny the evidence. It is clear, in fact, that Mami Korkor feels guilty for failing to meet her daughter's needs. Non-communication is both the consequence and the symbolic expression of their paralysing conditions.

Darko's novel raises the question of a daughter's development in relation to the mother's life. Bibio rejects the idea of being a mini-version of her mother, as she finds in her no acceptable model of womanhood. Here, the daughter attacks the mother as the tool of patriarchy, accusing her of colluding with the same power structures she is supposed to challenge. Bibio's hostile attitude towards her mother is mainly an expression of her rejection of a life she is condemned to live because of her mother's mistakes. She feels rage at her mother's powerlessness. The mother's victimisation does not only humiliate the mother, it mutilates the daughter who has no valid gender model to cling on to. According to Vivien Nice,

> In a nuclear family where mother carries the work and responsibility of caring without the power, we may wonder why our mothers are such martyrs to the needs of others and feel angry with her that she does not offer us a better model of independence and assertiveness. (Nice, 1992: 68)

However, what the daughter fails to see is the social system operating at her mother's expense. As Adrienne Rich asserts, 'It is easier by far to hate and reject a mother outright than to see beyond her to the forces acting upon her' (Rich 1977: 235). The mother–daughter predicament is aggravated by their economic status. Poverty, here, helps deteriorate an already crippled relationship. By refusing to accept the mother's position and mirror image, Bibio is not only revolting against her mother; she is revolting against society's exploitation of women.

The conditions of life have meant that for many poor African women like Mami Korkor little maternal energy remains at each end of the day which is channelled towards sheer physical survival. In the conditions of poverty and male absence, the mother fulfils the provider role and Bibio as the eldest and only daughter comes next in the line of 'natural providers'. *The Housemaid* shows that the mother assumes the father role but not necessarily the power and dominance associated with it. Father figures are either absent or unreliable, and the woman is by force responsible for child-bearing, child-caring and house-keeping. As Patricia Mohammed affirms, 'The centrality of women in their capacity as mothers does not necessarily translate into similar institutional or ideological centrality' (Mohamed 2001: 24).

Darko's critique is not directed at Mami Korkor's inability to take better care of her daughter, but at society's failure to guarantee a decent life for its members, especially for women, who appear still to be subordinated and subjugated in most contemporary societies. Darko's biting remarks in the novel are meant to uncover the ineffectiveness of legislation and social services in dealing with the growing problem of single mothers and employment in Africa. She focuses on the instability and collapse of a family structure in which a woman abandoned by a man, has to confront on her own the financial burden of a family. It is no surprise then that the survival of the family also depends on child labour. Therefore, to speak of the mother–daughter relationship in these terms is to attack the patriarchal and neo-colonial structures of present-day Ghana and to demonstrate the writer's participation in an act of radical revolt.

The idea of daughters who do not want to become like their mothers, but who inevitably do so, is a leitmotif in *The Housemaid*. In a society, which like most post-colonial African countries is still economically dependent on foreign aid for survival, money is worshipped by many above principles and values. Sekyiwa, Tika's mother, is totally illiterate and unscrupulous. She gets pregnant by a rich man and makes sure he sets her up in business. She mistreats him until one day he dies. The father's vulnerability and weakness allow a shift of power from father to mother. Sekyiwa is obsessed with money and teaches Tika to value it over everything else. Tika, therefore, learns to use her appeal to seduce men and secure financial support. Sekyiwa and Tika's manner of acquiring wealth by using their 'bottom power' (Nwapa, 1981: 126) compromises their moral integrity. Materialistic instincts are shown to prevail over dignity and morals.

Until now, the mother had been 'the guardian of tradition', especially for her daughter. In this novel, instead, social success and appearances are the only legacy Sekyiwa passes down to her daughter. Darko's 'truth' subverts stereotypical notions about motherhood which are shown to be one-sided and unacceptable, and presents motherhood and femininity as multi-faceted essences, which might incorporate excesses. The only role model Tika can follow is one which considers the female body in terms of its value as merchandise. Viewed along these lines, the mother–daughter relation assumes another dimension. In the novel, it is the mother who offers the model of prostitution and the marketed body as a basic approach to life. Motivated by money and greed, Sekyiwa is unable to fulfil traditional duties of maternity. Her only interest is to buy Tika's forgiveness for the death of her father. The status of the prostitute-mother plays a key role in the experience of for the daughter, who is presented with the image of woman's inevitable degradation. Refusing the mother's path would imply a new awareness on the daughter's part, an awareness that would lead to a movement of revolt, not only against the mother but also against men and therefore against the entire community. Unable to challenge her environment and what her mother represents, Tika follows in her footsteps. Obsessed with proving her success, she invests all her energy and dignity in her business, until one day she becomes pregnant. Tika decides to have an abortion but her mother desperately tries to talk her out of it: 'Tika please I urge you, keep this pregnancy [...]. I am desperate for a grandchild. Please reconsider aborting this baby. I beg you' (27). Tika refuses to bring a baby into the world as she fears it may become like her mother and herself and reproduce the same sort of relationship she is trying to free herself from: 'I won't keep this pregnancy. What if he grows to be to me what I have become to you?' (27). As indicated in the text, on one side, Sekyiwa is depicted as contradicting any ideas related to 'good mothering', as she is unable to fulfill her maternal role in providing sufficient love and a decent upbringing for her daughter. On the other side, she still adopts the role of 'keeper of tradition' which sees the woman as a biological reproducer of the nation. Her desperate need for a grandchild is in line with the cultural demands of the society for which a childless woman is not a woman at all (Ngcobo, 1988). Even in a society that is experimenting with woman's emancipation, professional success and wealth are not enough to justify a childless existence. However, Sekyiwa is not only concerned with models of respectability and reputation that come with the status of 'mother'. Sekyiwa sees in her grandchild the only possible way to make up for all the pain she has caused Tika and her father by playing the role of the perfect grandmother. Again, she is unable to discern what might be beneficial for her daughter's future, independent of whatever may be beneficial to herself. Tika, instead, shows no innate physiological need to have a baby. Moreover, the rejection of motherhood for Tika is both a rejection of her mother's authority and emotional abuse and of society's expectations.

Another example of mothers unable to mother daughters in the novel is Efia's mother. Efia is the housemaid of the title, who, with the sinister help of her mother and grandmother, tries to deceive Tika, by getting pregnant in order to claim Tika's protection and later her money. The plan is later discovered and Efia gives birth to a stillborn child whose body she then tries to conceal. Efia's mother's responsibility to safeguard her own daughter is here replaced by the mother's overt exploitation of the daughter's naivety. The two maternal figures, mother and grandmother, are so obsessed with money that they use Efia as a pawn for their interests. The grandmother seizes control of her daughter and the daughter in turn seizes control of Efia, thus creating a chain of oppression. The mother–daughter relationship here assumes a new frightening dimension: the mother is no longer a source of support but a source of oppression. The girl's youth and her body become instrumental to the grandmother and mother's plan of putting their hands on Tika's money. Emotional abuse is at the core of the mother–daughter–grandmother relationship in the text. The grandmother figure, a tie to the past and a symbol of resourcefulness and wisdom, the guardian of a certain order, has disappeared.

In all these examples, traumatic mother–daughter relations help to explain how the daughter got to be the person she is. Though Darko adopts a matrifocal structure in the novel, daughters are depicted as victims of their mothers' greed (Sekyiwa, Efia's mother) or powerlessness (Mami Korkor). Until now, in both Western and African societies, we were always assured that maternal love was inherent in every woman. Darko courageously points out that maternal love should not necessarily be thought of as existing naturally. In the case of African women, very few have dared consider such a possibility.

Bodies that matter in Ama Ata Aidoo's The Girl Who Can

Like Darko's novel, Aidoo's short story unfolds primarily within a world of women. The three-generation household here is represented by the grandmother, Nana, the mother, Kaya and her seven-year-old daughter, Adjoia. The father is mentioned only once in the text in an ambiguous way. As in *The Housemaid*, because of the matrifocal structure of the story in which the father is unknown, man has become a generic object. Aidoo's descent from a matrilineage helps to explain why female subjectivity and agency in her story are located in the contested socio-economic and political terrains of the woman-nurturing, matrilineal kinship system of the Akan of Ghana.

If in *The Housemaid*, mother and grandmother are shown to collude in the manipulation of the (grand)daughter Efia, in *The Girl Who Can*, the mother and grandmother represent two diametrically opposed forces. According to Naana Horne: 'Matrilineal kinship recognizes woman as the very source of intergenerational connectedness' (Horne, 1999). However, Aidoo's short story highlights that though 'intergenerational connectedness' is still a major component of matrilineal systems, cultural and social transformations have deeply affected the lives and experiences of women, prompting tensions and conflicts between generations. In *The Girl Who*

Can conflicts between the grandmother and the mother are generated by opposing ideas about the daughter's upbringing. The grandmother here represents the typical voice of tradition and a past in which people were judged not only according to their individual merits but also by their ability to contribute to the family and to the community. The younger generation, in contrast, is shown to be less tolerant towards these socialisation values.

The story of this relationship is told by Adjoia, the seven-year-old daughter who, with childish eyes, looks to her mother and grandmother for clues as to what it means to be a female in her environment. The mother, Kaya, and grandmother, Nana, are two maternal figures who oppose each other in the protagonist's gaze. In this way, the daughter becomes the intradiagetic narrator and is given a privileged insight into the world of grown-up women. The small child's innocent point of view offers Aidoo a good opportunity to criticise cultural practices in a game-like way by depicting the apparent confusion the daughter feels every time she hears Nana and her mother speak or when Nana laughs at her. Adjoia's comments make an impact on the reader and throw him/her off balance, as irony and satire are usually associated with adults. Here, instead, a child is shown to have more insight into the reality and possibilities open to women than women themselves.

The plot revolves around Adjoia's legs that are the object of much concern for Nana as she thinks, 'they are too thin. And also too long for a woman' (9). Adjoia's legs seem to be the cause of most of the mother–daughter tension, as Nana is unwilling to share Kaya's different point of view about Adjoia's body. The mother–daughter relation assumes a dual perspective, of two worlds, and three generations. As in her other works (*No Sweetness Here* 1970), Aidoo portrays differences in values and perception by presenting different generations of people in her stories. She therefore indirectly compares and contrasts the lives of her characters. Consequently, in *The Girl Who Can*, the reader is able to see immediately the impact, contribution and influence of the grandmother.

On the one hand, Nana is the one who takes over and adopts a position of control. She constantly silences her daughter, Kaya, by exercising the authority that society gives to old women as repositories of wisdom. Research indicates that in West African societies, the elders are honoured and command immense respect (Oppong, 1983). On the other hand, Kaya sides with her own daughter, but has little courage to challenge her mother: 'Oh mother!' (10). Nana and Kaya represent two opposing educational models for the African child today. For Nana 'If any woman decides to come into this world with her own two legs, then she should select legs that have meat on them: with good calves. Because you are sure such legs would support solid hips. And a woman must have solid hips to be able to have children'(9). Nana is the keeper of tradition and her gaze represents the gaze of the collectivity with its strengths and limitations. In *The Girl*

Who Can, the grandmother is concerned with the perpetuation and survival of her family.

Kaya does not share Nana's ideas about the female body, though she is not capable of contradicting her domineering and indomitable mother, who, in Adjoia's eyes, shows little compassion for her mother: 'I knew from her voice that my mother was weeping inside. Nana never heard that weeping. Not that it would have stopped Nana even if she had heard it' (9). Through Nana's overt complaints about Adjoia's legs, Aidoo voices the limitations that arise when the body is valued only for its reproductive potential and motherhood is to be obtained at any price. Mercy Amba Oduyoye asserts that: 'The livingness of the daughters of Anowa, is limited to their biology' (Oduyoye, 1995: 10). Women are not valued in themselves but only as valuable objects or means to an end.

School is another topic that generates conflict between Nana and Kaya. The child-narrator comments, 'Nana thought it would be a waste of time' (11), as Nana would say, 'Maybe with legs like hers she might as well go to school' (11). Adjoia's mother, in contrast, believes in the power of education as a means of social mobility and a way to escape the confinement she has been forced into in her life: 'She kept telling Nana that she felt she was locked into some kind of darkness because she didn't go to school [...]. I could always marry later and maybe...' (11). The importance of education is a recurrent theme in Aidoo's work. The above passage once again highlights the idea that marriage and motherhood are still something African women want to pursue but that neither marriage nor motherhood can be used to justify a woman's existence. Aidoo draws attention to the way women's sense of self is often plural, shaped by multiple roles and aspirations and to the way in which these multiple roles are often the arena of cultural conflicts between generations of women.

By adopting the point of view of the small child as narrator, Aidoo chooses a voice that differs from the adult's with the usual traditional inclination. Since in Aidoo's works the young narrators rarely confront their elders, Adjoia's comments on her grandmother and mother's attitude both towards each other and towards her are expressed through snatches of overheard conversation or internal monologues. Both techniques are used to uncover the pressures of one woman (Nana) on another (Kaya) to accept the traditional image often associated with the female body. To openly criticize the politics surrounding the female body in cultural practice represents a daring act for a woman writer, in particular for an African woman writer. The short story ends on a positive, determined note: Adjoia starts running for the junior section of the school. She wins first place each time, until one day she wins the cup for the best all-round junior athlete. In this context, the female body takes on great value as a sign of self-affirmation.

In most African stories, it is the grandchildren who learn lessons of wisdom and strength from the grandmother. Here, it is the grandmother who eventually challenges society's regulations and expectations by recognising alternative modes of being for her granddaughter: 'Thin legs can also be useful ... even though some legs don't have much meat on them to carry hips ... they can run. Thin legs can run ... then who knows? (13). Through the grandmother figure and the clash of cultural values between generations, Aidoo shows that though African cultures have firm foundations in tradition, culture is also dynamic and ever-changing. It is up to women across generations to bring about change.

Maternal love and the 'flight' from the mother: Nozipo Maraire's Zenzele: A Letter for My Daughter

Zenzele: A Letter for My Daughter, as the title clearly states, is a long, reflective letter written by a mother to her college-aged daughter, Zenzele, leaving her native Zimbabwe to study at Harvard, in the US. Although the novel is presented in letter form, conversations between mother and daughter occupy centre stage.

It is true that many of Zenzele's external and internal traits are revealed through descriptions and/or comments by her mother/narrator, but it is also true that Zenzele has a voice of her own. Most of the issues articulated by Zenzele indicate her curiosity towards life as demonstrated in her use of the first-person singular pronoun: "'I am not going to marry an African. I shall marry in America". "Honestly, Zenzele you watch too much television'" (33). These statements are bluntly directed to her mother in a provocative, at times rebellious, at times, game-like way which testifies to the traditional conflict between generations. What is expressed is the younger generation's eagerness to shake off the old system, which is perceived as synonymous with the exploitation of woman and with confined, limiting roles.

Zenzele feels love for her mother who has over the years provided her with care. On the other hand, her mother's inability to resist patriarchal forms of oppression causes frustration in the daughter. Like Bibio, Tika, and Adjoia, Zenzele looks to her mother to see what it means to be a woman, but growing into maturity she soon realises that the model her mother offers her is unacceptable. Like Mami Korkor, Zenzele's mother has hardly questioned patriarchal social and cultural hierarchies throughout her life. She has passively accepted the roles of devoted wife and all-caring mother that Zimbabwean society has carved for her.

The daughter realises that in order to chart a future of her own, in a direction she has chosen for herself, she must separate from her mother and what she represents. For Zenzele, this means studying abroad to achieve professional expertise and recognition in her field. For her mother, it means learning to accept and support her daughter's decision. What strikes the reader is that through Zenzele's questioning of traditional values, practices, and roles, the mother is forced to reconsider her own life. In this sense, the mother–daughter relationship is both enriched and enriching – the older generation feeling inadequate and obsolete as it struggles with the effects of change and modernity; the younger, idealistic and charging full force into the future. Through her daughter's provocative questioning of various forms of tradition, namely bride price, sexual exploitation, forced marriage and motherhood, Amai Zenzele, though already aware of gender disparities, is forced to revisit her position as a woman, even if she knows that the answers her daughter seeks are hers to find, 'I have made my contribution. I have nothing more to add. It is up to your generation to carry us the rest of the way' (39).

Her message is both harsh and moving. Not everyone has a chance to start over. For the older generation strongly rooted in its ideas, there can be little changing in life for the reason that any emancipatory messages oppose the ideological system that has guided it, for better or for worse, up to this point. Although she thinks it is too late for her to expand the limits of her own life, and although culture has already imprinted on her the sense of her limits as an African woman, she realises that 'the most important thing that a woman can do for another is to illuminate and expand the other's sense of actual possibilities' (Rich 1977). She thus tries to establish a strong line of love and confirmation that stretches from mother to daughter, from woman to woman across generations by providing her daughter with lessons of patience and tenacity.

Unlike the relationships between mothers and daughters in *The Housemaid* which feed themselves on rage and resentment, Zenzele's relationship with her mother, therefore, seems less fraught with tensions, with the mother here, not only fiercely partisan and supportive of her daughter, but also positively influenced by her daughter's 'fervent egalitarianism and sweet idealism' (37). Rudo Gaidzanwo, affirms that 'It is only rarely that there is overt tension and long-term antagonism between mothers and daughters in Zimbabwean literature' (Gaidzanwo, 1985: 15).

Through the daughter's questioning attitude, the mother confronts herself and recognizes the injustices lined up against women, injustices that the new generation is called to fight against. The inquisitive and curious Zenzele eventually shatters her mother's vision of the world into so many pieces that her mother is forced to admit, 'I no longer know what or who is the African woman, perhaps she is some synthesis of us both […]. Being an African woman is what you will make of it, Zenzele' (41). The mother is conscious she has provided the daughter with a contradictory model of womanhood, rebellious against neo-colonial forms of oppression though complicit with patriarchal power structures. The clash between traditional prerogatives and progressive aspirations is not resolved by the mother, yet she rightly perceives that the rules inherited from the past must constantly be re-evaluated by people in relation to their hopes and desires. On the other hand, through the mother's loving litany, the daughter is forced to recognise the importance of holding on to her roots while simultaneously occupying multiple locations.

In an interview 'We Speak Because We Dream', the Caribbean writer Merle Collins describes mothers and daughters as 'two different generations searching for solutions, often with similar ideas but with very different resources provided to bring these prevailing ideas to fruition at the time' (Brennian 1995: 37). Zenzele is shown to have both economic and cultural resources to realise her dreams. Her mother could count on neither of these. Though her life now is one of privilege, the mother has lived through colonialism and the struggle for freedom, whereas, as Karen Keim (2000) observes: 'Her daughter has experienced only the results of that struggle, such as material wealth and education' (168).

Economic freedom means that the daughter can escape family pressures and society's restrictive roles. Zenzele, who, at times, seems to function as her mother's alter ego (that is, her mother's less conventional, active, self-reliant side) is determined to get away from what her mother represents in her eyes, that is, what she does not want to be, the all-caring and obedient daughter and wife who has been forced over the years to put herself, her needs and desires aside in an environment hostile to the idea of female self-fulfilment and emancipation. Her decision to leave is the outcome of the critical awareness of both her limitations in her home and, on a larger scale, of the circumscribed nature of women's social roles in Zimbabwe. Expatriation for Zenzele seems to be a precondition for independence, where her mother can also be seen as her country, Zimbabwe, metaphorically speaking. The move from the sphere of family and secluded existence into society is a potentially liberating process which the daughter wants to experience and enjoy, since she feels suffocated and 'actively restrained as if her personal freedoms were being infringed upon' (25).

However, independence from both mother and mother country can be both a risky and enriching experience. The mother on her part can only try to warn the daughter against the dangers of giving up one's identity to embrace new ways of being. Amai Zenzele has learned this and other lessons in her life, stimulated by her daughter's questioning attitude. She then eventually comes to realize that although it is important not to forget who we are and where we come from, it is also necessary to be capable of arranging multiple layers of experience that will not replace existing ones but will coexist with them.

Nozipo Maraire, shows through Zenzele, that every daughter must seek out her own space, a world in which to create an individuality, a separate personhood. Nevertheless, through Amai Zenzele, she also identifies the necessity for the daughter to stay connected. The symbiotic bond linking generation upon generation of women helps to cement the historical and racial realities of matrilineage. In this sense, like Aidoo and Darko, Maraire correlates the theme of mother–daughter relations with the wider one of women's community.

Conclusion

Whether willing victims or accomplices of the system, mothers are shown to fuel their daughters' aggressiveness or separation through their inability (Mami Korkor) or unwillingness (Sekyiwa) to fight patriarchal and neo-colonial power structures. Darko, Maraire and Aidoo use the figure of the mother (and the grandmother) as the main conduit for the myriad limitations that patriarchal, colonial/neo-colonial societies impose on young women in search of a fulfilling identity of their own. Daughters' responses to mothers vary from passivity to open rebelliousness, resentment and distance. Their reaction is not only a reaction against the mother but also a reaction against society and community pressures and restrictions.

Darko, Aidoo and Maraire urge readers and critics to take another look at the texts to see how, in Obioma Nnaemeka's words, 'woman-on-woman violence and abuse show women as a group suffering from self-inflicted wounds' (Nnaemeka, 1997: 22), as they sometimes actively participate in oppressive practices and become instruments of oppression by subscribing to oppressive ideologies.

Each novel repeatedly raises the question of whether one can avoid one's mother's mirror image and free oneself from the saying, 'Like mother, like daughter'. The real question is clearly one of determining the nature and extent of this freedom. If Zenzele is not likely to reproduce her mother's position in society, Darko's daughter figures are. Social mobility and choices seem extremely limited for poor and uneducated women. Aidoo's The *Girl Who Can* demonstrates that even the older generation is capable of adjustments.

On a personal level, these works speak of the anger, guilt and difficulties which exist between mother and daughter in contemporary Africa, and the fact that anger can co-exist with connection. On a socio-political level, they function through careful intense analogy to create levels of meaning about neo-colonialism, race and sexual exploitation. Once again, African women writers demonstrate that the personal and the political are two sides of the same coin.

WORKS CITED

Aidoo, Ama Ata, *The Girl Who Can*. In Yvone Vera (ed.), *Opening Spaces: Contemporary African Women's Writing*, London: Heinemann, 1998. All references are to this edition and page numbers are given in the body of the text.

——. *No Sweetness Here*. London: Longman, 1970.

Brennian, Brenda. 'We Speak Because We Dream' interview with Merle Collins in Carol Boyce Davies (ed), *Moving Beyond Boundaries*, Vol. 2, London: Pluto, 1995: 31-42.

Darko, Amma. *The Housemaid*. London: Heinemann, 1998. All references are to this edition and page numbers are given in the body of the text.

Davidoff, Leonore and Catherine Hall (eds). *Family Fortunes: Men and Women of the English Middle-Class, 1780–1850*, Chicago: Chicago University Press.
Davies, C. Boyce and Ann Adam Graves (eds), *Ngambika: Studies of Women in African Literature,*. Trenton, N.J: Africa World Press, 1986.
Emecheta, Buchi. *The Joys of Motherhood*, London: Heinemann, 1979.
Foucault, Michel. *The History of Sexuality* Volume 1. Harmondsworth: Penguin, 1990.
Gaidzanwo, Rudo. *Images of Women in Zimbabwean Literature*. Harare: The College Press, 1985.
Gillis, John. *A World of Their Own Making: Myth, Ritual and the Quest for Family Values*, New York: Basic Books, 1996.
Greenfield, Susan. *Mothering Daughters*, Detroit: Wayne State University Press, 2002.
Horne, Banyiwa Naana. 'The Politics of Mothering: Multiple Subjectivity and Gendered Discourse in Aidoo's Plays.' In *Emerging Perspectives on Ama Ata Aidoo* Ada Uzoamaka Azodo & Gay Wilentz (eds.), Trenton, NJ: Africa World Press, 1999: 303–31.
Irigaray, Luce. *Sexe et Parenté*. Paris: Minuit, 1987.
Keim, Karen R. 'J. Nozipo Maraire's *Zenzele: A Letter for My Daughter*'. In Jean Margaret Hay (ed.), *African Novels in the Classroom*, London: Boulder, 2000: 167–77.
Maraire, Nozipo. *Zenzele: A Letter for My Daughter.* Harare: Baobab, 1995. All references are to this edition and page numbers are given in the body of the text.
Mohammed, Patricia. *Gendered Realities: Essays in Caribbean Feminist Thought*. Kingston: University of the West Indies Press, 2001.
Ncgobo, Lauretta. *Let It Be Told: Essays by Black Women in Britain*, London: Virago, 1988.
Nice, Vivienne. *Mothers and Daughters: The Distortion of a Relationship*, Basingstoke: Macmillan, 1992.
Nnaemeka, Obioma (ed.) *The Politics of (M)othering: Womanhood Identity and Resistance in African Literature*, London & New York, Routledge, 1997: 1–25
Nwapa, Flora. *Efuru*. London: Heinemann, 1966.
——. *One is Enough*, Enugu (Nigeria): Tana Press, 1981. All references are to this edition and page numbers are given in the body of the text.
Oduyoye, Amba Mercy. *Daughters of Anowa*. New York: Orbis Books, 1995.
Oppong, Christine. *Female and Male in West Africa*. Boston: Allen & Unwin, 1983.
Rich, Adrienne. *Of Woman Born: Motherhood as Experience and Institution*. London: Virago, 1977.

Transcending the Margins: New Directions in Women's Writing

Iniobong I. Uko

When in 1988, Narasimhaiah and Emenyonu edited the seminal volume titled *African Literature Comes of Age*, it symbolised a bold pronouncement of a milestone in the evolution of African literature in general. It indirectly foreshadowed the coming of age of female writing as well. This implied that new trends were also to characterise the writing of women in Africa. These trends involve such features as iconoclasm, the deliberate repudiation of all arch symbols of traditionalism and orthodoxy, as well as women's prescient critique of female subjugation, psychological brutality, individual inferiorisation and exclusion on gender lines. They also entail a vehement challenge to the female obdurate naivety and congenital passiveness that hitherto has dominated the configuration of African women in literary works. These features, and many more, comprise an ensemble of social and cultural forces that function as a catalyst that (a) questions the female episteme within the context of tradition, and (b) empowers women to impugn the authenticity of the eponymous tradition, which engender the grave schismatic, rather than the synergistic relationship between the sexes.

Evidently, the coming of age of African literature is identifiable by the true and pragmatic feminisation of the literary vision as a way of correcting absurd female images in African literature and culture. Here, the female writer explores the inner fibres of the androgynous ideal, thereby establishing and justifying the position of women. It is within this framework that this study finds authenticity and relevance, because it seeks to identify women's position in the socio-political schema as well as in the economic production and reproduction processes. In pursuing these, this chapter traces what obtains in select writings by African women in their goal of devising new templates for the signification and appreciation of contemporary African women, without necessarily evolving an ideological jacket or creed. To achieve its objectives, this chapter unavoidably engages in a double reading of history and culture, as well as other phenomena and practices, which the woman in Africa has to both appropriate and repudiate. The female writers in Africa whose works are examined in this paper are Flora Nwapa, Ama Ata Aidoo, Promise Okekwe, Osonye Tess Onwueme and Julie Okoh. This study across the genres (prose and drama) is deliberately intended to demonstrate that new directions are manifesting in the different genres of literature.

Prior to the last decade or two, the preoccupation of African women writers was to re-define African womanhood, represent an authentic personality different from that portrayed by male writers who dominated the literary scene in Africa and designed its landscape. Starting from the Eurocentric/colonial perception of African womanhood as seen in Joyce Cary's *Mister Johnson*, to Chinua Achebe's *Things Fall Apart*, the depiction is typical: the woman is an unthinking, uncritical and helpless being. In *Mister Johnson*, Bamu, Johnson's wife is portrayed as a model *ignoramus*. She knows nothing and can say nothing because she can think about nothing. After the ceremony of her marriage to Johnson, she

> is following Johnson out of the hut when he puts his hand through her arm, clasps her hand and conducts her through the crowd outside. Bamu does not like this. She wants to walk behind her husband, but she allows herself to be pulled along...(41)

This stereotype of the African female walking behind her husband is not unfamiliar. It has been variously recreated by African male writers, who always regard women as being led by men, thus justifying their second, subsidiary position. The only times Bamu expresses her opinion on issues, she seeks to remain within the stereotypic positions of women:

> 'We will eat now' [says Johnson]
> 'Very well, as you like. You are the husband.'
> 'You sit there and eat.'
> Bamu looks at the chair. 'But I can't sit while you eat.'...
> No, I must attend to you properly, like a wife.' (43)

Afterwards, while Johnson is lying relaxing, she brings 'a calabash of broth and gives it to him with a curtsey, turning her head politely to one side so as not to breathe on him' (43). Despite Johnson's misdemeanours as catalogued in the novel, Bamu at no point makes a comment, a reprimand, or an assessment of the circumstances that cause their frequent eviction from one location and resettlement in another. Her inability to think makes her unable to question their situation or criticise the inconsistencies in Johnson's childish, fun-seeking and irresponsible tendencies.

On the other hand, Matumbi, Sergeant Gollup's mistress is portrayed as the willing target of Gollup's drunken feats:

> ...if he beats Matumbi, he uses only his feet and fists...On Sunday,...he will sometimes thrash Matumbi with a stick, flog her or even batter her with a chair until she lies on the floor covered with blood...in fact, she has suffered no more, in four years of Sundays, than a broken arm, a split ear, and a few deep scars. Matumbi...has a strong affection for Gollup.
> ...

She is boundlessly greedy and lazy, she will not even scratch herself if she can get the small boy to do it. Her virtue is good humor. She will sit for hours apparently *thinking of nothing*...(25–126) [emphasis mine].

Of course, colonisation had little or no place for women. The positive aspects British colonisation in particular, were largely targeted towards men. Men served as assistants in the colonial offices, interpreters in the courts, workers in the churches, while women were condemned to domestic chores and featured only as shadowy beings that served the sexual and other needs of the men.

This depiction of the woman as a nonentity, with neither ambition nor concrete abilities might not really have been the thrust of the force that motivated African writers to correct the atrociously misconceived and misrepresented Africa, African landscape and values as well as African humanity, where hu*man*ity is contemplated as man, the male. It is not out of place, therefore that the first African literary work in English, the unbeatable classic of the 20th century African literature, Achebe's *Things Fall Apart*, consciously recreated the authentic Africa, African landscape and African hu*man*ity, in its portrayal of men of honour and valour – Okonkwo, Obierika, Ezeudo, Uchendu, and others. The obvious omission is in *Things Fall Apart* not consciously recreating a credible African woman who knows her own mind and even while married and performing nurturing roles, has her ambitions and contributes to the dynamics of economics in the micro and macro systems. Ekwefi, Okonkwo's second wife and Ezinma's mother seems to have a mind of her own – she leaves her first husband for Okonkwo, she is the only one who bangs on Okonkwo's door for his attention early in the morning. But her audacity contradicts the reality that she is a victim of Okonkwo's battering. Okonkwo suspects that a banana tree in his family premises is withering because it has lost its leaves. On inquiry, he discovers that his Ekwefi 'merely cut a few leaves' off it to wrap some food ... Without further argument Okonkwo gave her a sound beating and left her and her only daughter weeping. Neither of the other wives dared to interfere beyond an occasional and tentative 'it is enough, Okonkwo,' pleaded from a reasonable distance (39). This omission in Achebe's *Things Fall Apart*, in particular, calls into question Achebe's principle of duality, which implies that nobody can operate in isolation from others, that is, no man is an island, thus when one thing stands, another stands beside it. The obvious truism of this ideology makes it imperative that the female writers' sense of commitment must come alive in repositioning women within the mainstream of events, rather than have them quashed to the point of asphyxiation in the margins of the system.

From the above framework, this chapter suggests that African women have had to write their stories, not as an affront to the men, but as a recapitulation of the impeccable role of the symbolic *eneke-nti-oba* in Achebe's works. According to *eneke* the bird, when his friends asked him why he was always on the wing, he replied that since men have learnt to shoot without missing, he has learnt to fly without perching. Invariably, female writers in Africa have had to re-order the trends that perpetuate female inferiority, subjugation and silence. They try to re-assess the positions and roles, for example, of Okonkwo's wives in *Things Fall Apart*:

> Okonkwo was provoked to justifiable anger by his youngest wife [Ojugo] who went to plait her hair at her friend's house and did not return early enough to cook the afternoon meal.
> ...
> And when she returned he beat her very heavily. In his anger he had forgotten that it was the Week of Peace. His first two wives ran out in great alarm pleading with him... (30–1).

It is apparent that Okonkwo's wives merely operate from the fringes of the familial schema, while Okonwko dominates, sprawling his strict and rigid authority over his household:

> Okonkwo ruled his household with a heavy hand. His wives, especially the youngest, lived in perpetual fear of his fiery temper, and so did his children. (16)

It thus appears as if Eurocentric/colonial representations of the African woman serve as a model for the African male to perceive his female counterpart. These representations portray her as an outsider. The politics of the insider/outsider can easily be traced from the colonial value system that recognised African men and utilised their services and potential at the expense of the African women who were from then on condemned to domesticity and related activities. This paradigm was convenient for the African male who evolved a new sense of superiority over his female counterpart. These processes marked the genesis of the condescending and stereotypic images that compel women in Africa to be excluded from the centre and to be treated as outcasts in crucial socio-political processes.

The inter-gender polemics of women-as-outsiders in Africa involves such issues as the marginality, subjugation and relegation of women. They are marginalised within the praxes of professional, socio-political and economic self-acclaim; they are also subjugated to subservient roles and relegated to the performance of their biological roles and a life of domesticity. These constitute the major motivating factors for women's writing in Africa. Certainly, there is no disputing the fact that the pioneering feat by Flora Nwapa through the publication of *Efuru* in 1966 shook women from slumber and melancholic acquiescence to female stereotypes, gender discrimination and female invisibility. Nwapa paved the way for other women including Buchi Emecheta, Mariama Bâ, Zulu Sofola and Efua Sutherland, the group that Tess Onwueme describes as *literary foremothers*. According to Onwueme:

... the earlier works [of the literary foremothers] still, relatively, portrayed weak and helpless women, even though these writers were actually, rewriting and talking back to the male writers. (Personal Interview 8 June 2003)

In reaction to the diffident approach of envisioning African womanhood by the *literary foremothers*, and sometimes a concomitant negative portrayal of the African male (for which some of their writings have been criticised), some female writers in subsequent generations have made bold attempts at re-envisioning African womanhood. By doing so, they save African women's writing from the critique of *anti-sexist sexism*. Indeed, what this category of writers does is, as Onwueme articulates, 'to rewrite and represent women as individuals with conscience, able to question the system that marginalises and disempowers women' (Personal Interview 9 June 2003).

This act of writing described above, therefore, moves African women from the margins to the centre, that is, from being outsiders to becoming insiders, from being and feeling victimised and neglected to actually becoming the prime actors in all spheres of life in the society. The writers' vision is to give brains, critical sensibility and voice to the Bamus among contemporary African women (Joyce Cary, *Mister Johnson*). It also emboldens the Nnu Egos to resist being coerced by society into subjecting themselves to motherhood as the only means to the attainment of fulfilment and satisfaction. Motherhood here is considered in terms of having male children for the perpetuation of the lineage (Buchi Emecheta, *The Joys of Motherhood*). The Nnu Egos will consequently be able to resolve the issues raised by Emecheta in *The Joys of Motherhood*:

> God, when will you create a woman who will be fulfilled in herself, a full human being, not anybody's appendage? After all, I was born alone, and I shall die alone...When will I be free? (186-7)
>
> Sometimes seeing my colleagues, I wish I didn't have so many children. Now I doubt if it has been worth it. (202)

Clearly, societal constructs set motherhood and procreation as the woman's major sources of fulfillment, but contemporary African women are seeking new avenues for self-fulfilment, arguing that it is now untenable, obnoxious and unacceptable that womanhood is validated only through motherhood and procreation, where procreation implies the male-child principle.

It is significant that in exploring the new directions in women's writing in Africa, this paper first traces the contribution of Flora Nwapa to re-envisioning African womanhood and re-positioning the African woman from the fringes of the societal schema. Described by Emenyonu as Flora Nwapa's 'final legacy', Nwapa's play *Two Women in Conversation* does not only show-case the 'assaults on women (including domestic violence), and the dehumanization of womanhood by abusive patriarchy and feudalistic tradition' (Emenyonu, 2000: 209), but it clearly articulates contemporary African women's intrepid resolve to transcend the margins and actually take centre stage within micro and macro systems.

Juma and Niki, the modern, well-educated, sophisticated and independent women in conversation are the mouthpiece through which Nwapa makes very strong statements on the changing roles, positions and image of the African woman. Through the two women, the reader realises the implications of the notion of independence on contemporary African women: they have to be resilient, resolute and courageous to make (sometimes very hard) decisions. Juma recalls:

> I was busy.
> I worked and worked
> I went to school.
> I ministered to my husband
> I cooked, washed and ironed his clothes
> I took care of the children.
> He never lifted a finger to help.
> I did not even mind that;
> I rebelled only when he decreed
> We should have more children.
> I got myself some pills
> And took them religiously
> ... (97)

Such was the situation in the family before Juma's husband walked out and abandoned his family and children. Her husband neither gave her 'house-keeping money' nor money to buy things for an expected baby, which meant that Juma resumed work a week after she had their first baby (97).

On Niki's part, she married at the age of twenty-five, and her husband left her by the time she was thirty (103). The core of Nwapa's vision in *Two Women in Conversation* derives from Nwapa's desire to evolve strategies for the contemporary woman to cope with the strain of being in a marriage of bitterness, and the agony of separation and single motherhood. About the marriage of bitterness, Nwapa, through Niki, states:

> You musn't make a man feel
> That you know anything
> Above all
> You must not make him rich.
> ...
> Don't ever help him
> In his business
> Leave him to struggle
> If he makes it
> You share in the wealth ... (110–11).

However, both women agree that 'the institution of marriage will soon disappear from the face of the earth' (122), stressing that the contemporary African woman needs 'a man but not a husband' (114). This sense of independence emboldens the women to discuss freely the issues of divorce (137), abandoned wives/single mothers having lovers to ensure their emotional sanity (137), the evil of the *purdah* and its role in engendering unhealthy competition among co-wives (134).

Unfortunately, Flora Nwapa attained the consciousness and courage to take such a revolutionary position as gender issues in 1993 just before her death in October of that year. The explosive issues of African women's independence, sexuality, resilience and tenacity in this play indicate an obvious enhancement of the discourse she initiated in her previous works – the novels – *One is Enough*, *Women are Different* and others. The fresh sensibility of African women openly and freely discussing issues of sexuality, options in marriage, and other related matters is a remarkable new dimension in the writing of African women.

In Julie Okoh's play, *Edewede: The Dawn of a New Day*, Edewede's revolutionary impulse and leadership skills ensure her success in motivating the women of Otoedoland to rise against female stereotypes and all practices that perpetuate not just women's dependence on men, women's retrogression, undue silence and docility, but also the more lethal aspects of women's behaviour. In enlightening the women on the fatal implications of female genital mutilation or female circumcision, Edewede, the beacon of the women's struggle, along with Eriala (Mama-Nurse), a midwife, calls into question the tradition that insists on checking women's libido so that women would be passive partners in the sex act. She stresses that men rather than women gain from the practice of circumcision, stating:

> Our mothers practiced circumcision
> Because they knew nothing about anything
> Except for laws and taboos imposed on them
> To stop them from thinking for themselves
> So that from childhood, they learn
> To be shy, silent and docile
> Until they see themselves
> As objects for men's pleasure.
> ...
> ... they see any deviation from [this condition]...as a crime.
> But today, light has chased away darkness
> And women must change with time. (37)

Light here is perceived as the new awareness among women to choose, their determination to move from the margins and inaction to the centre so as to debunk the argument that 'the peanut is very delicate. It is the source of confusion, impurity and imperfection' (5), which should justifiably be 'carved out of its pod' through female circumcision.

However, contemporary women argue that women do not think with their genitals, thus female promiscuity cannot be checked through female circumcision. Recounting that this retrogressive practice has caused the infection, deformity, stigmatisation and death of many of its victims, the women decide to use their own resources to reinforce their insistence that the practice of female circumcision be stopped:

> Our bottom. Yes, our bottom is our power. As from this day lock it up until they [the men] crawl to us for reconciliation. (47)

This unprecedented female strategy of demonstrating rebellion against debilitating traditional practices against women achieves two immediate results. First, it engenders female solidarity; and second, it forces the men to critically re-assess the women's desire to expunge female circumcision from the society's value system. The women keep away from their husbands and homes, until the men concede to the women's proposal. By this victory, the women have overcome the evils of circumcision, and have transcended the periphery to re-position themselves at the centre.

Osonye Tess Onwueme's preoccupation in her epic play, *What Mama Said*, which is the climax of Onwueme's dramaturgy, is significant. She portrays the generational abuse, deprivation, marginality and oppression that the women and youth suffer in 'Sufferland', which produces enormous wealth that is appropriated and misappropriated through the connivance of the people's leaders and foreign partners. There is a high degree of unemployment, the government is both irresponsible and insensitive, and there is a general feeling of animosity among the masses towards their leaders. Omi, an unemployed college graduate, resorts to the humiliation of serving as Oceana's mistress and as a call-girl at the GRA/Oil Club where Oceana, the powerful foreign Oil Director lives. At the point of the women's rebellion against their leaders who represent capitalism, extortion and exploitation, Omi confronts Oceana openly:

> Like you too, I fix my price for my buyers. …You come to our own land. You take and take and also dictate the price? And still we have no right to say 'no'… To you, I fix my price: $5? $10? And all night long, everything adds up. (Vulgarly displaying her body…) You touch? $10. Suck? A double blow. And then the big one? … You think you can continue to pour and discharge all that for nothing? And then AIDS?…And then the other risk? Unwanted baby… All you want is just to kick us around and out… Not any more! You pour it? You pay for it! You pump it? You pay for it. You mess it up? You clean it up! (102-3)

The boldness of this 23-year-old in evaluating in monetary terms the worth of her sexual activities with Oceana may derive from her frustrations and hopelessness. She frees herself from restraint and what may be considered as decency, thereby rejecting the miserable fate of her mothers and grandmothers before her who where silent and were consequently devastated by the exploitative system. The awareness of what her foremothers experienced actually animates her to accuse her lover, Oceana of extortion:

> Paid me pennies all day and you want to kiss? … All day long you took my bra. My panties, you put under your pillow and you've been sniffing and sniffing

and touching and sucking ... And then you poured all that into... Don't you know it costs money? ... Nothing goes for nothing... You've sucked and drained enough. Now pay up! ... (103)

Omi's rebellion in *What Mama Said* indicates African women's resolve not to be exploited any more. That her fight is against the powerful foreign Oil Director shows that the women are determined to crush every form of obstacle on their way from the margins where they are mere pawns for male pleasures. Through Omi's provocative obscenity and vulgarity, a new vista of self-expressiveness is opened to foster the centrality of African women in the processes that are male-dominated.

Similarly, Promise Okekwe's prose in Zita-Zita laments the wasted potential and doomed fortunes of a country that is very rich but whose masses wallow in the anguish of poverty, disease and want due to the reckless self-aggrandisement, irresponsibility and insensitivity of the people's leaders. Okekwe pitches the essence of her satire within this framework. However, underlying this well-couched national tragedy is the development and search for self and identity by Zita-Zita who is motherless, spitefully used, treated and scarified by her step-mother's lover and stigmatised and pushed to the brink of insanity by the tumultuous pattern of her life. Zita-Zita becomes orphaned, roams the streets, is rescued and adopted by the first Lady, Her Excellency, Akuchukwu Igini (Aku). Zita-Zita is immediately integrated into the President's household at Aso Rock.

Promise Okekwe's *Hall of Memories* and *Zita-Zita* are two parts of one extensive story, whose significant feature is Okekwe's poignant description of sex acts involving, first, Zita-Zita and the President, His Excellency Michael Igini, who successfully seduces her; second, Zita-Zita and Vincent Mapo. The President, 'spread out [his] welcoming arms into which she [Zita-Zita] went,...she allowed his tender arms to guide her head on to his great chest...He cuddled her...' (91). And later:

> Her eyes met his warm eyes, full of candour. He pulled her face down to his and kissed her...(93)
>
> Michael took her face in his right palm and looked at her with pleasure.
>
> He closed his eyes and licked her tears until he found her lips which he kissed with unutterable tenderness which set fire in the secret places of her being. While he held her, loving her with an appalling innocence which repelled disbelief, he held her there, in the four-walls of his soul. And when it seemed as though the wine of her body was getting too much into his head, he held her apart because he wanted to love her with a cool head ...(96)

In spite of Zita-Zita's hitherto miserable life, and then having a son for the President, she refuses to marry him. Her resolve transcends all the prospects of affluence, love, name, prominence and protection that had eluded her thus far. Her dogged refusal to marry him derives from: (a) guilt for the hurt she causes Aku, and (b) the freedom she craves from the overwhelming and (seeming) irrational passion that Michael displays for her, which she fears might devour and engulf her. She allows the President to take custody of their son; she meets and marries Kazeem Zubir Ahom who she soon loses to Janet. However, Zita-Zita in losing Kazeem to Janet, also miscarries her three-month pregnancy by him. She rejects Kazeem's initiative of polygyny, and returns to Nigeria.

Zita-Zita, in Okekwe's novel by the same title, has progressed from a passive status to actually controlling the trends in her relationship with Vincent Mapo:

> All night his manhood stretched endlessly, hardened, heated up as his wine threatened time without number to burst the wine skin, but she contained him as he struggled to contain himself. And all she did was hold him as though by so doing she would calm the storm raging in him... he needed help. She was not full of pity for him ... (83)

> There she was, refusing to let him get intimate with her, there she was right in front of him, naked as the daylight. As his manhood stood in the salute to her regal build, she put his cream on her body, dressed up with careless abandon...(84)

Okekwe demonstrates Zita-Zita's evolution, in spite of her neurotic state, from the periphery to the centre, where the former implies self-pity, helplessness and hopelessness, and the latter alludes to self-confidence and esteem, critical consciousness of people and trends as well as total control of what is going on around her.

Ama Ata Aidoo in *Changes: A Love Story* deploys the sexuality of the vivacious Esi Sekyi to articulate the changing position of the contemporary African woman. Esi is career-oriented and has very little time for her family. Choked by the feeling of abandonment by his alluring yet illusive wife, Oko:

> ...flung the bedcloth away from him, sat up, pulled her down, and moved on her. Esi started to protest. But he went on doing what he had determined to do all morning. He squeezed her breast repeatedly, thrust his tongue into her mouth, forced her unwilling legs apart, entered her, plunging in and out of her, thrashing to the left, to the right, pounding and just pounding away. Then it was all over. Breathing like a marathon runner at the end of a particularly grueling race, he got off her, and fell heavily back on his side of the bed (9).

Esi reacts with calmness to what is described as marital rape and obtains a divorce while their daughter is raised by Oko's mother. Esi later becomes the second wife of Ali Kondey, the young charming and romantic business executive:

> Esi and Ali reserved their love-making for the comfort of Esi's bed...They would immediately fall into each other's arms and hold her welcoming kiss from the front door through the length of the sitting room, through her bedroom and on to her bed. ... (74)

Significantly, Esi's sense of independence is as astonishing as it is provocative: she enjoys 'walking around naked after love-making' (74), and she feels no shame in spending time with her close friend, Opukuya, in the lobby of Hotel Twentieth Century. They freely take alcoholic beverages while discussing such critical matters as marriage, divorce, motherhood, wifehood and careers. Caught in the web of his matrimonial life, Ali can hardly sustain the routine of his home (with his children and first wife, Fusena) – his office (work) – Esi's house. This weakness makes him merely a shadowy figure for Esi. Esi resents the fact that Ali's affections are manifested only in the numerous gifts that he showers on her over the period of their intense romance and eroticism:

> Esi decided she was just fed up... 'Ali, I can't go on like this.'
> ...
> 'This is no marriage...But if this is it, then I'm not having any of it', she added with such chilling finality that for a little while, Ali really did not know what to say. Then he turned, went back to the chair and picked up...his briefcase and turned to leave. 'If that's how you see it, then I'm going'. (158–9)

At this point, the marriage ends and Esi reverts to a lonely life, a situation Kubi, Opukuya's husband attempts to exploit. However, Esi's resistance is a testament to the fact that she is still in control of her emotions and sense of self: she may be actively sexual and titillating, but she would not be seduced by her close friend's husband. It is evident that Aidoo's *Changes*, winner of the 1992 Commonwealth Prize for Literature in Africa, marks the peak of the highly charged discourse on the position of women in contemporary Africa. Undoubtedly, African women have moved from the margins to the centre where they can make their own decisions, be their own critics and evolve viable taxonomies of socio-cultural, political and economic patterns by which womanhood may be perceived.

In conclusion, the new ways of capturing womanhood by African writers are reverberations of the prominent female stereotype of the prostitute, the whore, the temptress, in fact, the witch, whose activities are geared towards capitalising on man's helplessness to lead to his downfall. Contemporary women writers in Africa deconstruct and recreate the hitherto contemptuous stereotype of the voluptuous and sexual African woman; the stereotype that justified her exclusion in serious matters and credible activities. These writers utilise this stereotype as a loom on which to weave with hard and colourful yarn a not just attractive, but also very taut and resilient fabric that is a critically necessary adornment for contemporary Africa. This fabric turns out to be the woman, the African woman, whose sexuality is neither an epistemological evil nor a boisterous tendency as Jagua's in Ekwensi's *Jagua Nana*. Rather, as this study argues, her sexuality appropriates a catalysm for self-discovery, self-assertion and a holistic redefinition of African womanhood.

Essentially, this study to determine new directions in women's writing in Africa has been approached through a careful selection of some active writers and their current or most recent work. It is remarkable to note that contemporary African women writers are not only establishing the new woman who is free to love and express love; they also essentially surmount all sexist depictions and capture these in very succinct descriptions and picturesque portrayals. They show that though the woman may be said to be situated on the fringes, the borders, the margins, her strength and resilience keep her in control of the centre. Of paramount importance is the process deployed by the marginalised to transcend the peripheral positions and roles, and actually occupy the centre, to be relevant in the scheme of things and take control of crucial events. This study reveals the contours and modulations of self-writing – the women's excellent use of their bodies and sexuality, their transformation of hitherto negative stereotypes and stigmas into positive modes of female conception and perception. Herein lies the hallmark of new directions in women's writing in contemporary Africa.

WORKS CITED

Achebe, Chinua. *Things Fall Apart.* London: Heinemann, 1958.
Aidoo, Ama Ata. *Changes: A Love Story.* New York: Feminist Press, 1991.
Cary, Joyce. *Mister Johnson.* New York: New Directions, 1989 edition.
Ekwensi, Cyprian. *Jagua Nana.* London: Heinemann, 1961.
Emecheta, Buchi. *The Joys of Motherhood.* London: Heinemann, 1979.
Emenyonu, Ernest. 'Flora Nwapa's Final Legacy: Dramatic Elements in The Sycophants.' In Valentine U. James et al. (eds) *Black Women Writers Across Cultures.* New York: International Scholars Publications, 2000: 207–20.
Narasimhaiah, C. D and Ernest N. Emenyonu (eds). *African Literature Comes of Age.* Mysore, India: Dhvanyaloka Publication, 1988.
Nwapa, Flora. *Two Women in Conversation.* In *Conversations.* Enugu: Tana Press, 1993.
Okekwe, Promise. *Hall of Memories.* Lagos, Nigeria: Oracle Books, 2001.
———. *Zita-Zita.* Lagos, Nigeria: Oracle Books, 2002.
Okoh, Julie. *Edewede: The Dawn of a New Day.* Owerri, Nigeria: Totan Publishers, 2000.
Onwueme, Tess. Personal Interview. Eau Claire, Wisconsin. June 8, 2003.
Onwueme, Osonye Tess. *What Mama Said: An Epic Drama.* Detroit: Wayne State University Press, 2003.

Re-Thinking Nation & Narrative in a Global Era: Recent African Writing

Nana Wilson-Tagoe

Recent post-colonial theorisations of globalisation perceive it almost solely in terms of a trans-national convergence of cultures under the structures and pressures of a global economy. This culturalist view in which global flows in trade, people, knowledge and ideologies create 'third cultures' autonomous of national communities may distort the nature of cultural production in African worlds that still struggle with the after effects of an older modernity. The new global cultural economy is in the view of theorists like Apparadurai, a complex, overlapping disjunctive order that cannot any longer be understood in terms of existing centre–periphery models.[1] But in these trans-national imaginary landscapes where can we locate a modern African literature that continues to link nation, culture and narrative, yet centres on traumas of national collapse, trans-national movements and an increasingly global focus in social and economic relations? How do post-colonial Africans write their contradictory positions in this new phase of globalisation? How can we re-think the conjunction of nation, culture and narrative in this global era? How adequate are the theoretical models framed by resistance and hybridity for understanding this literature?

In focusing on three recent African novels that deal with global themes my aim is to examine relations between current theories of globalisation and the global themes explored in contemporary African literature. In a broad theoretical sense I want to explore the interaction of post-colonial and globalisation theories as interpretive frameworks for understanding cultural production in an age of globalisation. Two central questions frame my discussion: What does the discourse of globalisation with its emphasis on new postnational[2] global relations mean for those conceptions of nation and narrative that African literature has posited since its emergence? How may the selected narratives illuminate the theoretical literature on globalisation and at the same time question its conceptual terms? I approach these questions by distinguishing between two notions of the global: an earlier globality that was linked to an imperial capitalist system and its concepts of modernisation and a more recent notion of the global that is linked to the transformation of capitalism. The earlier globality had its specific manifestations. It created the hegemony of the single state with the authority to determine cultural value and collective identity. At the same time it consolidated class and gendered identities and integrated non-European histories into a global world dominated by Europe.

The more recent notion of the global is less clear since it is deployed in different ways in economic and social theory. But whether it is seen in materialist terms as the transformation of capital[3] or in culturalist terms as the globalisation of culture,[4] the common understanding is that the process radicalises notions of nation and culture as they were conceptualised in models of modernisation and in post-colonial visions of national communities. Apparadurai, the foremost cultural theorist of the new globalisation, has characterised the phenomenon in a series of statements:

> We are looking at the birth of a variety of complex, postnational social formations. These formations are now organised around principles of finance, recruitment, coordination, communication, and reproduction that are fundamentally postnational and not just multinational or international. [They] are more diverse, more fluid, more ad hoc...less organised, and simply less implicated in the comparative advantage of the nation-state.[5]

Cultural theorists of globalisation see the pressures that inspire this reshaping as originating from a global economy unhinged from its dominant structures and original formations in Europe and America. A 'disorganised capitalism,'[6] they argue, criss-crosses the West and other peripheral centres of technology and production and generates global flows in trade, people and knowledge, creating third cultures autonomous of national communities, histories and geographies. Such a disjunctive order, Apparadurai has argued, can no longer be understood in terms of the existing centre–periphery models that had structured the old globality; it demands instead an overhaul of analytical models that had conceived of society almost exclusively in terms of the bounded nation-state. The theorists themselves seem aware of the problematic nature of a global culture and the possible connotation of the globe as a single place, the unity within which the diversity of cultures can take place. For while Mike Featherstone argues rightly that the new globalising processes and their distinctive forms of social life challenge sociology's focus on society defined exclusively as the bounded nation state, he is also wary of a possible postmodern simplification of the phenomenon as simply 'opening up another space onto which can be inscribed speculative theorizations, thin histories and the detritus of the exotic and spectacular'.[7] On the other hand, Apparadurai's admission that what he calls global culture is fluid and heavily 'inflected by the historical, linguistic and political situatedness of different actors: nation states, multinationals and diasporic communities',[8] points a way forward to a context-based examination of the nature of global culture in non-European worlds.

Exploring my three selected novels on their own terms and in relation to some of these theoretical debates presents an opportunity to demonstrate how contemporary Africans locate themselves in these global flows.What are the determinants of these flows and what relation do the texts themselves stand to the national and the global? I situate the three novels – *A Squatter's Tale*, *By the Sea* and *The Translator* – in the contexts of these theoretical debates and in intertextual relations with earlier narratives of the nation in African literature. As narratives that deal in different ways with the shifting worlds of people in the global landscape, all three novels straddle the different contexts of the post-colonial and the global and therefore offer insights on the changing relationships between nation and narrative in a global era. What unites them is the foregrounding of global themes and a new shaping of home and nation from dislocated migrant locations. Such a perspective represents shifts in the positioning of nation and narrative that distinguishes them from earlier narratives of the nation and from the deterritorialised imaginaries posited in cultural theories of globalisation. In post-colonial African narratives global themes have almost always been subjected to the imperatives of national pedagogies. For most novelists of the 1960s and 1970s, writing the story of the colonised was either a way of constituting the modern community of the nation or a process of investigating its collapse. The global theme as a retrospective rephrasing of the narrative of capitalist modernity[9] or as an inscription of post-colonial hybridity,[10] was either absent or narrativised in oppositional terms. In most African texts nation, culture and identity were linked thematically to place, and place was seen as the determining context of cultural value. Even as relatively recently as Achebe's *Anthills of the Savannah*, where the novelist interrogates the nation and acknowledges that all certainties about it should now be suspect, the global theme, located in the global sensibilities of all the major 'witnesses', remains muted, subsumed in the novelist's need to imagine the nation as a geographic and culturally integrated space.

The global theme is equally distanced in Ngugi's *Devil on the Cross* even though the novel confronts an explicitly global theme by dealing with the impact of multinational capital on Kenya. The global configuration of multinational and local thieves is situated at the opposite end of the major characters' attempts to make meaning of their world despite the suggestion that the impact of the multinationals runs deeper in the nation than their antics in the cave demonstrates. In Ama Ata Aidoo's *Our Sister Killjoy* the protagonist's dialogues are less dialogues between Africa and Europe than dialogues between the nation's people. The anti-universalist perspective that frames Sissie's narrative of her European journey suggests an oppositional discourse even though ironically the most significant insights about herself and her nation derive from her experiences in Europe.

While in African literature the global theme merely hovers on the fringes of the national narrative, it constitutes the very basis of other post-colonial theorisations. Indeed, the two divergent perspectives that underlie post-colonial theory and mark its different phases both hinge on the relative positioning of the global and the national. Theorists like Stuart Hall and Homi Bhabha have always characterised the post-colonial as essentially anti-foundational and transnational. For these theorists the re-narration of the story of colonisation from a post-colonial perspective does not create the bounded nation outside the context of the global. Rather, it displaces the 'story' of capitalist modernity from its European centring to its dispersed 'peripheries' and presents new ways of conceptualising the relationship between them. The focus here is on how the global and the local reorganise and reshape one another. The decentred narrative introduces new sites of identity that redefine conceptions of the European nation and its Eurocentric time.[11]

I explore the three novels against this theoretical background in order to create a context for identifying and explaining shifts in conceptions of nation and narrative in recent literature on the global experience. How for instance, do these novels fit in the divergent perspectives I have outlined? How does the cultural theory of globalisation illuminate them and how do the novels themselves call these theories into question? Though theoretically the new global economy is seen as dislodged from its original location and dispersed through multiple centres and peripheries, the globalising process is ironically still perceived as the flow of meaning from centre to periphery or at best, as a 'peripheral corruption scenario in which the centre offers its high ideals and its best knowledge, and where the periphery first adopts them and soon corrupts them'.[12] Yet as Simon Gikandi argues in an illuminating essay, globalisation is not primarily a mode of transformation of cultural or structural relations in the West itself but a 'result of the transformations in both First and Third Worlds'. The third world itself is the source of the cultural energies and the tragedies that have brought new migrants to the West.[13] It is thus the conditions of this mutual interplay that will ultimately test Stuart Hall's claim that what he calls the mutual reorganisation of the local and the global really means 'a decentring of capitalism nationally' and the 're-articulation of native cultures into a capitalist narrative'.[14]

Ike Oguine's novel, *A Squatter's Tale*, situates itself within the ramifications of such mutual impacts. Centred on the personal story of a young Nigerian banker, the novel encompasses the history of an entire generation of Nigerians, unanchored, rudderless and adrift in a nation that provides no meaningful forms or standards for living their lives. Because the relatively few reviews of the novel read it primarily as a narrative of Nigerian immigrant experience in America, the context of globalisation, far more crucial to its deeper meanings, is often deflated. Yet this connection is important not only because the Nigerian government's pseudo-free market policies create forced displacements of people inside Nigeria and draw local forms of life into the world system but because the novel's own structure of interspersing local and global spaces demands this connection. Unlike earlier narratives of the 1960s and 1970s Oguine's novel confronts the global not as a threat to the nation's integrity and cultural consolidation but as an aspect of its global history and its continuing transformation in a new transnational and decentred global order. The transnational world of corporate finance in Nigeria has historical roots in a global order that dates centuries back in colonial times. Its cultural economies weave an image of a dynamic investment octopus with arms in all the major financial centres of the globe. Yet for all its fashionable veneer and sleek vocabulary it cannot re-write the capitalist narrative or escape the larger corruption of the Nigerian nation itself.

Oguine's self-reflexive narrator continually makes the link between the global and the national, suggesting their inseparability but at the same time distinguishing the Nigerian nation's peculiar crisis within the global economy. His narrative dramatises a disjuncture between the possibilities of global culture and the trans-national fantasies and failures of the Nigerian banking elite. Their inability to harness capitalist 'greed'[15] and energies for transforming themselves in the global economy presents a less celebratory narrative than we find in the theoretical literature on globalisation. Oguine's narrative places contemporary Nigeria within the framework of the global world economy but explores different scenarios and problems that call both the assumptions of the nation and theories of globalisation into question. When Stuart Hall and Homi Bhabha read post-colonialism as an essentially transnational and transcultural global process they talk in diasporic terms of a global re-writing of nation-centred imperial narrative and of the global and the local reciprocally reorganising and re-shaping one another. Oguine's novel however, narrates the global from the context of national crisis, suggesting that we do not all experience the global in the same way; that Nigeria's location in the global economy is disjunctive and requires different modes of interpretation. In his novel the movement of people and the conditions of migrancy are inspired not by emergent transnational social forms but by the deformation of the Nigerian nation itself. His protagonist, Obi, flees Nigeria only to escape degradation, poverty and shame. In America his struggles are defined by his conflictual relation to both America and the disintegrating nation back home, and it is the productive tensions generated in this relationship that point to new ways of conceiving his place in both worlds.

In the theoretical literature on globalisation such transnational movements are seen as dimensions of global cultural flows that can be liberating and productive. In Oguine's novel however, these possibilities can be gleaned only in gaps within the narrative. Migrant stories may enact the expansion of individual horizons of hope and fantasy (as Apparadurai imagines) but they do not encourage the growth of a wide range of progressive transnational alliances. Such possibilities are lived rather in confusing fantasies and in the tragic lives of migrants diminished or disoriented by their experiences: characters like Nebraska Man and Justin, presented as metaphors of the dystopic side of global flows and as symbols of roads not to be taken in the narrator's bid to claim a space in mainstream America.

Globalisation is a process marked by instability and disjuncture. The disorienting and illusionary lives of migrants may enact this disjuncture yet at the same time provide spaces for re-thinking nation, location and identity. The satirically dramatised scene of Nigerian migrants attempting to claim space and political affiliation by presenting themselves as both American and ethnic may be a pathetic and risible portrayal of the kind of transnational alliances imagined in Appadurai's 'ethnoscapes,' but it is also a caricature of what may be possible in an ideal global culture. The carnival character of the dramatisation and the narrator's ironic insights force us to read the scene on multiple levels. We grasp the deceptive self-representations of the migrants, their simple versions of ethnic identity and the Republican politician's utter indifference to their aspirations. The migrants create a fantasy of themselves as a group actually involved in global commerce and business, aspiring to power and inclusion in their new world. But the Republican politician only knows of the powerful presence of Chinese and Vietnamese migrants in Silicon Valley and cannot envision a Nigerian version of global affiliation. Yet within the gaps of the narrative and beyond the carnival atmosphere we also glimpse the possibilities of those multiple centres and global flows celebrated in the theorisations of globalisation.

The protagonist's decision to make his life in America but live both inside and outside its culture may be connected thematically with this earlier drama since it is also about how one constructs oneself in a wider global world. The decision does not obliterate the Nigerian nation from his consciousness but it diminishes its claims to be the sole source of culture and identity for him. At the same time his focus on the present may appear to be consistent with a global culture that is nationless, but Obi's relation to his nation and to America is far more complex. He may reject the idea that culture and identity are fixed to particular national spaces, that the Nigerian nation guarantees his economic freedom and well being, but the nation still exists in his consciousness as stored memories that may shape his responses to the new space. His in-betweenness must in this case be distinguished from the concepts of culture and nation that have shaped post-colonial nation formation since the nationalist project.[16] It is also not the intervening space theorised by Bhabha as the revisionary 'beyond', the site of hybridity and translation.[17] It is literally the state of being in both worlds, of appropriating America but not forgetting Nigeria. It is a position that has not yet developed into a particular ideological vision. For even as a self-reflexive narrator, Obi still has to transcend the sexism that leaves his view of women superficial and blinkered and he must learn to see beyond America's prosperity and recognise layers of disorientation and 'madness' behind the material well being of characters in the new space of America. Obi's commitment to the 'here and now' is sealed with a Nigerian ritual of libation, suggesting continuing links between old and new spaces. But the continuity suggested is far more complex than it appears. The ceremony is performed by the dying Uncle Happiness, a failed migrant 'who had never arrived in America' whose 'soul had never learnt (was perhaps incapable of learning) ... how to follow doggedly the immigrant's mountainous path'.[18] It is thus the young migrant (armed with his stock of books, his maps and his new horizon of aspiration) who is left to translate and re-invent the old links. We leave him at this intersection of histories, simultaneously lodged between the possibility of either translating old memories in the new space or encountering what Iain Chambers has called, the 'languages of powerlessness'.[19]

Whatever illumination *A Squatter's Tale* offers on global spaces and their impact on conceptions of nation and narrative, it cannot claim to represent a homogenous experience let alone a paradigm. The global canvass encompasses a heterogeneity of circumstances and positions and is as Apparadurai has conceded, 'inflected very much by the historical, linguistic and political situatedness of different sorts of actors'.[20] Thus while Oguine's protagonist marks his new identification with the United States by privileging the 'here and now', the two narrators of Abdulrazak Gurnah's *By The Sea* come to terms with exile by assembling and sifting through memories and histories. Published in 2001 and centred on the experiences in Zanzibar, Europe and England of two generations of Zanzibar migrants, Gurnah's novel encompasses a much larger global space than *A Squatter's Tale* yet foregrounds realities and dynamics that predate the contemporary scenario of globalisation. When theorists of globalisation challenge us to measure contemporary experience in relation to new global flows in trade, people and cultures, they talk mostly in terms of transcending traditional boundaries of the nation-state and of re-thinking relations between nations along transnational lines.

Gurnah's novel however, demands that we re-think the global in relation to an earlier globality in the Indian Ocean that precedes European modernity, to the politics of colonialism and nationalism and to the realities of kinship and religion. In exploring the global in this comprehensive way Gurnah situates his novel between a limiting postcolonial notion of hybridity[21] and narrow definitions of nation-ness in postcolonial Zanzibar.[22] His strategy of locating contemporary narratives of displacement in their wider historical contexts provide a grounding for engaging both colonialism and post-colonial nation formation, the twin situations at the heart of the migratory flows in his novel. This particular focus explains why in spite of a suggestion that the narrator's life-saving flight from Zanzibar 'has shut one narrow door and opened another into a widening concourse',[23] this possibility can be imagined only in relation to the future. For in the late twentieth-century context in which the book is set it is the crisis of modernity and nationhood rather than any emergent postnational social forms that generate the movement of people and the condition of exile. The criss-crossing of contrasting histories and narratives of exile take us through the different terrains of Zanzibar, Europe and Britain as the characters narrate their different histories and journeys. Since the older man's story covers a wider and older history of the Indian ocean and is (in spite of suppressions and personal biases) a re-telling of the dramas of Zanzibar's history as it has impacted on him, it is in their light that we must place the younger man's more fraught and alienated narrative.

The narrative of Latif, the younger migrant, takes us through the kinds of histories frequently encountered in theorisations of the post-colonial condition. For even as a somewhat settled migrant in England he sees himself as an "Other" of the West and is constantly negotiating his historical presence in an imperial world. He is a man unable to move forward, plagued and paralysed by memories and longings for a home he had carelessly left. Against this fraught and alienated narrative the sixty-five-year old Saleh Omar presents an elaborate and layered history whose seductiveness lulls us into glimpses of an old world Zanzibar and its ancient and historical links with the entire east coast, Persia, Arabia and ancient Egypt. Behind the fascinating Arabian Nights evocation however, lies a paradoxical story of slavery, colonialism and a sombre history of postcolonial violence and national collapse. Omar may well declare that his narrative does not strive to illuminate 'our condition' and 'our times', but his account of centuries of trading and commerce and the intermingling of people and cultures around the Indian Ocean recalls a pre-colonial world in which identities were fluid and negotiable. British colonial mapping and classification introduced a new order and modernity to this region but also a grammar of territorialisation, hierarchies and nationness in whose confines the region was forever transformed and shaped. Omar's narrative makes a connection between this mapping and the traumas of post-colonial nationhood that are implicated in his situation of exile. Colonial political and economic institutions tended to follow this colonial pattern of stratification. It was the style of British administration, Anthony Clayton has argued, 'to prefer to see people in compartments. Asians were to be traders, Arabs junior officials and Africans, indigenous or mainland, were to be labourers'.[24] Omar's narrative in spite of its personal thrusts and its uncertainties about the precise relation of events and their causes, bears witness to the paradoxes and tragic repercussions of these colonial arrangements. 'I crave to utter [these words]', he declares, 'to display them as judgments of my time and of the puniness of our duplicitous lives'.[25] More than this, his narrative draws out implications. It demonstrates that contrary to our conceptual assumptions, nations, especially those within ethnic settings, are not natural givens but fragile collective projects that may not always be emancipatory or protective of individual freedoms and interests. To the younger migrant, alienated and paralysed by feelings of loss and a longing for the 'smells and sounds' of the homeland, these stories offer a possible absolution, a chance to lay the ghosts of the past to rest and to re-invent himself from the new constellations that these histories assume in the present.

In 'Patriotism and its Futures',[26] Apparadurai sees the crisis of the nation-state as a spur to the emergence of social forms that would compel us to think postnationally and to create national forms that are largely divorced from territorial states. In Gurnah's novel however, such diverse and fluid solidarities across national structures may only be imagined in the 'widening concourse' that the relative safety of exile makes possible. The novel writes against the kind of nation it narrates, a nation that is ethnically defined, that acts in the name of the people yet works to the advantage of the powerful. Indeed there is a sense throughout the narrative of a phenomenon of displacement and global placelessness generated by the contradictory assumptions of just such a nation. Omar knows that he and his fellow refugees at the detention camp are not just the flotsam and jetsam of political life, floating between the certainties and stabilities of nation-states, but victims of the nation itself, 'fleeing places where authority required full submission and grovelling fear...' enforceable with daily floggings and public beheadings.[27] Such common circumstances may create bonds and sites of struggle. But they may not. Omar may find that his life is deepened by the lives and stories of his fellow refugees in the detention centre, but at Celia's Bed and Breakfast neither the horrors of individual displacements nor the indignities of exile creates common sites of struggle among exiles. Apparadurai would argue that this lack of transnational solidarity occurs because 'no idiom has yet emerged to capture the collective interests of many groups in translocal solidarities, cross-border mobilisations, and postnational identities', that

> The incapacity of many deterritorialised groups to think their way out of the imaginary of the nation-state is itself the cause of much global violence because many movements of emancipation and identity are forced, in their struggles against existing nation-states to become anti-national or anti-state and thus to inspire the very state power that forces them to respond in the language of counter nationalism.[28]

Gurnah's novel, however, suggests other thrusts and directions. In reconstituting 'place' through the narratives of Saleh Omar and Latif and implicitly foregrounding the protagonist's stock of old memories and religious values, he upholds those categories that nation-states often subsume and globalisation theories diminish, in this way differentiating his protagonist's location in the new space of exile. It is from memories, personal histories and religious and cultural lore that both migrants see their old worlds in new critical lights and draw strengths for the 'widening concourse' that exile opens up. In exile Saleh Omar may be conscious of 'a discontinuous state of being'[29] but he confronts this not by losing himself in postnational yearnings but by a simultaneous awareness of the two settings of exile and home. In enacting a kind 'homecoming' through different forms of narratives, he defies the loss signified by exile but at the same time looks forward (no doubt with anxiety and trepidation) to the 'widening concourse' opened up by his new 'global' space. The paradox of his own personality and life perhaps best sums up the simultaneous dimensions he acquires in exile. On one hand, he is a man fascinated by maps. He can reach across imagined places on the globe and bring them alive through the stories he re-tells. On the other hand, he is interested in furniture, which at the very least 'weighs us down and keeps us on the ground, and prevents us from clambering up trees and howling naked as the terror of our useless lives overcomes us... keeps us from wandering aimlessly in pathless wildernesses....'[30] It seems to me that it is this paradoxically dual apprehension that characterises Omar's response to exile, leads him to recognise his discontinuous state yet stops him from reconstituting his broken life into some kind of wholeness and tribal pride. Edward Said has argued that there is a unique pleasure in this kind of dual apprehension especially 'if the exile is conscious of other contrapuntal juxtapositions that diminish orthodox judgements and elevate appreciative sympathy.'[31] *By the Sea* gestures towards such directions. It ends with hints of a new cross-cultural relationship for the young Latif, and for Omar a chance of new sympathies between him and Rachel's parents, themselves migrants with an intricate family history of journeys and odysseys.

It seems then that what Apparadurai sees as postnational yearnings in situations of displacement and exile is qualified and complicated in Gurnah's foregrounding of a 'home', seen in his novel as a community of language, culture, and religious lore that mediates our apprension of the widening spaces of exile. In his essay on 'Globalisation and the Claims of Postcoloniality' Simon Gikandi remarks that many of the codes we use to explain the global phenomenon can be anterior to the people who live through the transnational experiences.[32] The emerging differences between between theory and representation in the new narratives I explore reveals a continued focus on place, nation and religion. The crucial point to make though is that all three categories are rethought and positioned differently in these new narratives of journeys and exile. To rethink place or nation in terms of travel is to question the naturalising biases of these categories and to be aware of the mediating role of other places, other worlds, other people and identities in our experience and understanding of home and nation in a global era. Leila Aboulela's novel,

The Translator presents us with such simultaneous dimensions even though the narrative appears to privilege an Islamic discourse. Her protagonist's personal history represents a variant of the kind of transnational movement that Apparadurai attempts to theorise in his essays. Born in England of Sudanese parents, Sammar, the protagonist, returns to Sudan with her parents at the age of seven, travels to Scotland with her student husband in her twenties, returns to Sudan after her husband's sudden death and is literally coerced into returning to Scotland because as both her aunt and her mother-in-law imply, it is the civilised place where her future prosperity lies. Sammar spends four years in Scotland working as a translator, isolated, paralysed by her displacement and constantly plagued by memories of home.

The intervention that sends her back to Scotland is significant in this novel because it breaks a traditional pattern of female dependency and affords Sammar the agency and political space for looking critically at the spaces of home and exile. In a much wider thematic sense it enables a simultaneous placing of a European and an Islamic /African world in a mutually dialogic relation. It is perhaps only within a love relationship that the narrative's symbolic conversion of the West to the enduring values of Islam could be effected. For paradoxically, contrary to her mother-in-law's views and to the general assumption that culture flows from the West to East, the narrative reverses this assumption and works to convert the 'West' to the meaning of Islamic faith. Sammar falls in love with her employer but leaves him and returns to Sudan when he is unable to convert to Islam. But ultimately, buoyed by his love for her, Sammar's lover works his own way into a genuine conversion and travels to Sudan to ask for her hand. The processes through which this conversion is achieved follows the trajectory of the deepening love between the two players, Sammar and Rae. East and West meet sensitively through them not in the polarised way in which Mustafa Said and his white women friends feed into each other's fantasies and prejudices in Tayeb Salih's *Season of Migration to the North*, but in an exploration of the possibilities of cross-cultural relations in a global world that still privileges Western perspectives.

The inter-textual dialogues with *Season of Migration* are implicit throughout Aboulela's novel. The crucial section of her protagonist's return to Sudan appropriates a similar section in *Season of Migration* in which Salih's narrator attempts to obliterate the wider impact of his European journey by re-situating himself unproblematically in the familiar world of his childhood. In forcing his narrator to confront the contradictory import of Mustafa Said's European journey, Salih counters his illusions about continuity and leads him to recognise the problematic nature of home, the inroads made by colonialism and the fragmentation of self that the colonised psyche suffers in colonial encounters. In *The Translator* Aboulela takes on Salih's fundamental ironies about our illusions of home but invests these with paradoxes crucial to her particular thrust. Her protagonist evokes the sights and smells of home and the everyday acts that give purpose, stability and continuity to life. But these co-exist with another evocation of the nation as corrupt and already crumbling. Sammar believes, in spite of her new self-understanding, that her life is here: 'Her future was here where she belonged...The sun and dust would erode her feelings for him. She must pull his words out of her head like seaweed and throw them away... Here. Her life was here.'[33] Yet such a view is also an illusion since her life has already been shaped in wider dimensions that complicate the notion of home itself. For it is through their cross-cultural relationship that both Sammar and Rae transform themselves – she from feminine dependency to agency and voice, he from detached academic to committed believer in Islam. Aboulela refuses a tragic ending to this East–West encounter, but the narrative's happy ending is not achieved through sentimentality. Colonial and post-colonial realities are present as are the historical and cultural differences stacked against their friendship. For even as a sympathetic analyst of Islam and a liberal academic Rae still shares the common Eurocentric view of modernity and globalisation as essentially Western derived and controlled. His view of Islamic terrorists as irreversibly caught up in the Western modernity they fight, is quietly deconstructed when his own conversion to Islam demonstrates that the flow of culture can move in both directions.

In this kind of cross-cultural connection place and nation are centred rather than discarded. It is Sudan itself (its glaring imperfections unsparingly foregrounded) that gives Sammar the foothold and spiritual centre to see Scotland and see herself beyond the dividing lines of 'Otherness'. Geoffrey Nash has observed that the religious consciousness of Sammar is at the heart of the novel.[34] The crucial point, however, is that this consciousness along with the sense of home and nation is sustained as Iain Chambers would argue, 'across encounters and clashes with other histories, other places, other people.'[35] They are thus no longer totally unique but touched and shaped by these encounters. Islam itself is quietly appropriated in a feminist cause as the trajectory of Sammar's self-discovery reveals inconsistencies between religious principle and social practice that may militate against women's gender interests. As a widow in Sudan, married to Ali Yasseen, Sammar might have lived uncritically with these inconsistencies. Touched by other frontiers and histories that run through her life, she can negotiate received ideas about reputation and the politics of the veil, recognising her own complicity in maintaining the status quo. For ultimately Sammar too must learn, as her lover finally converts to Islam, that the true meaning of conversion is when it is inspired by conviction and faith not when it becomes an expedience that makes marriage socially acceptable. These processes of self-discovery are made possible by the location of both characters at the intersections of histories and spaces. The simultaneous dimensions that such locations afford means that histories, memories and religion cease to be confined to particular times and spaces and become 'transnational' in the sense in which they deflate orthodoxies and encourage plural visions.

Such transnational mediations give a different colouring to the metaphors of home and nation in these narratives of global experiences. On one hand, they are the footholds from which national subjects negotiate wider global spaces. On the other hand the interaction of old and new environments means that local contexts are no longer orthodox and homogenous but mediated and translated. The relationship between space, culture and nation changes in these narratives but so too does the meaning of globalisation as it is theorised in Cultural Studies and Postcolonial theory. The idea (vigorously refuted by Anthony D. Smith) that today's emerging global culture is 'tied to no place, draws from everywhere and nowhere'[36] and renders the nation state obsolete, is complicated by the persistence of forms of national affiliations in these global narratives from Africa. Such differences in representation have more to do with the different histories of the nation in Africa. The nation-state may have emerged at a particular stage of technological, economic and literary development in Europe,[37] but in Africa it emerged in different circumstances, and the concept was invested with the varied aspirations, needs and longings of a people struggling to shake off years of colonial domination. The apparatus of the nation was thus more than simply the structure of the state; it was linked to the myths, symbols and religious lore of pre-colonial communities as well as their shared memories and their expectation of continuities between generations. As Anthony Smith argues in relation to ex-colonial and other societies, such 'values and symbols shaped the culture and boundaries of the nation that modern elites managed to forge'.[38] These contexts should not only explain the different relations to nation and community in the selected narratives; they should also affect our theorisations of global culture itself.

NOTES

1 Arjun Apparadurai, 'Disjuncture and Difference in the Global Cultural Economy.' in Mike Featherstone (ed.), *Global Culture: Nationalism Globalisation and Modernity*, p. 296.
2 Apparadurai explores three meanings of the term 'postnational' that may be summarised thus: The emergence of alternative forms for the organisation of traffic in resources, images and ideas is encouraging the spread of national forms that are largely divorced from territorial states and are rendering the nation-state obsolete. See *Modernity at Large: Cultural Dimensions of Globalization*, Minneapolis; London: University of Minnesota Press, 1996. 169.
3 See Roland Robertson, 'Mapping the Global Condition: Globalisation as the Central Concept', in Featherstone, *Global Culture*, 14–30.
4 See Apparadurai, *Modernity at Large*.
5 Apparadurai, p. 167.

6 Apparadurai, 'Disjuncture and Difference in the Global Economy', p. 296.
7 Featherstone, 'Global Culture: An Introduction', in Featherstone, *Global Culture*, p. 2.
8 Apparadurai, 'Disjuncture and Difference in the Global Cultural Economy', p. 296.
9 See Stuart Hall, 'When Was "The Postcolonial"? Thinking at the Limit', in Iain Chambers and Lidia Curti (eds), *The Postcolonial Question. Common Skies, Divided Horizons*, (London and New York, 1996), 250.
10 See Homi K. Bhabha,*The Location of Culture*, pp. 1–18.
11 See Stuart Hall, 'When Was "The Postcolonial"?', p. 250.
12 Ulf Harnnerz, 'Scenarios for Peripheral Cultures', in *Global Culture*, 108. Hannerz's essay actually calls this perspective into question.
13 Simon Gikandi, 'Globalisation and the Claims of Postcoloniality', *The South Atlantic Quarterly* 100:3. (Summer 2001), 645.
14 Hall, 'When was "The Postcolonial"?', p. 259.
15 In a somewhat ironic statement Oguine's protagonist sees capitalism as 'greed' but accepts it has built nations and civilisations: '[we] had possessed enough greed to transform our country, to make it nearly as "civilised" as the wealthy nations of the world. But it was a greed that turned inwards, like acid biting the walls of an empty stomach.' Ike Oguine, *A Squatter's Tale*, p. 104.
16 The link between nation, culture and identity has been a fundamental assumption in nationalist thinking in Africa. African writers have continually searched for modes of narration that would explore the significance of this link.
17 Bhabha, *The Location of Culture*, p. 4. See also pp. 5–18.
18 Oguine, *A Squatter's Tale*, 138.
19 Iain Chambers discusses the implications of living inside and outside the situation at hand in *Migrancy, Culture, Identity*, p. 6.
20 Apparadurai, 'Disjuncture and Difference in the Global Cultural Economy', p. 296.
21 When theorists like Hall and Bhabha read the post-colonial as a transnational and reciprocal re-shaping of global/local relations they think in terms of the ex-colonial's capacity to rupture the narrative of Western dominance. But the notion of hybridity that derives from this rupture still limits the ex-colonial to the narrow space of the colonial encounter in spite of Bhabha's claim that such a rupture marks the enunciative boundaries of a range of other dissonant, even dissident histories and voices. See Bhabha, *The Location of Culture*, p. 5.
22 Anthony Clayton gives a good account of how the post-colonial nation-state that emerged in Zanzibar soon after independence privileged Arab landowners and how after the revolution there was a systematic purging of Omani Arabs. Gurnah's novel captures an aspect of this post-revolutionary purging. See Anthony Clayton, *The Zanzibar Revolution and its Aftermath*.
23 Abdulrazak Gurnah, *By The Sea*, p. 1.
24 Clayton, *The Zanzibar Revolution and After*, p. 15.
25 Gurnah, *By the Sea*,p. 212.
26 Apparadurai, *Modernity at Large*, pp. 158–77.
27 Gurnah, *By the Sea*, p. 46.
28 Apparadurai, *Modernity at Large*, p. 166.
29 See Edward Said's discussion of the nature of exile in *Reflections on Exile: and Other Literary and Cultural Essays*, p. 186.
30 Gurnah, *By the Sea*, p. 3.
31 Said, *Reflections on Exile*, p. 186.
32 Gikandi, 'Globalisation and the Claims of Postcoloniality', p. 644.
33 Leila Aboulela, *The Translator*, p. 144.
34 Geoffrey Nash, 'Re-sitting Religion and Creating Feminised Space in the Fiction of Ahdaf Soueif and Leila Aboulela', *Wasafiri* 35, Spring 2002, p. 30.
35 Chambers, *Migrancy, Culture, Identity*, p. 4.
36 Anthony D. Smith critiques this perspective in 'Towards a Global Culture?' in Featherstone, *Global Culture*, p. 177.

37 Benedict Anderson examines the modern nation in Europe from this perspective in *Imagined Communities*. But see E. J. Hobsbawm's observation that even in the context of Europe it is important to reckon with those hopes, interest, needs and longings of ordinary people that gave a particular colouring to the notion of nationhood. See E. J. Hobsbawm, *Nations and Nationalism Since 1780. Programme, Myth, Reality*, p. 10.

38 Anthony D. Smith, 'Towards a Global Culture?' *Global Culture*, p. 180.

WORKS CITED

Aboulela, Leila. *The Translator*. Edinburgh: Polygon, 1999.

Achebe, Chinua. *Anthills of the Savannah*. London: Heinemann, 1987.

Aidoo, Ama Ata. *Our Sister Killjoy: Or Reflections From a Black-eyed Squint*. London: Longman, 1977.

Anderson, Benedict. *Imagined Communities*. London: Verso. 1983.

Apparadurai, Arjun. 'Disjuncture and Difference in the Global Cultural Economy'. In Mike Featherstone (ed.), *Global Culture: Nationalism, Globalisation and Modernity*. London: Sage, 1999: 295–310.

———. *Modernity at Large: Cultural Dimensions of Globalization*. Minneapolis and London: University of Minnesota Press, 1996.

Bhabha, Homi K. *The Location of Culture*. London: Routledge, 1994.

Chambers, Iain. *Migrancy, Culture Identity*. London: Routledge, 1994.

Clayton, Anthony. *The Zanzibar Revolution and After*. London: C. Hurst, 1981.

Featherstone, Mike. 'Global Culture: An Introduction'. In Mike Featherstone (ed.), *Global Culture: Nationalism, Globalisation and Modernity*. London: Sage, 1999.

Gikandi, Simon. 'Globalisation and the Claims Postcoloniality' *The South Atlantic Quarterly* 100: 3 (2001): 626–58.

Gurnah, Abdulrazak. *By the Sea*. London: Bloomsbury, 2001.

Hall, Stuart. 'When was "The Postcolonial"? Thinking at the Limit'. In Iain Chambers and Lidia Curti (eds) *The Postcolonial Question. Common Skies, Divided Horizons*. London and New York: Routledge,1996: 242–60.

Hobsbawm, E. J. Nations and Nationalism Since 1780. *Programme, Myth, Reality*. Cambridge: Cambridge University Press, 1990.

Hannerz, Ulf. 'Scenarios for Peripheral Cultures'. In Mike Featherstone (ed.), *Global Culture: Nationalism, Globalisation and Modernity*. London: Sage, 1999: 107–28.

Ngugi wa Thiong'o. *Devil on the Cross*. London: Heinemann, 1982.

Oguine, Ike. *A Squatter's Tale*. London: Heinemann, 2000.

Said, Edward. *Reflections on Exile: and Other Literary and Cultural Essays*. London: Granta Books, 2001.

Salih, Al Tayeb. *Season of Migration to the North*. Trans. Denys Johnson Davies. London: Heinemann, 1969.

Smith, Anthony D. 'Towards a Global Culture?'. In Mike Featherstone (ed.), *Global Culture: Nationalism, Globalisation and Modernity*. London: Sage, 1999: 171–91.

A Last Shot at the 20th-Century Canon

Bernth Lindfors

In 1985 I introduced a simple arithmetical scheme for measuring the literary stature of writers from anglophone Africa both comparatively and diachronically. Since this elegant blunt instrument is not yet widely known, and since I now intend to extend its scope up to the end of 1999, it may be well for me to rehearse once again the ground rules governing the reduction of fine literary distinctions to the less subtle certainties of round numbers.

My objective was to provide verifiable answers to several tantalising questions: Who are the major authors in anglophone African literature today? How can the reputation of one be measured against the reputation of another in an objective manner so that the relative importance of each can be ascertained quickly, accurately and dispassionately, without the least trace of subjective bias? How, in other words, can we determine scientifically who stands where in the pecking order established by the preferences and prejudices of public opinion? How can we quantify qualitative discriminations?

As one approach to resolving such issues, I devised a Famous Authors' Reputation Test that records the frequency with which an author and his works are discussed in detail in print by literary scholars and critics. A score is thus arrived at that can be compared to the scores achieved from the same data base by other authors. Those who score highest can be said to have gained wider recognition than those who register a lower number of substantive citations. The Famous Authors' Reputation Test ensures that an author's fame will be assessed not intuitively or ecstatically but purely mathematically. Plain numbers will determine the final ranking.

The database from which statistical information has been drawn in this quest for objective analysis is the most comprehensive one I could lay my hands on – namely, my own bibliography *Black African Literature in English: A Guide to Information Sources* (Detroit: Gale, 1979), and its five supplements, *Black African Literature in English, 1977–1981* (New York: Africana, 1986), *Black African Literature in English, 1982–1986* (Oxford: Zell, 1989), *Black African Literature in English, 1987–1991* (Oxford: Zell,

1995), *Black African Literature in English, 1992–1996* (Oxford: Zell and Currey, 2000), to which I will now add the data from the latest three-year compilation, *Black African Literature in English, 1997–1999* (Oxford: Zell and Currey, 2003) – volumes which together attempt to list all the important critical books and articles (in whatever language) published on anglophone Black African literature from 1936 to 1999. The first volume (hereafter cited as BALE I), covering the earliest forty years of academic productivity, contains 3,305 entries; the second (BALE II), covering five additional years, contains 2,831 entries; the third (BALE III), covering another five years, contains 5,689 entries; the fourth (BALE IV), covering the next five years, contains an impressive 8,772 entries; the fifth five-year supplement (BALE V) contains an extraordinary 13,652 entries; and the sixth supplement (BALE VI), covering only three years but bringing the record up to the end of the 20th century, contains 9,293 entries. Each volume thus records a proportional increase in critical activity, testifying to the tremendous growth of scholarly interest in this literature in recent times. The expanded database now contains a total of 43,679 books and articles produced over a 64-year period. This is not a small or inconsequential corpus of criticism.

But while these six volumes seek to be as comprehensive as possible, they remain to a degree selective: certain materials of marginal interest are deliberately omitted. For instance, brief reviews of books and of stage performances, political biographies of statesmen who happen to be writers, and newspaper reports of the non-literary activities of famous authors are excluded, but not review articles, biographical materials and newspaper items possessing some literary significance. No creative works – novels, stories, plays, poems, anthologies – are recorded unless prefaced by a critical introduction. The intention throughout is to provide thorough coverage of major scholarly books and periodicals as well as selective coverage of other relevant sources of informed commentary.

In each volume the bibliographical corpus is divided into two parts, the first organised by genre or topic, the second by individual author. Annotations are appended to some entries, mostly to identify the authors with whom the article or book is primarily concerned. The general rule of thumb is to note all authors who receive at least a page or two of commentary. If many authors are mentioned but none is discussed at length, the annotation indicates that the work is a survey. 'Et al.' (and others) is used whenever a work briefly treats additional authors.

A concerted effort has been made to list each item in the bibliography only once and to provide numbered cross-references to it in all other sections to which the item belongs. For example, an article on Nigerian drama discussing J.P. Clark-Bekederemo, Ola Rotimi and Wole Soyinka in some detail (i.e., devoting at least a page to examination of each writer) but treating other Nigerian dramatists in a cursory fashion (i.e., discussing them in less than a page each) would appear in the drama section in Part

Chart One

1. Soyinka	9091	19. Abrahams	792
2. Achebe	6585	20. Farah	782
3. Ngugi	4081	21. Rotimi	742
4. Saro-Wiwa	2093	22. Ngema	732
5. Armah	1621	23. Okara	716
6. Head	1574	24. Osundare	646
7. Tutuola	1464	25. Okri	605
8. Clark	1117	26. Awoonor	588
9. Emecheta	1109	27. Rive	578
10. Ekwensi	1082	28. Marechera }	544
11. Mphahlele	1050	29. Serote	
12. Brutus	982	30. Plaatje	531
13. Osofisan	905	31. Equiano	527
14. La Guma	894	32. Mbuli	508
15. Nwapa	879	33. Amadi	487
16. Aidoo	851	34. Ndebele	437
17. Okigbo	849	35. Omotoso	426
18. Okot	812	36. Sutherland	407

One with an annotation reading 'Clark, Rotimi, Soyinka, et al.' The number of that entry would then be included among the cross-references following the individual sections in Part Two listing books and articles devoted exclusively to Clark, Rotimi and Soyinka respectively. On the other hand, a specialised article on only one author – e.g., 'Pidgin English in Soyinka's Plays' – would be recorded under Soyinka in Part Two with numbered cross-references appearing in the topical sections on 'Drama' and 'Language and Style' in Part One. So each author treated in the bibliography has a special niche in Part Two where all the books and articles dealing with him or her alone are listed, after which numbered cross-references provide leads to all other items in the bibliography that offer substantive commentary on his or her work. A good many of these cross-references may yield no more than a few pages of sustained criticism, but certain of them – book chapters, lengthy monographs or doctoral dissertations focusing on only two or three writers, for instance – may provide much more exhaustive treatment of specific texts than do some of the individual articles.

Nonetheless, in devising a scoring system for my Famous Authors' Reputation Test, I have decided to award three points for every discrete entry on an individual author and one point for every cross-reference. This seems to reflect the balance between the two categories more accurately than does a straight one-for-one system that would tend to inflate the scores of authors who are frequently cited but seldom examined with

112 A Last Shot at the 20th-Century Canon

Chart Two

1. Soyinka	1,475	19. Marechera*	154
2. Achebe	988	20. Plaatje	131
3. Saro-Wiwa	599	21. Koigi*	130
4. Ngugi	521	22. Mazrui*	129
5. Tutuola	478	23. La Guma	127
6. Head	330	24. Dangarembga*	123
7. Nwapa*	290	25. Equiano }	121
8. Mbuli*	270	Okigbo	
9. Aidoo*	235	27. Manaka *	118
10. Emecheta	232	28. Mhlophe	109
11. Armah	225	29. Clark	108
12. Farah*	211	30. Mphahlele	101
13. Osundare*	197	31. Rotimi	98
14. Osofisan }	191	32. Ike*	97
Ngema*		33. Mda* }	96
16. Okri	173	Brutus	
17. Singh*	171	35. Mutwa*	93
18. Ekwensi	161	36. Bandele*	91
		37. Ndebele	90

any care. An author who is known but never studied intensively may be a significant minor reference point in African literature, but it is unlikely that he or she commands the kind of respect that reflects genuine distinction. Literary critics and scholars tend to gravitate toward those writers whose works interest them the most. They do not waste too much time on second-rate talents.

Chart One is a list of the eighteen authors who achieved a score of at least 800 on the Famous Authors' Reputation Test and then a list of eighteen others who achieved a score of at least 400. According to statistics gleaned from more than six decades of critical commentary, these thirty-six names are those most consistently chosen as worthy of serious attention, the figures on the left constituting what could be called a High Canon and the figures on the right a Low Canon.

But since such a list may be biased toward older writers who have been on the scene a long time, it may be interesting to look at the figures derived from the latest volume alone in order to see who among writers young and old has emerged as important in the eyes of scholars and critics in more recent years. Chart Two thus gives the scores for eighteen writers who gained more than 160 points between 1997 and 1999 and then lists nineteen others who earned at least 90 points during the same period. Asterisks have been placed beside those names making the most striking

A Last Shot at the 20th-Century Canon   113

Chart Three

	1976	1981	1986	1991	1996	1999	FINAL
1.	Achebe	Achebe	Soyinka	Soyinka	Soyinka	Soyinka	Soyinka
2.	Soyinka	Soyinka	Ngugi	Achebe	Achebe	Achebe	Achebe
3.	Tutuola	Ngugi	Achebe	Ngugi	Saro-Wiwa	Saro-Wiwa	Ngugi
4.	Clark	Armah	Armah	Armah	Ngugi	Ngugi	Saro-Wiwa
5.	Ngugi	Tutuola	Clark	Saro-Wiwa	Head	Tutuola	Armah
6.	Ekwensi	Mphahlele	Okot	Head	Ngema	Head	Head
7.	Okigbo	Ekwensi	Head	Ekwensi	Emecheta	Nwapa	Tutuola
8.	Abrahams	Okot	Brutus	Clark	Osofisan	Mbuli	Clark
9.	Okara	Clark	La Guma	Emecheta	Mphahlele	Aidoo	Emecheta
10.	Armah	Awoonor	Ekwensi	Osofisan	Armah	Emecheta	Ekwensi
11.	Mphahlele	Abrahams	Rotimi	La Guma	Brutus	Armah	Mphahlele
12.	Okot	Okigbo	Tutuola	Osundare	Nwapa	Farah	Brutus
13.	Brutus	Brutus	Emecheta	Iyayi	Rive	Osundare	Osofisan
14.	Awoonor	La Guma	Okigbo	Tutuola	Okri	Osofisan	La Guma
15.	La Guma	Head	Mphahlele	Farah	Serote	Ngema	Nwapa
16.	Nzekwu	Okara	Awoonor	Mphahlele	Aidoo	Okri	Aidoo
17.	Aluko	Emecheta	Abrahams	Rotimi	Farah	Singh	Okigbo
18.	Liyong		Okara	Brutus	Ndebele	Ekwensi	Okot
19.			Aidoo	Okara	Osundare	Marechera	Liyong
20.				Marechera	Tutuola	Plaatje	Abrahams
							20. Farah

short-term gains. These are evidently the most upwardly mobile celebrities at the moment, but it remains to be seen whether any of them will have the kind of staying power that some of their numerically superior colleagues have already manifested.

Since some reputations have waxed or waned over time, I am presenting in Chart Three a diagram that may help us to see the diachronic patterns more clearly. The lists of names show the position held by the top seventeen to twenty authors in each of the successive volumes as well as the position that the top twenty hold today in the rankings derived from the cumulated data in all six volumes.

An author's rise or fall in reputation can be gauged by the trajectories produced when lines are drawn connecting his or her name in each list, with the final cumulated ranking representing where in the grander scheme of things that author stands today in relation to all others past and present. It is clear, for example, that Soyinka and Achebe have always been at the very top, that Ngugi and Armah made impressive early gains

Chart Four

1976	1999
1. Achebe	1. Soyinka
2. Soyinka	2. Achebe
3. Tutuola	3. Ngugi
4. Clark	4. Saro-Wiwa
5. Ngugi	5. Armah
6. Ekwensi	6. Head
7. Okigbo	7. Tutuola
8. Abrahams	8. Clark
9. Okara	9. Emecheta
10. Armah	10. Ekwensi
11. Mphahlele	11. Mphahlele
12. Okot	12. Brutus
13. Brutus	13. Osofisan
14. Awoonor	14. La Guma
15. La Guma	15. Nwapa
16. Nzekwu	16. Aidoo
17. Aluko	17. Okigbo
18. Liyong	18. Okot
	19. Abrahams
	20. Farah

and have more or less held their positions, that Saro-Wiwa has had a meteoric rise, that women writers – notably Head, Emecheta, Nwapa and Aidoo – have been making remarkable gains recently, that Osofisan and Farah have achieved some visibility, that Mphahlele, Brutus and La Guma have been holding their own, that Tutuola, Clark and Ekwensi have been creeping down, that Okigbo, Abrahams, Okara and Okot have suffered steeper declines, and that Awoonor, Nzekwu, Aluko and Liyong have fallen off the chart.

Another diagram (Chart Four) which ignores the five-year fluctuations between 1976 and 1999 and charts individual trajectories from beginning to end of this entire period, enables us to isolate dominant trends in these diachronic patterns more readily. On this simplified chart it is plain to see whose reputation has risen, whose has fallen, and whose has held steady.

However, if we look more closely at Chart Three, taking into account the organisation of entries in the database, it is not difficult to explain some of the seismic ups and downs we see represented there. Entries under 'Individual Authors' in Part Two of each volume of BALE are divided into four categories: (1) Bibliography, (2) Biography and Autobiography, (3) Interviews, and (4) Criticism. If an author is newsworthy – that is, if he or she attracts a great deal of attention in the press or in periodicals as a result of notorious deeds (e.g., the winning of a prize, the losing of a freedom, the taking of a stand, the engagement in a controversy, the ending of a life) – there are likely to be numerous entries in the Biography and Autobiography subsection, each of which will garner the author three points in the final score, the same number of points that are awarded for a critical book or essay on the author's work. Thus, Wole Soyinka's Nobel Prize, coming at the end of 1986, was sufficient to catapult him well ahead of Chinua Achebe, with whom he had been running almost neck and neck in BALEs I and II. Indeed, had it been possible to list every newspaper article published on Soyinka's winning of this prize, the gap between Soyinka and Achebe, not to mention all the rest of the anglophone writing community, would have been much wider. Similarly, Ngugi's detention in 1978 and his subsequent political activities both in Kenya and abroad, the deportation trial of Dennis Brutus in 1982-83, Soyinka's campaign against the Abacha regime in the 1990s, and the deaths of Okot p'Bitek, Alex La Guma, Bessie Head, Flora Nwapa, Richard Rive, Efua Sutherland, Zulu Sofola and Amos Tutuola attracted considerable biographical commentary that added significantly to their total numbers. The single most newsworthy individual in the 1996 compilation (i.e., BALE V) was Ken Saro-Wiwa, whose judicial murder in Nigeria in 1995 led to extensive press coverage both at home and abroad. Saro-Wiwa had already risen faster from obscurity than any other writer in anglophone Africa in the preceding five-year span, when he had ascended sharply to position five on the list, due in large part to the popularity of his serialised television comedy Basi and Company in Nigeria,

Chart Five

1. Soyinka	1,436	16. Ekwensi		126
2. Achebe	1,298	17. Osofisan	}	122
3. Ngugi	744	Saro-Wiwa		
4. Armah	348	19. Rotimi		109
5. Head	319	20. Plaatje		97
6. Tutuola	195	22. Equiano		96
7. Emecheta	184	23. Marechera		93
8. Clark	178	24. Brutus	}	91
9. La Guma	158	Osundare		
10. Abrahams	148	26. Mphahlele		84
11. Aidoo	147	27. Okri	}	81
12. Farah	137	Dangarembga		
13. Okigbo	135	29. Amadi		80
14. Okot	133			
15. Nwapa	128			

his frequent media interviews, and his activism on behalf of the Ogoni people, but it was his trial and hanging in 1995 that propelled him still higher to the third spot in BALE V and to fourth place in the cumulative rankings. One expects, however, now that he is no longer a dynamic presence on the literary and political scene, that he will gradually lose ground to other luminaries in the years to come.

As a corrective to these biographically inflated statistics, it may be well to create an alternative scale of measurement that takes into account only the critical books and articles devoted exclusively to a single author. This may give us more reliable information on an author's standing as a literary artist for it will measure only his reputation as a writer, not his notoriety as a public figure. Instead of being a Famous Authors' Reputation Test, this will be strictly an Authors' Reputation Test. Fame will not skew the numbers. Here then is one more chart (Chart Five) in which only a single point has been awarded for each book or essay published exclusively on a black African author since 1936.

As in Chart One the same three names are at the top, but Saro-Wiwa and Ekwensi drop out of the top ten, Brutus and Mphahlele drop out of the top twenty, and Ngema, Awoonor, Rive and Serote not only drop out of the top thirty but along with Mbuli, Ndebele, Omotoso and Sutherland slip entirely out of sight, their meagre numbers no longer justifying a prominent place in the literary hierarchy. These may be some of the writers who benefited most from public curiosity about their lives rather than their writings; certainly the murders of Saro-Wiwa and Rive, the deportation trial of Brutus, the arrest of Mbuli for bank robbery, and the death of Sutherland helped to raise their profiles in Chart One. Similarly, the successful film and television career of Anant Singh, the imprisonment and subsequent run for public office by Koigi wa Wamwere, and the death of Matsemela Manaka may have boosted the biographical portion of their respective scores in Chart Two. These were newsworthy writers who garnered a lot of publicity in the popular media.

Chart Five also reveals which writers earned greater respect based on their writings alone: for instance, Abrahams and La Guma moved up to the top ten, Aidoo, Farah, Okigbo and Okot gained places in the top fifteen, Equiano and Plaatje made substantial gains, and newcomer Dangarembga suddenly climbed into visibility. These, along with the consistent front runners, may be among the most durable names on the list for it is their books rather than their personalities that command attention.

In order to examine recent trends in critical activity, it may be useful to add one more chart (Chart Six) showing which writers scored highest in the latest three volumes of Black African Literature in English, i.e., those covering the thirteen years between 1987 and 1999. Again, only critical articles and books count in this chart, and only one point has been awarded for each entry.

Chart Six

1. Soyinka	940	15. Marechera		91
2. Achebe	810	16. Osundare		86
3. Ngugi	498	17. Dangarembga		81
4. Head	277	18. Okri		80
5. Armah	223	19. Plaatje		78
6. Emecheta	168	20. Okot		73
7. Saro-Wiwa	119	21. Equiano	}	72
8. Nwapa	118	Rotimi		
9. Farah	117	23. Abrahams		63
10. Aidoo	114	24. Ekwensi		59
11. Osofisan	108	25. Okara	}	
12. La Guma	105	Okigbo		
13. Clark }	98	27. Amadi		55
Tutuola		28. Brutus		54

What is most noticeable here is the rise of critical interest in women writers, who now occupy four of the ten top rungs of the ladder. It used to be said that African women writers were being ignored by literary critics; that evidently is no longer the case. What may have helped Head, Emecheta, Nwapa and Aidoo to ascend in the ranks is not only the increasing attention given to women's studies in universities throughout the world but also the impressive collections of essays that have been published on their works, edited and written mostly by women scholars. This phenomenon may reflect a significant change in the discipline of African literary studies: women are now making their presence felt both as authors and as critics.

Other African literary figures conspicuous by their rapid ascent are Saro-Wiwa, Farah, Osofisan, Marechera, Osundare, Dangarembga and Okri. Meanwhile, some of the older, established figures in the so-called 'first generation' of anglophone African writers have descended in the ranks, Tutuola and Clark moderately, Ekwensi, Brutus, Mphahlele, Okigbo and Okot more precipitously. Perhaps some of these former luminaries are losing their lustre, outshone by several of the younger, brighter stars.

However, even a relatively high total score on these charts now or for an extended period is not necessarily an irrevocable passport guaranteeing permanent entry into an anglophone African writers' Hall of Fame. Time marches on, and if a writer's works do not sufficiently interest or engage future generations of readers after that writer is gone, he or she will eventually lose relative standing, a fate that will be reflected in a downward trajectory on later charts.

The only writers at this point who appear destined to become permanent fixtures in the pantheon of African letters are Soyinka, Achebe and Ngugi. The dramatic disparities between this front-running troika and the rest of the pack are now quite apparent. Indeed, it is unlikely that anyone will catch up to them in the near future, for at each five-year interval so far they have put greater distance between themselves and their followers. In any construction of a canon of anglophone African writing, works by these three writers would have to rank high. Their reputations are very great and growing. Their impressive statistics demonstrate that they are by far the most important anglophone black African writers of the 20th century.

This is not to say that there is no hope for younger writers whose names do not yet appear on any of the charts. On the contrary, as demonstrated in Charts Two and Six, several newcomers have made striking gains in recent years, and one may expect a handful of them to keep rising in the ranks. But the only way that they and others can continue to ascend or to hold their own in future tabulations is by regularly being the subject of critical scrutiny – that is, by frequently being written about. The Famous Authors' Reputation Test shows no mercy on writers whose works and lives do not attract commentary. The unexamined literary career is not worth much in a noisy marketplace of ideas. To be famous, to be reputable, to be deemed worthy of serious and sustained consideration, an author needs as much criticism as possible, year after year after year. Only those who pass this test of time – the test of persistent published interest in their art – will stand a chance of earning literary immortality.

And the progress of such pilgrims towards final canonisation can be assessed as easily and accurately with statistics gleaned from a citation index as with any other divining instrument. Simple numbers may not tell us the whole truth and nothing but the truth, but they can reveal something of the truth in an objective and unbiased fashion. Indeed, quantification may be the best possible method for dispassionately measuring and comparing literary reputations. To arrive at an honest, trustworthy, scientifically constructed canon, all we need to do is count and de-cipher the relevant numbers.

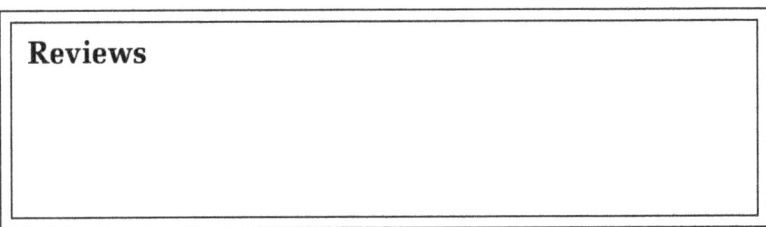

Reviews

New Fiction from West Africa

Grace Ukala, *The Broken Bond*
Ibadan: University Press, 2001, 256 pp., $9.95/£5.95; ISBN 978 030 533 5

Lekan Are, *The Challenge of the Barons*
Ibadan: University Press, 2001, 154 pp., $9.95/£5.95; ISBN 978 030 742 7

Dwaboyea E. S. Kandakai, *The Village Son*
Accra: Sedco Publishing Ltd., 2001, 138 pp., $9.95/£5.95; ISBN 9964 72 177 3

All distributed by African Books Collective, Unit 13, King's Meadow, Ferry Hinksey Rd, Oxford OX2 0DP www.africanbookscollective.com

The publishing industry in many parts of Africa is going through a crisis of faith. With the success of African writers in the 1960s and the 1970s came calls (often from the up and coming writers) for the setting up of indigenous African publishing houses (where such had yet to be founded) and the patronage of such houses by writers who tended to think that being published by foreign houses added a lot to their international leverage. Today, three decades later, the place of the publisher in the practical economics of literature is only just being addressed. In recent years, the Association for African Literature has begun to foreground more and more the input of African publishers (based in Africa or elsewhere) in its sponsored discourses of literary production. A central figure in the new assignment of roles is Kassahun Checole, the publisher of Africa World Press who, at a roundtable on Yoruba metalanguage at the Association's 27th annual conference in Richmond, Virginia in 2001, talked about the risks and the leaps of faith he sometimes takes in publishing in East African languages. At the 28th conference in San Diego, Heinemann staged an elaborate return to mainstream publishing of African literature with a celebration of what it dubbed '40 Years of Distinction in African Publishing'. Highlights included a luncheon, a lecture by Ngugi wa Thiong'o on the role of Heinemann's African Writers Series in fostering nationalism, and the presence of Becky Clarke, a Heinemann literature editor, who tirelessly distributed fliers and pamphlets and fraternised with delegates.

(Circumstances at Heinemann, referred to elsewhere in this section, have since changed. Adepitan's vivid account catches an historic moment. JG)

The call for indigenous publishing of African literature was probably most clamorous in Nigeria during the 1970s. There were a number of reasons for this. Unlike East Africa with its East African Publishing House which gave a fillip to the careers of writers like Okot p'Bitek and Ayi Kwei Armah, Nigeria had no national equivalent, no central publishing house devoted to the discovery and broadcast of original talent. The huge, unspeakable irony of Nigerian literature (which until then accounted for perhaps about one-third of sub-Saharan African literature) was that virtually everything was achieved outside of government patronage, indeed outside of any awareness by the government of its responsibilities in such cultural matters. The only vehicle of cultural exchange with an active participation of government was the redoubtable *Nigeria Magazine*, which published reports by Nigerian academics in the culture vanguard.

By the 1970s the major figures in Nigerian literature had made their mark. Wole Soyinka had published widely and variously with, for example, Methuen, Faber, Penguin, and Cambridge University Press. Chinua Achebe, since *Things Fall Apart* (1958), had enjoyed an almost exclusive publishing franchise with Heinemann. The African Writers Series which that house made into an institution was also edited by him, and several of the major figures in African literature today, including Ngugi, trace their 'induction' into the Heinemann house of fame to the series' patron saint. By the late 1970s there was a glut in Heinemann's list of titles, many of which were chosen not so much for quality as for representational spread.

The writers who were emerging in the early 1980s clearly didn't find it in their best interest to have any truck with a series. Aspiring writers, including Ben Okri, wrote articles (See 'The Problems of Young Writers', *The Times*, Lagos, 1978) criticising the prevailing relations in African publishing which privileged established writers to the detriment of new ones. By the beginning of the '80s, Femi Osofisan, Kole Omotoso and Niyi Osundare had resorted to even more drastic measures: they would not publish with any foreign houses. The ideological premise was that indigenous publishers such as Ethiope, Nwamife, Onibonoje, Aromolaran and Olaiya Fagbamigbe, who were publishing primers and potboilers and high school textbooks and struggling almost in vain against juggernauts such as Oxford University Press, Longman and Heinemann, needed support.

By the middle of the decade more publishing concerns had sprung up. They included Fourth Dimension, Spectrum (founded by Joop Berkhout) and Malthouse Press. This was the closest Nigeria ever came to engendering a publishing culture. Berkhout's Spectrum canvassed scripts from sinners and saints alike, paid advances and ensured that new publications were effectively launched. Major figures in political life, soldiers, socialites, Frederick Forsyth and Princess Elizabeth of Toro among them, basked in the glitz of media attention as their contributions to the Spectrum catalogue were released. From the mid-'80s Malthouse rose to the challenge with an eye on newer talent, even though they also published established writers including J. P. Clark-Bekederemo and Osofisan.

A certain character does seem to be emerging about locally published books, however: the quality of production is falling. At the same time books are over-priced, in a development that no longer takes cognisance of one of the major reasons why indigenous publishing was encouraged in the first place. But nothing is as damaging, nothing as incalculable in its negative advertisement value about recent works of literature published 'from home' as the desperation with which, it would seem, inferior manuscripts are published, with little evidence of basic editorial intervention. Of course, there has to be a higher cadre of writers somewhere out there, or we might as well all pack up and call it a day. But when mediocre fare ends being the subject of serious attention in first-rate journals we need to raise the alarm. Is it for want of something serious and tutored enough to invest time in? Is it a kind of cultural subversion or the age-old clash between the mercantile profit motive and the greater need to avoid selling a whole continent short before the world?

If the charge that a lot of the new writing from many parts of Africa is inferior and lacking in tutored seriousness and craft is easy to misunderstand, let it be said right away that this is not a call for every aspiring African writer to sound like Soyinka. Nonetheless there must be something very worrisome about a body of literature that seems to be regressing into the very milieu of the tradition of Onitsha market literature without the naivety and unified sensibility of the exponents of that pioneering tradition. In work after work, regardless of age or exposure (travel, education, acculturation, etc.) the samples of literature from virtually every corner of the continent are scandalously inferior and are liable to do irreparable damage to whatever little gains were made by the writers who came before. It may be that every culture has a certain level at which the very bottom of its barrel is scraped, but not half as assiduously as we seem to be doing, nor with the same desperate desire to present the same as evidence of what contemporary African writing is about!

Grace Ukala's *The Broken Bond* dives into the steamy life of the Nigerian nouveaux-riches with the crusading sense of indignation that many Nigerians readily recognise. But as with many Nigerians, the mystique of wealth and affluence, especially as it shapes feminist values, gets the better of heroine and author alike, not necessarily in that order. Important decisions are made based on offers of a 'Mercedes Benz 200' as a reward for the birth of a son. In a gratuitous concern with the supernatural (a common feature in many of the recent novels) Ukala claims in her preface (a fine expository piece, except that it takes you back to the old tradition of Onitsha market, with its abundant advice and the promise of a happy life thereafter if the reader learns from the novella) that: '... in *The Broken Bond*, the heroine, Belinda, unlike Ogbanje in *Dizzy Angel,* tackles the witches head-on'. Behind this opposition of good and evil lies the Pentecostal fervour sweeping across the continent; as a window onto spiritual experience it is not only rich but can also admit of heightened levels of interpretation, but our writers wallow in it. They are part of it and hope to awe their readers with the force of its unsullied truths!

Ukala's novel is a string of linear, episodic narratives that take the heroine Belinda from a life of penury on page one to the proud owner of a Mercedes Benz by the end of her story. Her brother, Johnbull, and father, Bello, are cobenefactors; the love of her life, Henry, is not: he shoots himself as a result of insane anger at the broken bond of love. Belinda's husband, Chief Ojo, is also a loser: he barely survives wounds from Henry's gun while his two sons, trained abroad, both die within seconds of each other when Ukala unleashes a scourge of sudden deaths. The town of Agbor, where part of the novel is set, might have been rendered with greater subtlety. Blessed with rugged terrain, a rolling landscape and a critical location as a meeting point of Yoruba, Edo and Igbo elements Ukala can only struggle with the land's significance in her depiction of characters. Crucial landmarks symbolising the very nature of ethnic oppositions in the town are tamely cited once or twice. Benin City, the other locus of action, fares no better.

Lekan Are's *Challenge of the Barons* attempts to secure a place beside Soyinka's *The Interpreters* and Chukwuemeka Ike's *Toads for Supper* in the tradition of the West African university novel. The intrigues in Are's novel pitch progressive African academics against white expatriates in a predominantly US-funded institution. As it turns out, the winds that blast against Onaola Jungu's soul (and he is clearly the author himself, complete with his pedigree as a scion of 'a stock of warriors in the Ibadan of yesteryear') come not from the expatriates but their African lackeys. There are a number of initiatives credited to the hero that are praise-worthy. For example, he selflessly establishes a kola nut nursery from his own pocket for the greater research good of his department and university. The rest is just haughty falconry, as they say. There is too much self-celebration and too much valorisation of a self-perceived sense of worth and significance. More than a half of this 'novel' is really a personal dossier, including report cards from elementary school where Gunju 'was a brilliant pupil who shone like a bright star'. Hopefully the Nigerian nation will at some point define its myriad problems to include the affront posed to the humble task of nation building by the egotist in each of us.

Dwaboyea E. S. Kandakai's *The Village Son* is supposed to have been written in the 1970s. But there is an unevenness to it, which suggests that it was begun at that period, abandoned and then completed much later. Unfortunately the long delay seems to have damaged many things about the novel. The book begins with energy and a lyrical flourish, by the middle the readers can only wonder whether they are still reading the same author. There is a headlong rush about the pace of the story, unmitigated by the absence of chapter divisions or any other kind of structural demarcations. The novel struggles to paint an idyllic image of Liberia, much of which admittedly may be a carry-over from the optimism of the pre-Samuel Doe and George Taylor era. It is disappointing that little is said about the country's contemporary human dilemmas. Yet the verdict has to be that works from Africa's trouble spots need to be encouraged, and we must hope that new initiatives in publishing will cater for them.

Titi Adepitan
Department of English
The University of British Columbia, Canada

124 *Reviews*

Issues in Recent African Writing

F. M. Archibong, *Boko*
Ibadan: Spectrum Books, 2000, 59 pp., $8.95/£4.95; ISBN 978 029 110 5

Laury Lawrence Ocen, *The Alien Woman*
Kampala: Fountain Publishers, 1999, 145 pp., $11.95/£6.95; ISBN 9970 02 181 8

Mary Abago, *Sour Honey*
Kampala: Fountain Publishers, 1999, 122 pp., $9.95/£5.95; ISBN 9970 02 147 8

Kaleni Hiyalwa, *Meekulu's Children*
Windhoek: New Namibia Books, 2000, 119 pp., $9.95/ £6.95; ISBN 99916 31 712

S. N. Ndunguru, *Divine Providence*
Dar es Salaam: Mkuki na Nyota Publishers, 1999, 118 pp., $9.95/£5.95; ISBN 9976 973 53 5.

All distributed by African Books Collective, Unit 13, King's Meadow, Ferry Hinksey Rd, Oxford OX2 0DP www.africanbookscollective.com

There are disturbing trends in African literature. These trends have been apparent at least for the last two decades, but as the generation of African writers with an international reputation grows older it is inevitable that attention will shift to the quality of writers and writing that will come after them. The 1980s and the 1990s heralded the arrival of a new breed of African writers who in ordinary circumstances would be described as constituting a new generation. But they came labouring under too many anxieties. The political landscape was becoming more and more desperate; before they learned how to write many were co-opted into the vanguard of literature as an instrument of protest, and that was all they wrote.

Those who argue, as many do that African literature, particularly Black African literature is in good health err when they point to the few isolated examples of writers who have published a decent title or two. The turnover that goes into identifying such tokens is huge, and whole nations and crucial moments in contemporary African history are the casualties in a situation that makes heroes out of curious exceptions to an unseemly norm. It is time to face the truth: there exists a huge gap between both the quality and fervour of writing which made the 1960s the golden age of African writing and now. The decline in the quality and environment of education and non-existent policies on culture by many African governments have contributed to stunting the growth of African literature.

It would appear that in addition to the ravages of contemporary African life new African writing is tearing up under the tremendous stress brought on it from the 1980s on. The 1980s were characterised in many African countries by an extraordinary situation which made the African writer, as it were, the last line in the defence of liberty. In taking up literature as a tool and a weapon we never took care to point out that literature also had a responsibility to insist on its own self-contained meaning, outside of the particular occasions that might seem to generate it at any given time. In a panel discussion at an

Association of Nigerian Authors conference in 1992, this reviewer argued that literature had a responsibility to detail and to preserve the interplay of the various facets of culture and life. The contribution was greeted with an uproar for not tagging along behind the prevalent opinion that the main task of literature was to wage a war against corrupt Nigerian generals by calling them names. A reporter went a step further to write that the panelist 'could not understand what the fuss was about' with protest literature and human rights. It should not be difficult to imagine why much of what issues forth from African pens is vitiated by its own motivation: concerned with the desire to be seen making a point against 'the system', not much room is left for anything else.

Of course the point is not that African literature should distance itself from social matters. Such tasks are undertaken and such responsibilities are already coded, perhaps in far greater measure than many realise, into the very structure of relations between art and society on the continent. But even social commentary needs some polish, some skill, and there can't be much to admire in it when it becomes an invitation to all comers who think they have 'a message'. The same is evident in the reliance on traditional material in the samples of new writing considered here. There is something very retarded about the fixated gaze on the African past, and three or four out of every five young writers are likely to belly-flop into it because it seems to be a captive area of the imagination. When writers such as V. S. Naipaul wonder at what point African literature will move away from painting images of a frozen African past in work after work we might console ourselves that he is one writer who has never had anything good to say about the continent. Furthermore, since his examples are invariably taken from the generation of Achebe, it might be sensible to assume he could not have been charitable about what was clearly an historical necessity. The truth, however, is that new writers keep grinding out versions of *Things Fall Apart*, imagining that they are Achebe and that the rest of the world, inundated with television images of Africa as a jungle, is dying for an account of the latest ritual or superstition from the continent.

The only thing that is more deplorable than this state of affairs is the confusion of literary tawdriness with more serious business. Possibly because we have yet to systematise the different functions of the literary critic a lot of very poor works keep coming to the fore. In the newspapers of countries such as Nigeria fierce debates rage about standards. Writers and critics are increasingly self-indulgent because father figures are out of sight and the rule of thumb, and a little worse, have become the norm. A literary historian has a duty to take notice of every single title – perhaps – that is published, but not so the critic who has to be seen to insist on some standards. It is a different question altogether whether such standards will ever be acceptable to all, but when people (writers and critics alike) disagree it helps the ground clearing that needs to be done if it is seen that their premises are determined by knowledge and generosity of spirit. It is sad that at a time when the only incontrovertible gain that post-colonial theory has won for itself is a stronger, more prominent identity for regional literatures on the global stage, Black

African literature does not seem to have much to offer apart from what already went before. African literature *is* in decline and the way out is not by publishing anything in endorsement of a dubious ebullition.

F. M. Archibong's *Boko* is an example of the kind of complications that we have been trying to describe. The play's theme of incest comes with the sensationalism that used to be found in the old Nigerian television drama series *For Better, For Worse*. Three siblings, two brothers and a sister, somehow become involved in a love triangle, and each comes forward in turn to invest this soggy, dripping, contrived association with the old Greek tragic convention of the discovery – and in language that clearly shows that the playwright still believes that Greek drama is the way to go! Archibong's talent lies in his ability to transport himself back and forth in time, as he imitates this time the language of *Oedipus Rex* and *The Gods are not to Blame*, that time the language of the witches in *Macbeth*, or of Lear and Prospero, with J. P. Clark-Bekederemo's *Song of a Goat* tucked in somewhere in-between. Consider the following:

> Long ago, in the dark wasp-nest of a village called Ekput, a land not far from the forgotten cave of Arochukwu, this land where dearth of love and flatigiousness rank, is where I was born. (*pause*) There, unknown tribulations exiled me and my mother when I was a baby. (16)

And

> **Eze**: Go gently... That is the name of my father! Were you told of a brother?
> **Mbori**: Two that I cannot trace... A warring twin with no names mentioned. (*pause*) Except a birth mark on the left breast of the junior. He was said to be of great strength and brave in pride of courage.
> **Eze**: O strange exaltations, I am of that untold soldiery, an unknown brother! Look at this breast and welcome a brother.
> **Mbori**: Romance of paternal lineage. (17)

Then Boko, the third brother-husband-lover and Orestes-wannabe walks in, 'serving himself a drink from the bar'! On the next page he declares:

> **Boko**: You wrong me, brave friend. Have I named myself your accuser? If ever I hold my wife suspect (*sic*), she leaves... Take my word for good... Of all the fears on earth, fear the woman who is a wife... for if the man should be of base degree, he will hunt for your life! (18)

I'faith, the play speaketh not in verse and the real time of dramatic action doth not last till the Twelfth Night. A pox on that! A serious pox, methinks, because verse would have helped a few pages later when Boko spills forth once more: 'Felicity betrayed! Immoral jade, that I had discerned your incontinence by your smoothened face! Good it would have been for me to live a celibate, than to trade passion with one dead to honour. O woman, let this hair be a witness if this rend of heart be not avenged. Akan! Akan! Akan!' (21)

Language is the greatest pitfall of the upcoming generation. There simply is no awareness of it, and no help will come from blurb writers like the one for Laury Lawrence Ocen's *The Alien Woman*, who offers: 'The writer uses language in a distinctive manner – it is simply intriguing. I can only echo Gabriel Okara's comment: 'English words; African speech' (sic). There is promise of cultivated talent in the young novelist from Uganda, but there is nothing, at least on the evidence of the novel under review, to warrant the gratuitous comparison with Okara. The older generation of African writers always took their mastery of language beyond plain *command* to *control*: those coming behind them still need to be told that no praise about verbal craft is due without the latter; regrettably, not much evidence is available even of the first. A sentence such as the following cannot possibly aid such a transition: 'But unfortunately, on his way to the States the plane encountered a tragic crash which led to its absolute wreckage and his death' (59). By the same token, Ocen's novel might have been credible as a conscious experiment in the magical realist tradition if he were not, like the two other East African novelists considered in this review, writing about the magical and the fantastical with the credulousness of one who himself has no alternative realist frame of reference.

Mary Abago's *Sour Honey* tells the story of a village girl whose dreams of a future life of intellectual pursuit are given short shrift by the all-consuming ardour of a man old enough to be her father. The plot does not lose much for having antecedents, nor does the story line become trivial for tracing out what must be the experience of many a village girl. The problem with Abago's story is its heavy autobiographical load. Which is not to say that the author went through the more dramatic of her heroine's experiences. There is no doubt, however, about the over-identification in the novel; it is not difficult to conjecture that Maria, the heroine whose 'brilliance' is praised so much is an alter ego for Mary Abago herself, and a lot of the material that holds the novel together could have done with a lot more mediation and self-distancing. Abago is the most promising of the novelists under review; her strength is in her narrative positioning.

Authorial identification is a strong pillar for young writers to lean on, but it should not become a crutch. Aspiring writers who are not aware of its pitfalls are likely to go for its emotional appeal – in form of pity – while trying to underscore the harshness of experience. When such experience comes from the very backwaters of a well-known theatre of war and strife such as Angola, playing up private miseries may pale before the more portentous consequences of history, to which the reader may already be privy. Stories of war and its consequences told from a personal angle will of course always carry their plaintive appeal (which is no less heart-rending than any other), but they need a lot of skill to achieve. That is the shortcoming of *Meekulu's Children*, the otherwise very poignant novel by Kaleni Hiyalwa. When black literature from southern Africa eventually comes into its own, its writers will have deserved the glory that comes from the enormous task of tempering the brutality of war and strife into more permanent forms of artistic recall. It is not an easy process, and novels like *Meekulu's Children* ought to be read to see from what humble beginnings such journeys of national healing may take off.

S. N. Ndunguru's *Divine Providence* is a mixed bag of African ethnography and Christian pulpit morality. Even though the author does not knock down one set of values for another there is no doubt that he's out, in the words of Milton, to 'justify the ways of God to men' – and women. A good deal of the ethnography is forced down the throat like bitter medicine, the Christian morality justifies itself because, like manna from heaven, it is just divine providence. *A propos* of the first, consider the following:

> 'Aunt, have you buried my child?' Hossana asked.
> 'Yes, Sister Madovena and I buried it last night.'
> 'Where?'
> 'You don't have to know that. Our tribal custom forbids a mother to see the grave of her baby who dies at birth....' (3)

The niece, born and bred in the same culture as her interlocutor, is having the custom of her land explained to her by her aunt for the benefit of the reader. Like the other East African writers under review, there is a distinctly oral feel to Ndunguru's novel, meaning that the story line has not been tempered in any way by formal or stylistic interventions on the part of the author. It is difficult to call this an advantage or an achievement. All three East African novels *narrate* their stories; Ndunguru's, by an author in his sixties, comes with the additional, all-knowing avuncular smack that seems to draw its certitude about life from the knowledge that such a string of contrived situations and scenarios that litter the novel is the very foundation on which the Christian faith is built. It is time for East African fiction to work its way back up to reckoning.

Titi Adepitan
Department of English,
The University of British Columbia, Canada

Scholarship in African Universities

Okot p'Bitek, *The Defence of Lawino,* trans. Taban lo Liyong
Kampala: Fountain Publishers, 2001. 115 pp., $11.95. ISBN 9970022695

Felicia Okah Moh, *Ben Okri: An Introduction to his Early Fiction*
Enugu: Fourth Dimension Publishers, 2001. 160 pp., Price not stated;
ISBN 9781564598

K. E. Yankson, *The Rot of the Land and the Birth of the Beautyful Ones: The World of Ayi Kwei Armah's Novels*
Accra: Ghana Universities Press, 2000. 19 pp., Price Not Stated; ISBN 996430260.

Taban lo Liyong's new translation of *Wer pa Lawino*, written by Okot p'Bitek and first rendered in English by the author himself as *Song of Lawino* raises more issues than it resolves. An uncharitable reading of this new translation will be that it is a gratuitous effort that ends up simply transferring money from one writer's estate to another. But that will be skirting the larger issues of intellectual property, the oral tradition and that increasingly blurred zone of copyrighted translations from the oral which this work brings to the foreground. Serious as they are, and deserving of much more attention than have been thus far accorded to them, these questions are not what this review is about. These truly important issues pale into insignificance when placed beside the even larger literary/critical question of the ontological status of the texts which we deal with in African literature, the primary mode and language in which they exist as objects of academic study.

One of the founding principles on which literary studies established itself as a respectable academic discipline was what has come to be known as the 'intentional fallacy'. It was only by bracketing off the intentions of the author and affirming the primacy of the text in its original language and form that the study of literature could cut itself loose from other disciplines concerned with the study of texts. All the conceptual and methodological tools of the discipline have therefore been grounded on this idea of an original document in an original language that demands close reading in and for itself, without final recourse to the intentions of the author. Conventional literary scholarship has thus tended to treat translations and re-renderings such as updating the language of a Shakespeare play as somewhat less than the real thing. In spite of the influence of new theories of intertextuality and various kinds of post-structural/postmodern approaches which regard the notion of originals with deep suspicion, the idea of an original text – if only as final arbiter in literary analysis – has remained. But this is precisely where African literary scholarship has been less than certain about its object of study.

African writers – at least in the early nationalistic phase of modern African literature – never tired of insisting that while they write in English or French or Portuguese, as the case may be, they think and compose in their own mother tongue. This is rather like saying that their writings were in effect translations; that the 'originals' which African literary criticism should take as its object of study existed at some primary level in a different language, different from that reproduced in the text before us. A substantial part of the scholarly/critical analysis of African literary texts focuses on how the English or French text analysed appropriates and approximates the linguistic structures of some other language, which is usually the author's first language. Here, it should be noted, we are not simply speaking of the writer's intentions before the production of the text but of the language that informs the writing itself. Not only does this destabilise the ground of conventional literary scholarship which 'naturalises' the connection between language and literary expression, it recasts African literary study as the study of simulacra from which we can retrieve no originals in the public domain. Given this early insistence on the centrality of 'translation', it is surprising that translation remains one of the under-theorised areas of African literary scholarship. Taban's work thus refocuses our attention on an issue about which critics have been embarrassingly silent.

In the preface to this re-translation of Okot's *Lawino*, Taban gives his reasons for embarking on the project. The major thrust of his argument is that in the original translation Okot 'went for drama, humour, and the striking figures of speech' rather than representing the deep philosophical current and understated sarcasm that runs through the Acholi original. This, he claims, is because 'Song of Lawino is addressed more to the English and English-speaking Africans' (xv). The objective of this new translation is to 'return the discussion to where it was: Lawino discoursing on African ways of life to fellow Africans without too much consciousness about the presence of the whites'(xvi). It is of course debatable whether 'the presence of whites' can be ignored in a poem like this which would surely not have been written without that presence; a poem in which the white presence and imitation of the ways of the white man is so central that it is the motive force of the entire piece. Aside from this and the obvious paradox of the new translation pursuing this objective of downgrading the 'white presence' in another English translation, what I find particularly curious is the idea of returning the discussion to where it was. Where, we may ask, is this uncontaminated point where the discussion was before it was deflected from its course? Taban seems to think that this pure point of reference is the Acholi 'original' but this 'origin', as we can well see from the poem, is already overdetermined by the white presence. But Taban's view again is that this primary fact and the secondary question of the subsequent 'journeys' of the poem from this source – a term, I prefer in this context, to the more definitive notion of an original – in Acholi to English and the history of commentary and criticism that has shaped our reception of the text till this day is of no consequence to the discourse of culture and colonialism enunciated by Lawino in the 1950s. Accordingly, he says:

> Since I embarked on the translation, I have never revisited Okot p'Bitek's *Song of Lawino* at all. I wanted my translation to bear the burden of Lawino's Acholi version and not to be coloured by Okot's mannerisms and poetics of translation. I would have cheated if I had tried to rework Okot's version but not ventured to make my own. (xii)

This may broadly be true and every translator is or course free to make their own choices but one cannot avoid the feeling that Taban has 'cheated' the reader and also the text by 'pretending' that the fifty-odd years since *Wer pa Lawino* did not exist; that since its first appearance an English translation – a translation which has since become a classic of African literature – has not intervened to reshape and refigure the original. This not only reduces over five decades of discourse and critical labour to naught but also voids those years in terms of the social, political and historical currents which have made Africa and the world a very different place from what it was in Lawino's day. Indeed, it is Okot's positioning of his text in relation to the dominant discourses of colonialism and cultural nationalism in the 1950s and 1960s that made it such a significant cultural statement. Instead of 'translating' this classic statement into the language of the global realities and struggles of the 21st Century, Taban relocates it even further back. Rather than Okot's song with all the connotations of celebration and a lyrical run of passion and emotion, we are given the legalism of a defence complete with all the futile sophistry of good/bad or superiority/inferiority that has long since ceased to define the relationship between cultures in a post-modern world of cultural consumerism. (It is difficult to walk the streets of any of the major metropolitan centres of the world and not see that 'cultures' have become one of the consumer items of choice available and put on display.)

Taban's anachronistic discursive positioning marks and – in my opinion – mars his translation in comparison with *Song of Lawino*. Even though this translation is supposedly based only on the Acholi version, it is inevitable that readers and critics will look at this text in comparison to Okot's English version. And in any such comparison, I am afraid, the earlier version appears much more consistent in objective and execution. The stylistic shifts between formality and colloquialism, the archaic diction which again and again draws attention to itself, the translation of the names of Acholi musical instruments into 'lyres' and 'castanets', the use on one occasion of the word 'fire-tops' for stoves, are all instances of a less than consistent approach to translation in this version. To read this poem is to be constantly reminded of the earlier English version and beyond that of the Acholi source of these 'translations' and to invite comparisons. And this perhaps will be the enduring value of Taban's translation for literary scholars: that it highlights once again the question of orality, language, translation, the boundaries between originals and simulacra which seem to me to be central to the study of African literature and the evolution of a poetics of this literary tradition.

Felicia Oka Moh's book *Ben Okri: An Introduction to his Early Fiction* and K.E. Yankson's inaugural lecture, 'The Rot of the Land and the Birth of the Beautyful Ones: The World of Ayi Kwei Armah's Novels', are not directly related to these concerns. Both works, however, raise an issue which may be tangentially related and this is the question of the state of scholarship in African universities. The fragile state of many African economies further compounded in recent years by the effects of the IMF/World Bank structural adjustment policies has brought many African universities almost to their knees. In many cases the infrastructure for academic production has been so crippled by years of political corruption, mismanagement and neglect that libraries and laboratories are a sad echo of what they used to be in the first two decades of the post-independence era. To draw an unfortunate analogy, many African universities have – like Taban's translation – been pushed further behind than they were in those glorious days.

Moh's book which – from the note of gratitude to her chief supervisor in her acknowledgements – is obviously based on a her dissertation for an academic degree in a Nigerian university relies entirely on newspaper articles and interviews for secondary material on Ben Okri's works. These articles are not even immediately available. In her own words, she has to rely on the regional British Council office and help from her students to 'hunt for' them. Though not as explicitly stated, Yankson's inaugural lecture proceeds in a similar vein. Here there is absolutely no mention of – let alone reference to – Ayi Kwei Armah's novels after the publication of *The Healers*, his last novel to be issued under the Heinemann African Writers Series. Indeed, Yankson refers to these novels as 'Armah's five published novels' (1) as if Armah has written nothing else since, that his literary career ended more than two decades ago. Yet Armah is alive and still working. Yankson goes further by doing away completely with that nicety of academic convention – the bibliography of works cited. His reading of Armah's work is conducted within the narrow confines of the reflectionist paradigm of early African literary criticism; a reading that shuttles back and forth between the fictional world of Armah's novels and the socio-economic and political realities of contemporary Ghanaian society. The thesis is a simple one: there is a rot in the land and its agents are the diseased souls and the land awaits the birth of the 'beautiful ones' whose agents will be the healthy souls.

In comparison to Yankson's limited, reductionist reading of Armah, there is a sense of genuine endeavour and integrity in Moh's book despite its limitations. Very honestly, she lays bare these limitations of working in an environment in which books are unavailable not just in her acknowledgements but also by labelling her work 'An Introduction'. The title also informs us that this is not only an introduction, it is more precisely an introduction to Okri's earlier fiction – even though she devotes a chapter to *The Famished Road*. Within the limits it sets itself, the book comes off well. It provides a background to Okri's work by giving some biographical information on the author and locating his fiction within the tradition of the African novel of the city. Its conventional 'lit. crit.' approach is likely to make it a very valuable text for teaching Ben Okri's short stories and novels to students at the higher school level.

Harry Garuba,
Centre for African Studies, University of Cape Town

Alessandra Di Maio. *Tutuola at the University: The Italian Voice of a Yoruba Ancestor*
(including an Interview with Tutuola and an Afterword by Claudio Gorlier)
Rome: Bulzoni, 2000, 192 pp., €12,92; ISBN 88-8391-544-2

Alessandra Di Maio's unusual book catches the lively atmosphere and intellectual vivacity that characterised Amos Tutuola's stay in Palermo, Italy, during October 1990. Invited as a visiting professor by the local university, the Nigerian novelist gave a series of lectures on African literature and Yoruba traditions which, avoiding any kind of academic stiffness, evolved into a captivating experience for both students and scholars, and turned out to be a unique literary event.

Drawing on his ground-breaking masterpiece *The Palm-Wine Drinkard*, originally published in 1952, Tutuola's seminar tackled the different notions of Nigerian folklore, creative writing and African myths. In order to introduce such topics to a Western audience, Tutuola operated as a cultural mediator and provided recognisable socio-cultural models. Indeed much effort was devoted to helping the audience picture the typical elements that make up African frames of reference, ranging from the starchy yam tuber to the frothing palm-wine served in sub-Saharan countries, from cowries to the meaning of names. 'Tutuola', apparently, means the 'gentle one'.

The fascinating result is shown in this volume published with the support of a Turin-based branch of the National Research Council (CNR), the Centre for the Study of the Literatures and the Cultures of the Emerging Areas (CSAE). It has the power to bridge the gap between different cultures.

While dealing with the treasure of African stories, oral traditions and religious beliefs, Tutuola's starting point was to identify the difference between myths, which 'mix up certain things and uncertain things' (35) and legends, which, according to Tutuola, 'always tell the truth of what happened in the past' (41). In his unsophisticated style, he points out the complex nature of the African world, where the mundane is juxtaposed with the manifestations of gods by means of rites and customs. Because of this the tales and proverbs he employs to define the Yoruba heritage are populated by peculiar characters such as the personification of Death, creatures who can change their shape, or uncanny devices such as *juju* (explained as a charm to protect oneself from evil spirits). The function of the stories is not simply to beguile children by the fire: indeed the stories constitute a well-rooted and valuable segment of African culture that has moral significance and pedagogic dimensions.

The structure of Tutuola's fiction combines a miscellany of riddles, religious beliefs, and folktales. In his lectures, the novelist lists fourteen central motifs that reverberate throughout his work. These included, the relationship between the Yoruba language and English, the local customs of social gatherings, the perception of curses, jokes and spells. Though impressed by the written word – 'when I saw a book, it was just like magic for me how it was produced' (48) – he pointed out that his narratives stemmed from the oral tradition. As a young boy, the artist from Abeokuta learnt and collected stories and jests. These later became elements in his creative jigsaw.

Imagination is another key term as it indicates both the Yoruba cultural background and the artist's idiosyncratic viewpoint. When commenting on his major novel, the author identifies himself with the protagonist and this peculiar oscillation of subjects betrays the role of the singer/performer in African culture who violates the rigid paradigms of the Western canon. The practice of storytelling can, he claims, be 'textualised' because 'novels contain invented stories' (51).

The editor of the volume, Alessandra Di Maio, supplies explanatory notes and renders the book, which is also enriched by an updated and exhaustive bibliography, a precious tool for intercultural education. The closing interview with the writer, conducted by Claudio Gorlier, a distinguished Italian Africanist, takes the opportunity to illuminate some rhetorical mechanisms of African literature and culture. It also provides information about the identity of Tutuola, man and artist, and throws light on the context in which he emerged. For instance, the influence of British culture dating back to the colonial period is acknowledged, and yet there are strong warning notes against simplification in his statement that 'not only European literature teaches to write, or how to be a writer' (165).

Questions raised concerning the elements of Yoruba heritage retained in some South American countries bring up the concept of religious syncretism and reminds one of the issue of the slave trade. In Tutuola's vision the substance of religious beliefs is intermingled with the earthly experience of the living so that the notion of the afterlife becomes a parable for the harshness of life in a continent entirely exploited and abused by colonialism. In Tutuola's words '... hell in the story means a place of sacrifice and punishment. The heaven I mention in the book is all about Africa' (163).

Esterino Adami
University of Turin, Turin, Italy

Robert Muponde and Mandivavarira Maodzwa-Taruvinga, eds, *Sign and Taboo: Perspectives on the Poetic Fiction of Yvonne Vera*
Harare: Weaver Press, 2002; Oxford: James Currey, 2003, 236 pp., £14.95; ISBN: 0-85255-584-9. Distributed by African Books Collective Ltd in the United States; ISBN 0-77922-004-9

Yvonne Vera has produced a significant body of work in a short period of time. Since the publication of a short story collection in 1992, she has written five novels and edited an anthology. This first critical collection on Vera's work, written by scholars from Southern Africa, Britain and the Americas, examines the fiction largely within its Zimbabwean context.

In the section 'Language, technique and imagery', Vera's work is interpreted using theories of art forms other than the literary. Jane Bryce's persuasive essay analyses the influence of film and photography in Vera's aesthetics. Controversially, in her discussion of the camera eye point of view in Vera, Bryce compares Vera's technique with that of the anthropological filmmaking of Jean Rouch, arguing that both bring what is usually hidden or secret into view.

Jessica Hemmings' essay combines an academic interest in textile design and literary criticism to produce an unusual article on the role of cloth in Vera's fiction. Hemmings was working on a PhD on Vera and her essay appears to be work in progress. The problem is that the design history she is applying to Vera's work does not provide adequate theorisation of literary texts. To compensate for this, Hemmings is over-reliant on her own practical criticism of Vera's novels. Nevertheless, her close readings draw the reader's attention to the language of Vera's work.

In other sections of the book, Maurice T. Vambe and Kizito Muchemwa analyse Vera's use of orality and ritual. Vambe is more critical of Vera's historical reconstruction than Bryce, arguing that Vera, in her appropriation of spirit possession in *Nehanda*, represents black women as speaking with one voice, and ignoring contradictions in their experiences. Rather than presenting a critical realist perspective on pre-colonial Zimbabwe, Vera presents a Shona society with a traditional idyllic past which, ironically, not only 'normalise(s) the colonial discourse' (130) it attempts to deconstruct but also fails to challenge a male-dominated discourse of nationalism. Muchemwa too takes issue with Vera's rewriting of history. He argues that her reconstructed orality is essentialist and sits uneasily with the hybridity and postmodernism of her novels.

In contrast, Nana Wilson-Tagoe argues that Vera uses dialogism in

Nehanda to represent history through the voices of those on the margins. In her convincing article, Wilson-Tagoe makes the important distinction that Vera's novels are 'narratives out of history' rather than 'narratives of history' (160). According to Wilson-Tagoe, in *Nehanda*, Vera represents a world in crisis in which history itself is contested as it is rewritten in ways which challenge the official version. In a stimulating reading of *Under the Tongue*, Wilson-Tagoe shows how Vera, through writing incest into a narrative set during the liberation struggle and through presenting multiple perspectives, moves beyond retelling women's history to interrogating gender and power relations.

Wilson-Tagoe contrasts Vera's foregrounding of Nehanda's *chimurenga* role with the emphasis the historian Terence Ranger places on the male medium Kaguvi. Ranger is the author of an essay in this collection which offers a historian's commentary on Vera's *The Stone Virgins*. The essay's significance lies in the auto/biography it relates as Ranger explains the influence he and Vera have had on each other's work. Ranger rightly asserts that *The Stone Virgins* breaks new ground as the first novel by Vera to confront history directly and also as the first Zimbabwean novel to delineate the horror of both army and dissident violence in Matabeleland during the early 1980s.

Large claims are made for Vera in this book, particularly by those critics, arguing from a feminist perspective, who see Vera as a pioneering writer, breaking the silence of traditional taboos and bearing witness in a newly created historical discourse. The essays, as a whole, demonstrate that Vera is worthy of this acclaim. The variety and quality of the essays in this well edited collection suggest that it will be the definitive work on Vera for some time.

Pauline Dodgson-Katiyo,
Anglia Polytechnic University, Cambridge, UK

David Murphy, *Sembene: imagining alternatives in film and fiction*
Oxford: James Currey/Trenton, NJ: Africa World Press, 2000, 275 pp., £14.95; ISBN 0-85255-555-5

It is interesting to speculate as to why David Murphy's excellent monograph on Sembene's extensive output of novels, novellas and films should be only the second published full-length study of his work. Here is one of the most widely read and studied writers from francophone Africa, the acknowledged founding father of African cinema, now over 80 years old, and yet he had to wait until 2000 for the recognition afforded by a serious book-length discussion of his work.

In the interview granted to the author of this volume it is abundantly clear that Sembene has little time for literary critics and even less for academic literary theorising, yet this is only one of the most recent of some forty published interviews he has given during his long career. The number of articles published is similarly extensive, as is the number of theses devoted to him, mostly in North American universities. Why then so few monographs? It has to be because of his unrepentant Marxist stance, and his very unfashionable conviction that Communism still has something to contribute to the future of Africa, even more than ten years after the collapse of the Soviet bloc, and the demise of most of the continent's Marxist-inspired régimes. Yet this very marginality, and the incisive critical eye it gives him in representing the cultures of his native Senegal and sub-Saharan Africa, is what allows him to 'imagine alternatives', as Murphy puts it, and the current failure of the neo-colonialist and global capitalist model to offer viable solutions to Africa's problems makes this capacity more precious than ever.

Sembene is often reductively pigeonholed as a 'committed' writer, but he denies creating a 'literature of slogans' and Murphy is at pains to highlight the questioning of modes of representation which underlies all his work, whether literary or cinematic. For Murphy, the high point of this is his 1976 film *Ceddo*, which offers a radical re-appraisal of Senegalese history that presents the successive attempts of traditional rulers, slave traders, Catholic missionaries and Islamic imams to dominate the country as so many layers of ideological perversion of the will of its people. In a similar fashion his 1992 film and novel *Guelwaar* show how religious rivalry serves to mask the neo-colonial dependency of Senegalese society on international aid programmes. Murphy's detailed and very well-documented analyses of these and other earlier texts draw on many less familiar Senegalese writers and commentators to illuminate the subtlety of Sembene's questioning of received versions of Senegal's colonial and post-colonial history, as well as the true focus of his political commitment, which is to make this questioning available to his less well-resourced compatriots, whether in print or through the medium of film, which allows him to address them in their own language. The ramifications of this project are explored by Murphy in a series of thematic chapters each centring one or two representative texts, whether cinematic or literary. An exception is the chapter 'Mothers, daughters and prostitutes' that considers the revolutionary representation of women, one of the most characteristic and wide-ranging features in Sembene's works.

Murphy's study is a major and most welcome contribution to the understanding of one of Africa's greatest contemporary artists, and one which will be an unavoidable reference point for all future studies of his work.

Peter Hawkins
Department of French, University of Bristol, UK

The Igbo Novel

Igboanusi, Herbert. *Igbo English in the Nigerian Novel*
Ibadan: Enicrownfit Publishers, 2002, 136 pp., including index; £14.95/$24.95; ISBN 978-34225-6-1

Herbert Igboanusi is a professor of Linguistics at the University of Ibadan and the author of *The Igbo Tradition in the Nigerian Novel* (2001), *A Dictionary of Nigerian English Usage* (2002), and an edited collection of papers, *Language Attitude and Language Conflict in West Africa* (2001). The ten chapters of *Igbo English in the Nigerian Novel* reflect Igboanusi's grounding in M. A. K. Halliday's linguistics. They provide an interesting, albeit descriptive overview, akin to Oluwole Adejare's *Language and Style in Soyinka: A Systemic Textlinguistic Study of a Literary Idiolect* (1992).

In *Igbo English in the Nigerian Novel*, Igboanusi usefully examines Igbo English, staying close to seasoned writers of international reputation, such as Chinua Achebe, Cyprian Ekwensi, Buchi Emecheta, Chukwuemeka Ike, thus avoiding the pitfalls that A.A. Nwankwo, for example, would create for a linguist. Igboanusi is not silent on this point, as his proposal for future developments is that

> The future speaker of global English should enjoy the freedom of being able to bend and shape English language in order to reflect correctly his life experiences. This freedom does not advocate that teachers of English be more liberal in their acceptance of what constitutes correct usage, nor does this liberty aim to encourage laxity or incompetence in the use of English. (97)

The creative work of Simon Armitage (England), Robert Kroetsch (Canada), Tom Leonard (Scotland), Peter Carey (Australia), Toni Morrison (USA), Kerri Hulme (New Zealand) and countless others demonstrates the fulfilment of both of Igboanusi's criteria for English, though the effects of popular software limitations on vocabulary and the effects of the media's linguistic 'policies' are likely to have a greater effect on English language developments, to our great misfortune, than creative writings or the establishment of a comprehensive language policy (102).

Igboanusi examines Igbo writers' roles in the development of Igbo English (IE) and, less comprehensively, in the development of Nigerian English (NE), through literary interpretation of the writers' 'borrowing, coinages, loan-blends, translation equivalents, semantic extension, collocational extension, and colloquialisms' (2). Igboanusi's inclusion of Amadi (Rivers State) and Emecheta (Delta State), while fulfilling his mandate 'that the literary tradition cuts across all the linguistic and cultural areas of Igboland' (3), is controversial in its intra-Nigerian colonialism; his book does not define, historicise, nor theorise the Igbo 'state' and its development. Indeed, one could argue that the selection of authors has more to say about Western educational influences upon a strain within the development of Nigerian English than it has to say about the indigenous influences on English. Publishers' mandates and editorial direction/guidance to writers is another area of research from which

Igboanusi's study would benefit. Of his 17 primary texts, only two have Nigerian publishers – Ike's *Toads for Supper* and Saro-Wiwa's self-published *Sozaboy.*

The fractious nature of Nigerian society and its micro-communities requires more careful and detailed work. Igboanusi's study, within these limits, is a useful addition to the scholarship that is describing and constructing a vital component of Nigerian English.

Craig McLuckie
Department of English, Okanagan University College, Canada

Drama and Poetry by Wole Soyinka

Wole Soyinka, *King Baabu*
London: Methuen, 2002, 107 pp., £7.99;
ISBN: 0-413-77175-X

Wole Soyinka, *Samarkand and other Markets I have Known*
London: Methuen, 2002, 80 pp., £9.99; ISBN: 0-413-77255-1

King Baabu is a satiric, allegorical representation of Nigeria's General Sani Abacha's rule. The play defies straightforward classification because it mixes diverse dramatic techniques: burlesque, lampoon, story-telling, and all sorts of over-the-top dramatic devices, in the manner of Alfred Jarry's *Ubu Roi,* to create a single, unambiguous effect: gut-wrenching disgust for the decadence, intellectual poverty, greed, and mindless brutality that has come to be seen as the distinguishing characteristic of the Abacha years.

What makes an allegory interesting is its ability to stand on its own, to capture our attention even if we are not aware that it is an allegory. *King Baabu* is the story of General Basha Bash's transformation from an oafish military general into an even more oafish self-declared monarch and the transformation succeeds mainly because of Soyinka's ability to take us deep into a certain type of character: the all-grabbing dictator whose greed knows no limits and whose progression from one sensual excess to the next, up to his prophesied end in the 'union of woman and beast', leaves us amazed. *Ubu Roi* is based loosely on Shakespeare's *Macbeth,* and from his constant allusions to the latter Soyinka expects his audience to come to *King Baabu* with an impeccable knowledge of Shakespeare. Thus from the very opening of the play a similarity is suggested between Bash's character and that of Macbeth – both are military generals, both are brave and loyal. In both plays the men are introduced just after performing a bloody deed in which they have yet again proved their mettle and have been rewarded by their leaders with the title of the men they have just helped to undo: Macbeth becomes the Thane of Glamis and Bash becomes the Chief of Army Staff. But that is just the first step in both men's transformation – soon, under the urging of their virago wives, they will usurp their leaders' positions. Bash is a caricature of the brave, even sometimes noble Macbeth, just as his wife Maariya is a caricature of Lady Macbeth.

Here is our first glimpse into Bash's character, he is replying to his wife's charge of lack of ambition: 'If I hearing you right, you saying we going to die paupers. Now how that possible when this very moment we moving into all this new and sumptuous bordello, and with blood of former occupant making that special design on wallpaper... Now we have his mansion, I wearing his general's stars and stripes and long service medallions on personal orders of my commander-in-chief, Field-Marshal Potipoo...' (6) This scene introduces the first usurpation and annexation, the late General Uzi's post and mansion we soon realise are symbols for the whole nation that Bash will soon annex.

Soyinka skilfully undermines his hero by portraying his crude speech, his pant-wetting cowardice and his greed, making us lose all sympathy for him from the first scene. By the end of the play, we are totally disgusted with him.

The play is about transformations: from Basha Bash to Baabu, from the loyal, stupid general to the usurper-leader and finally to the patriarchal monarch. More important to the plot however is Maariya's character: a grasping, jealous barracks woman, always urging her husband on. She is the brain of the family, the engine that drives the play's plot from one step to the next. Potipoo's leadership is short lived, Maariya makes sure of that. She, more than her husband, realises the unconstitutionality of Potipoo's position, he is a usurper and her husband made him what he is, why therefore can't her husband take the plum position himself. As she says, '...All is fair in love and war – that's what they all say. Fair is foul and foul is fair...' (10).

Soyinka's intent, from the outset, is clearly to show the military in politics as nothing but a bunch of adventurers, opportunists who prey upon each other and upon the nation as a whole, as a result of which the ordinary man suffers. Nothing in the play establishes that more than the first meeting of Potipoo's ruling council, the 'Supreme Council for Advance Redemption'. The military has invited the usual 'people's representatives', chiefs, union leaders, religious leaders, as members of the council, all in an effort to gain legitimacy and show that: ' ...ours will be the final military coup d'etat in our nation' (12).

Although Soyinka's writings, creative and journalistic, have always been consistent in condemning all forms of despotic and irresponsible regimes in Nigeria and Africa as a whole, yet at no other time was he as strident and energetic in his condemnation as during Abacha's reign which lasted from 1993 to 1998. This period saw him go into exile and dedicate almost all of his time to creating pro-democracy propaganda. *King Baabu* is more direct in its handling of its subject matter than his other works that treat a similar theme, *Kongi's Harvest*, for instance. The play, from the first scene to the last, is an unremitting deconstruction and demystification of despots and despotism; it takes most of its material from history, the life and times of Abacha, and extends it as a metaphor for similar regimes of terror.

Soyinka depends on his audience's acquaintance with Abacha lore, since the names of his characters are supposed to act as introduction to their behaviour. Basha's avatar is obviously Abacha. His secretive Chief Security Officer's name, 'Fatasimu', is a near anagram of Abacha's real life CSO

Mustafa. Abacha's wife, Maryam becomes 'Maariya'. However, the force of the message is not abated even if one comes to it without a knowledge of its antecedents. This to a large extent is due to Soyinka's ability to make his characters rotate with an energy of their own. The play's ambit is ambitious, almost every aspect of a despot's progress is touched upon: the violent power takeover, the quest for legitimacy which usually includes bribery, promises of immediate return to civilian rule, often with the general as the sole presidential candidate, the corrupting of intellectuals such as the Tutor into spin doctors, the ruthless repression of all opposition (in one gruesome scene King Baabu orders the hands of an entire village chopped off to ensure that they never vote or cause trouble again), and finally the recourse to witchcraft which helps to perpetuate a myth of indestructibility.

King Baabu's transformation is into a monarch, not a politician. Under one of the many empty programmes worked out by his spin doctors, Tikim and Tutor, titled 'Reinvent the Continent', they agree that first they have to reinvent the nation, and the best way to do that is to turn Basha into the monarch of Guatu, because 'The whole world is saying – no more military rule. Good. We don't rule by the Army. But nobody can raise a voice against monarchies because they still have kings and queens even in European countries' (39).

Perhaps the most dramatic moment of the play, and the single most insightful exposure of Baabu's character, is at the impromptu coronation ceremony. His greed, his intellectual poverty, and his instinctive, almost Falstaffian, cunning are all on display as he stands before the people. He appeals to them to accept him as their leader, even though, as he himself admits, he has nothing to offer. *Baabu* means 'nothing' in Hausa.

This is a very interactive scene, with the spotlight shifting from Baabu and his entourage on the stage, to the crowd in the gallery. The inclusion of the crowd, of course, gives Soyinka a chance to present to us the essential character of the people. They are hungry, poor, powerless, and politically naive, ready prey to the next fast-talking and promise-gushing leader, fickle.

King Baabu is one of Soyinka's most pessimistic plays, at no point does he offer any hope. He makes it clear that military rule is an aberration, a tampering with 'nature' which in the end leads to Baabu's death, but the person that vanquishes Baabu is Potipoo, his former boss. The cycle is complete. Often we see the playwright struggling to contain his message within the dramatic, fictional bounds, and in this he is not always successful. The failure is most apparent at the end of the play when Maariya rants on and on about pretenders – but of course this is a play rooted in history, as were lots of other plays by the author.

Samarkand and other Markets I have Known should be read as a companion volume to *King Baabu*. Parts of it are really continuations of the discourse in the play, translated into poetry. For instance, take these lines, from the poem, 'Exit Left Monster, Victim in Pursuit':

Long, long before he slipped
Viagra
Down his throat, and washed it down
With 3-Barrel rotgut,

His favourite gargle from Iganmu,
Libelled home-made brandy as in
Home-made democracy, the Gunner
Was a goner (21)

Again, the subject (Gunner) here is Abacha/Basha; the aphrodisiac, rhino horn powder in *King Baabu*, has here become Viagra. Again the dominant theme is the downward spiral of a despot, *'the Gunner/Was a goner'*. Despite the poem's seriousness of theme, Soyinka never misses an opportunity to play with words, 'Gunner', 'goner', and 'libelled' for 'labelled'.

It can be said that writers of Soyinka's generation, in the forefront of African literature for over four decades now, have lost the ability to surprise, their repertoire is fairly predictable. Politics and religion have always been Soyinka's primary fields of concern, and his work acquires especial poignancy when the two meet. This can be seen in *Death and the King's Horseman*, for instance, or *The Bacchae of Euripides*, or *The Trials of Brother Jero*, or in the 35-page pamphlet, *Being and the Credo of Nothingness*, or, in fact, in most of his work.

Samarkand is Soyinka's fourth collection of poems. The blurb on the dust jacket says it 'spans the poet's recent experience of exile from Nigeria as well as the journeys that have followed his Nobel Prize for Literature award'. The poems closely follow the trend of events that have happened in the life of Nigeria in the time delineated above, from Abiola's death to Abacha's death, to the rise of Islamic fundamentalism.

The collection opens with a bold declaration of intent in the multi-layered poem, 'Ah, Demosthenes'. The story of the apostrophised, Demosthenes, is taken from Plutarch's *Lives of the Poets*. Demosthenes is said to be a stammerer who cured his ailment by placing hot pebbles on his tongue and forcing himself to speak slowly and distinctly, until at last his stutter was cured.

I shall ram pebbles in my mouth
Demosthenes
Not to choke, but half Dolphin, half
Shark hammerhead from fathoms deep
Ride the waves to charge the breakers
They erect,
Crush impediments of power and inundate
Their tainted towers –
I shall ram pebbles in my mouth. (3)

We are being prepared from the outset to expect a 'charge' against the 'impediments of power'. And this is going to be done with 'pebbles in my mouth', that is, beautifully. But then, like some ferocious animals are said to throw themselves about to work up anger before moving to attack, incrementally the poem masses fervour, the mild pebble is substituted for 'nettles' in the second stanza, and *'werepe'* in the third, then 'ratsbane', then 'fingers down the throat' and, finally, 'hemlock'.

Throughout the poem Soyinka chooses his words carefully, each symbol carrying within itself multiple meanings. From the name Demosthenes we can isolate a root word, '*demos*' which means 'people' in Greek, and suddenly the poem is transformed, especially when we come to these lines in the fifth stanza:

> This stuttering does not become the world,
> This tongue of millions fugitive from truth –
> I'll thrust all fingers down the throat. (4)

The *demos* are clearly the 'millions fugitive from truth' for whom the poet-persona's 'fingers down' their throats will give voice.

The collection is made up of only twenty poems, some of them quite long, divided into five sections with such emblematic titles as 'Outsiders', 'Of Exiles', 'Fugitive Phases', 'The Sign of the Zealot', and 'Elegies'. The writing includes lyrical, haunting lines in 'Elegy for a Nation' written for Achebe's 70th birthday:

> There are wonders in that land, Chinua
> Are you wired? Tuned to images of cyber age?
> Severed hands will soon adorn our walls
> And Conrad's *Heart of Darkness* be fulfilled. (74)

And the awkward, 'his targets – women (Kudirat et al)/ Octogenarians – Alfred Rewane – and…', in 'Exit Left, Monster…' (22)

The collection's centrepiece, its *pièce de resistance,* is definitely the title poem, 'Samarkand And Other Markets I Have Known', dedicated to Naguib Mafouz. At eleven pages, it is the longest poem in the collection, and yet not once does it falter. This is Soyinka straddling the areas that he knows perhaps better than any other living poet: the mythical, the religious, and the political.

'Samarkand' espouses a Utopian vision of peaceful coexistence, its message is Christian in its 'lamb and lion coexisting' entreaty. The central symbol is that of the world as a market place/ temple, '….Each stall/ Is shrine and temple…' The market is the ultimate place of free expression, just as a temple should be, nobody is ever barred from a market place, 'Let a hundred thousand/ Flowers diffuse exotic incense and a million/ Stars perfume the sky, till the infant cry of Truth/ Resound in the market of the heart…'

The enemies of Utopia are those who seek to control the mind, in the market place as well as in the temple. Images of the once glorious Samarkand shackled under Marxism are used to symbolise the loss of freedom and free will. The poem ends on a note of hope: zealots will come and go, but the truth remains eternal,

> One market day, in the *souk* of Cairo,
> The zealot's counterfeiting hand did not triumph.
> *The moving finger writes, and having writ* … the mind
> Survives to sing the way on the Golden Road
> Where dreams of Samarkand outlive
> Tomorrow's market day. (59)

Helon Habila
University of East Anglia, UK

Ghanaian Poetry and Fiction

Kofi Anyidoho. *PraiseSong For The Land*
Accra: Sub-Saharan Publishers, 2002, 112 pp.; ISBN 9988 550 45 6

Ayi Kwei Armah. *KMT: In the House of Life*
Popenguine: Per Ankh Publishers, 2002, $18.00; ISBN 2 911 928 06 7

A new collection of poems from Ghanaian poet, Kofi Anyidoho, is always a welcome event, a chance to hear again in the mind's ear a new articulation of the English language as it is teased and woven to express the experience and hopes of the peoples of Africa.

This volume, however, offers a significant innovation in the publication of modern African verse. It offers, in addition to the printed text, recordings on CD and audio cassette of the poet's own performance of his work, thereby providing the reader/hearer the uncommon opportunity in our time of access to the 'full burden of [the poet's] voice', a chance to experience something of the intimacy of the oral performance.

The mission to regain in our time the power of the oral performance has been a central enterprise of Anyidoho's. Never a believer in poetry as an art form for the aesthetic contemplation of the solitary reader, Anyidoho writes poetry meant for performance to a communal audience, indeed sometimes with musical accompaniment, and in the case of 'Memory and Vision' in this anthology as part of a dance drama. He has always regarded the printed text alone as an insufficient transmission of his poetic message. And for that reason the recordings which accompany this volume would represent for him an important recovery of the fullness of his message.

The poetry itself shows considerable variety of theme and style. Many of the poems, public in theme, deliberately recall the poetic mannerisms of Anyidoho's last collection, *AncestralLogic and CaribbeanBlues,* and express in a variety of tones, ranging from complaint to defiance to exhortation, the racial and Pan-African concerns which animated the earlier collection. The poet in fact sometimes relies for the effect on the same clever juxtaposition and play on resonating African names which was a feature of the earlier anthology:

> The Asante the Azande and the Mande
> The Mandingo and the Bakongo
> The Basuto the Dagaaba and the Dogon. (27)

In these poems, the poet, speaking for all peoples of African descent, pictures himself in a characteristic image as the dog who caught the game but must wait under the table for scraps from the master, just as the African who gave birth to civilisation is now an abject beggar in the marketplace of the world.

But a new note of impatience and anger is struck in the title poem, 'PraiseSong for the Land'. The persona surveys the African's unhappy lot and for once does not simply blame the Western exploiter, but blames himself for his lack of pride and endeavour, and calls upon Africans to put aside the perennial begging bowl and take more pride in themselves and their heritage:

> How many times
> Have we not gathered the garbage of the rich
> And dumped the rot upon our sacred groves?
>
> And have we not begged and wept enough? (59)

Lines like these make it a matter of regret that in our time poetry is read only by a few, despite the efforts of Anyidoho and others in Ghana to make poems part of popular entertainment and instruction. The pride in ourselves as Africans which is strongly evoked in these lines should inform the consciousness of Africa's leaders in the global marketplace. In this way, we would not forget our cultural treasures even as a global radio seeks to drown us in tidal waves of American hip-hop music. Nor would our leaders so quickly betray the needs of their own people in abject acquiescence to the demands of the Bretton Woods institutions and multinational corporations.

This tone of critical or even satirical introspection in which the poet questions his own society instead of merely railing at the enemy abroad, though always present to some degree in Anyidoho's work, is more pervasive in this collection. Thus alongside the celebration of Africa's resilience, we find comic portraits of Africa's politicians with their deceptive antics and perennially empty promises:

> ...this New
> Generation of InfantMen
> all dressed in camouflage
> lost among their own arguments. (81)

Inevitably, however, some of the satire is directed at America, supreme global power, where the poet not only studied but has returned many times as guest of one university or the other. The United States comes across in these poems as a Godless hysterical and restless nation where excessive affluence engenders eccentricity:

> A woman comes in with a child
> and buys icecream for her Dog. (88)

My favourite poems, however, are the ones which speak of personal relationships, though of course the line between the personal and the public is not always easy to draw in the work of this poet for whom public issues often determine the character of interpersonal sentiment. Of the poems dealing with the joys and anxieties of personal relationships, I find 'Dreams in Babylon' to be the most moving, perhaps because it provides a contemporary, African variation on an archetypal theme – the poet expressing love for and anxiety over the uncertain destiny of an offspring in a troubled world. One is reminded, for instance, of W.B.Yeats' 'A Prayer for My Daughter'. In this version, the anxiety arises from the unclear destiny of a child born into the dissolving traditions of the emerging 'global village', and who, furthermore, has to deal at a tender age with the agony of looking and sounding different in new settings because her itinerant father is constantly on the move. It is a powerfully moving poem.

Altogether, the collection offers a wide variety of moods – from the dirge-like tones of the tribute to Efua Sutherland, the proverbial utterances of 'Agbakpe', the personal pathos of 'Dreams in Babylon' to the rousing Pan-Africanism of 'Memory and Vision' and the satire of 'Lake Forest'. *PraiseSong for the Land* is a most satisfying volume.

The transition from Anyidoho's collection to Ayi Kwei Armah's novel, *KMT: In the House of Life* is made logical by the interest the two writers share in the history and destiny of African peoples everywhere. Indeed the following lines from Anyidoho's poem, 'Memory and Vision' could serve as the epigraph to Armah's novel:

> Somehow somehow we must
> Recall that we are a People
> Who once rode the Dawn
> With Civilization's Light
> Still glowing through our Mind.
>
> And if today we seem lost among Shadows
> We must probe the deep Night of our Blood
> And seek out our Birth-Cord
> From the garbage heap of History's crowded Lies. (26)

Seeking out the buried truth of Africa's past and reclaiming it from the morass of lies accumulated over centuries of distortion is precisely what Armah undertakes in this unique novel which offers a new definition of the historical novel as a genre. Armah offers a re-creation of the way of life of the ancient Egyptian scribes, a community of thinkers and writers who recorded the thoughts, the values, the beliefs, the scientific observations of this ancient civilisation, and recorded also the trends and divisions which caused that fine culture to disintegrate.

The novel provides a wealth of information about ancient Egypt and includes the correction of some familiar misconceptions. We learn for instance that in the view of these scribes, writing before the rise of the pyramid-building Pharaohs with their exploitation of religion, Re, Ast, Jewty, Hathor, etc, are not deities, but *netchers*, principles by which human intelligence structures and gives order to an otherwise chaotic universe. 'Believe in them,' the novel says, 'and you will kill your intelligence with the poison of blind faith. After that you will live enslaved to priests and kings and manipulators' (219). We learn many of the common names of the ancient Egyptians, their idea of love and marriage, how divorce was effected, their creation myths, their scientific knowledge, and, above all, how they were transformed from an open, sharing community into a rigidly hierarchical, slave-owning society and into vain builders of pyramids.

In the novel, the information about Kemt or ancient Egypt is translated from ancient hieroglyphic documents given to the main character, Lindela, and her companion by custodians in the village of Iarw, somewhere in what seems like West Africa. The people of this village and of another village in the neighbourhood seem to be descended from migrants from the ancient Nile valley; and in the two villages we see the perpetuation of the division between 'keepers' and 'sharers' which led to the migration of the scribes away from Kemt. But it is not just possession of these ancient documents which links the people of Iarw with ancient Egypt, but also their names, such as Hor and Astw, and some of their gestures, such as when 'the couple, raising their hands at the same time, in a wordless gesture turned up their palms, then suddenly turned them face down and patted the mat'(129). Here as in his previous novel, *Osiris Rising,* Armah suggests cultural continuities between ancient Egypt and parts of present-day black Africa.

Why has Armah chosen to present this extensive information about ancient Egypt, obviously the fruit of laborious research, in the form of a novel? There are several answers. A novel gives life to mere information and also allows the writer room to imagine and speculate. Above all, the novel, being a more popular form of writing than the merely discursive, provides wider dissemination of its information. In this way, the wealth of information contained in the novel is wrested from the grasp of a closed circle of specialists and, potentially, made available to a wider readership. *KMT: In the House of Life* thus tries to live up to its own message that knowledge should not remain the property of a privileged few, but should be made available to all and be used for the general good. Through the novel, Armah seeks to make knowledge about ancient Egypt a matter of general knowledge in Africa. One wishes, once again, that more Africans could read literature in English.

Furthermore, the novel tries to make this knowledge about Egypt relevant to the African situation in the era of globalisation and the ever deepening diminution of Africa's status in the world. Armah argues that the African intellectual has, since the advent of colonialism, been the victim of an education that has denied African achievement. African intellectuals who have tried to challenge Africa's conquerors in this denial of the accomplishments of black people have been made to pay a very heavy price for their daring. Thus in the novel, Biko, a young friend of the protagonist is driven out of school, in a pivotal moment in the novel's plot, and ultimately to suicide just for pointing his European teacher to a passage in Aristotle in which the Greek philosopher describes the ancient Egyptians as very black. In the white teacher's typically racist view, ancient Egypt, the cradle of civilisation, could not possibly have been inhabited by black people.

As a result of an education which has suppressed their curiosity about themselves, and of course as a consequence of impoverished Africa's marginal role in a global economy designed to keep the continent subservient, African intellectuals have been obliged to use such knowledge as they possess to ensure their survival as individuals in their under-resourced countries and institutions. They organise conferences not with the goal of helping find solutions to the continent's problems, but merely to talk endlessly about these problems in order to ensure a continuous inflow of sponsoring funds from the donors in Europe and America. One of the most amusing moments in the novel concerns a satirical paper which one of the protagonists writes on the goals and methods of African intellectuals as they scrounge survival on the international conference circuit, using their knowledge not to bring relief to the continent, but to ensure personal gain. The African intellectual, as Armah sees him or her, is in league, like the African politician, with Africa's enemies in order to be able to pick up the crumbs from the Euro-American table.

KMT: In the House of Life redefines a meaningful purpose for the African intellectual. The intellectual in Africa must first seek such knowledge as will help free the continent from bondage to the West. This means rejecting a great deal of such knowledge about Africa as has been put out by Western scholars because such knowledge, based on racism, seeks only to confirm European dominance over a subservient Africa. The revolutionary African intellectual will not find answers to Africa's problems in any imported ideology or educational tradition. Africa's salvation lies in her own ancestral wisdom, particularly in the concept of *Maat*. In a very real sense, *KMT: In the House of Life* continues a project announced in *Osiris Rising,* the preceding novel. In that work, Armah suggests that a study of ancient Egypt should be a central part of modern African education. This new novel enables the reader to walk among ancient Egyptians and learn directly from them.

This is, in my view, an important novel for anyone, particularly any African, interested in the structure and wisdom of ancient Egyptian society. In the era of the African Renaissance, an essential part of Africa's awakening or re-awakening comprises rediscovering and reclaiming that ancient past which has been systematically misappropriated – just as Europe in the Renaissance rediscovered and reclaimed her Classical heritage. It is argued by some that Armah's Manichean division of the world into *us* (black people) against *them* (others, particularly the West) is retrograde or at best irrelevant in the era of NEPAD when a multi-racial and multi-cultural Africa seeks constructive engagement with the rest of the world. But, surely, African or black people, if they are to be more than mere junior partners, must engage the rest of the world from a position of self-belief, seeing themselves as significant contributors to the progress of humanity. For Armah, Egypt or Kemt is the source not only of this self-pride but also of the values that will redeem the continent.

A.N.Mensah
Department of English, University of Botswana

Ama Ata Aidoo, *The Girl Who Can and Other Stories*
Oxford: Heinemann, 2002. 151pp., £6.99; ISBN 0435 910132

This collection of fourteen short stories by the well-known Ghanaian writer, Ama Ata Aidoo is a revised edition of an earlier version published in Accra by Sub-Saharan Publishers in 1997 (reprinted 1999). Several of the stories have also appeared individually in various forms in scholarly and literary publications across the globe. This new publication [almost the last, JG] in the Heinemann African Writers Series is a welcome addition. It includes three new stories, 'Her Hair Politics – a very short story', 'Comparisons or who Said a Bird Cannot Father a Crab?' and 'Nutty'.

These stories are a delight to read. They are written in Aidoo's typical conversational tone, with the reader drawn into the stories as though being let into some secret or a conspiracy. Several of the stories are dramatic with quick exchanges between characters, as for example in 'She-Who-Would-Be-King', 'Her Hair Politics', 'Choosing', 'Some Global News', 'About the Wedding Feast', and 'Nutty'. Often she takes us into the thoughts of the main characters as they reflect on their lives and make decisions. This style is effectively employed in *Lice*, a powerful story of :

> just a woman,
> an ordinary wife with a normal marriage,
> ignored, double-timed –
> a harassed mother,
> a low-paid teacher in a rotten,
> third world educational system. (93)

She frequently makes use of verse. Later in the same story she writes:

> They scurried among them
> Like frightened mice
> In a tropical forest,
> Forever surprise in their eyes,
> Yet
> Still managing to
> Fuss,
> Like all mothers

> And from her mother:
> 'My Child, don't complain
> so much. Always remember
> that it doesn't matter how
> bad your situation is, someone
> nearby is wishing they were you.

Aidoo, as in all her writings, is concerned in these stories with pertinent social issues in her community and beyond, especially as relates to women. In 'Some Global News', 'Nutty', and 'Nowhere Cool', she engages with the experiences of Africans in the West. She treats sensitive issues with humour and in a matter of fact manner. For example, in the first two she examines racist prejudices with exceptional candour without being offensive. 'Choosing' examines the dilemma of the African writer seeking to make a living out of her writing. 'Heavy Moments' and 'She-Who-Would-Be King' consider the ability of women to achieve in areas traditionally thought of as male domains and some attitudes which such women invariably encounter. 'Lice' and 'Comparisons' expose some frustrations of working women in marital relationships, juggling several roles at the same time.

A number of the stories have an interesting time structure, with past events juxtaposed and compared with current ones. For example in 'Comparisons or Who Said a Bird Cannot Father a Crab?', a husband and a father are compared, and the phrases, 'Back Then', 'Today' or 'This Morning' are used throughout the story to indicate shifts between the past and present.

There are hints of biographical material in some of the stories. 'Nowhere Cool', for example, opens with a dialogue between the writer and her daughter Kinna, giving the impression of an actual exchange:

> Kinna: *(of five years old)* Mama, Mama, why do you look so quiet?
> AAA : Hmm...I am thinking.
> Kinna: Are you thinking again?
> AAA: Yes.
> Kinna: Mama, do people have to think all the time?
> AAA: Yes, child, it looks like we have to. All the time! (136)

Taken together, these stories are a feast of story-telling at it's best with a mélange of prose, poetry and drama. They have been written with passion, and are deeply felt by someone who is '(thinking) all the time'.

Awo Mana Asiedu,
School of Performing Arts, University of Ghana, Legon

Samuel Duh. *One More Time*
Accra, Ghana: Ghana University Press, 1999, 232 pp., £6.95/$11.95;
ISBN 9964-3-0262-2

Distributed by African Books Collective, Unit 13, King's Meadow, Ferry Hinksey Rd, Oxford OX2 0DP www.africanbookscollective.com

Once upon a time, a certain young man from Ghana, an indigent graduate student of engineering somewhere in North Carolina, called Kwame Afriyeh fell in love with Ginger, a white woman from a very wealthy family. Prior to meeting Kwame, Ginger had had her share of bad luck with black lovers, and had vowed not to date black and foreign men. Her plan is derailed by Kwame's charm and his promise to love her 'for ever'. They agree to get married despite the cultural and social differences between them. As one might have guessed right from the beginning, the 'for ever' does not last. However, that is not the main problem with this novel.

The novel makes a commendable attempt to challenge some of the age-old stereotypes and prejudiced attitudes many Africans have encountered in the United States, but this is at the expense of the narrative. The major structural fault in *One More Time* is the series of unconnected seminar-like sections during which the plot is put on hold, much to the irritation of the reader. Samuel Duh has ruined a fairly interesting interracial love story with lectures on African culture in all its ramifications. For example, at various times in the novel, Kwame Afriyeh provides Ashanti perspectives on African life (27–40;

45–9; 56–61), on racism (83–103), on culture, customs and beliefs. Anecdotes, often in the form of traditional African tales, describe customs and rituals linked with family life (188–95), with birth (183–8), marriage (69–78; 149–55), witchcraft (158–70) and death (195–8).

Discussions on African culture, many of which are held at parties or in Ginger's apartment, end up leaving the reader confused and bewildered. While some of the talk may impress those who are ignorant of Ashanti marriage customs, other readers will find them tedious. Readers may also question the eagerness of a father to hand over his daughter to a man he has never met, and whose family he barely knows (134). And this behaviour is in sharp contrast to Kwame's excited explanation of his ethnic group's marriage customs.

The novelist's handling of Angelina, a girlfriend from Ghana whom Kwame introduces to Ginger as his 'cousin', is another indication of the book's poor construction. The first time one hears anything about a girlfriend in Ghana is a cursory reference and no name is mentioned (32). When Angelina arrives, some ninety pages later (125), Duh has not prepared the reader adequately for her. She seems to have been manufactured as the solution to a financial problem (126).

It is rather simplistic to have Kwame tell his fellow Ghanaians of Angelina's imminent arrival just a few days before she turns up. Members of this same group, that includes Ben, have seen Kwame with Ginger several times and seem to have sanctioned the relationship. It is very shallow for them to switch allegiance so easily.

Certain sections of the novel would benefit from tighter editing. For example, what exactly does the writer mean by 'protection'? Did Angelina know Ben was 'protecting' Kwame (137) after they have collected her from the airport? What is he 'protecting' her from? Is this, one wonders, Duh's way of implying Kwame's mental confusion? 'Protecting' sounds as it might be a direct translation from Twi, and might possibly refer to Ben providing an alibi for his friend.

One wishes Duh had focused more on developing the main plot – the love triangle featuring Kwame, Ginger and Angelina – instead of treading paths already worn out by anthropologists and historians. Dragging a reluctant reader through a myriad dreary tales of African mumbo jumbo in the midst of telling a love story makes *One More Time* a tiring experience. One is so irritated that one wants to scream, with apologies to Flora Nwapa, 'Once Is Enough!'

Olabisi Gwamna
Division of Languages and Literature, Iowa Wesleyan College, US

Nigerian Fiction

Nwankwo, Kate I. *Fatal Greed*
Enugu: Fourth Dimension, 2002, 116 pp., £6.95/$11.95; ISBN 978-156-476-8

Afolayan, Sunday. *Beyond the Silent Grave*
Ibadan, Abuja, Benin City, Lagos, Owerri: Spectrum Books, 2001, 251 pp., £6.95/$11.95; ISBN 978-029-281-0

Martins, Stella. *Our Moment in Time*
Enugu: Fourth Dimension, 2002, 98 pp., £8.95/$14.95; ISBN 978-156-500-4

Nwankwo, A[gwuncha] A[rthur] *Season of Hurricane*
2nd ed. Enugu: Fourth Dimension, [1993], 1998, 257 pp., £6.95/$11.95; ISBN 978-156-424-5

Nwankwo, A[gwuncha] A[rthur]. *Reckoning at Storm End*
Enugu: Fourth Dimension, 2002, 119 pp., £6.95/$11.95; ISBN 978-156-506-3

Aniagolu, Emeka. *Black Mustard Seed*
Enugu: Fourth Dimension, 2002, 312 pp., including a glossary of Yoruba, Hausa and Igbo words, £11.95/$19.95; ISBN 978-156-487-3

All distributed by African Books Collective, Unit 13, King's Meadow, Ferry Hinksey Rd, Oxford OX2 0DP www.africanbookscollective.com

Onitsha market literature, which flourished from the close of the Second World War until the beginning of the Nigerian Civil War, reflected an unconscious belief in 'shared assumptions' and a hoped-for compatibility in 'world outlook'. The Marxist aesthetician Mikhail Lifschitz understands the desire of the market traders to write when, in *Marxism and Art*, he asserts: 'Artistic modification of the world is ... one of the ways of assimilating nature. Creative activity is merely one instance of a realization of an idea or a purpose in the material world; it is a process of objectification.' In this process the early Onitsha pamphleteers were content with a small financial gain, so long as they had the opportunity to educate the community morally. This pedagogical intent represented an objectification of their world view to promote the basis for an eventual communal understanding.

Kate Nwankwo's *Fatal Greed* is for younger adult readers. In its pedagogic emphasis it continues the tradition of the early Onitsha pamphleteers and series such as Macmillan's 'Pacesetters'. Ngozi, the antagonist, makes her own destiny; it is juxtaposed with the book's dedication and primary message: 'To Almighty God, Divine Authority, the Strength of My Life'. This morality tale persistently offers a Christianity that requires, to counterpoint the Onitsha pamphleteers and Lifschitz, blind adherence to one's lot in life: 'She raised her hand in supplication and prayed God that they should live happily ever after and they lived happily ever after' (116). Of course, the act of praying is a form of intervention that undermines acceptance of one's fate.

Told over two generations, the book thumps forth its message, at times in clichés: 'she reasoned that east, or west, home is best' (52). Sequencing of narrative revelations is flawed (53), and an abundance of errors in manufacture (copy-editing) are present. These include: incorrect diction: 'matched' for machete (3), 'scaly wag' for scally wag (4), misplaced punctuation (6), missing participles (12), redundancy: 'Ngozi thought ... Ihemma, who wasn't aware of what Ngozi was thinking' (54), and confused syntax: 'you ye forgotten that the doctor said' (27). There is a plethora of '~'s that appear to result from the lack of the appropriate letter when manually setting pages (31). There are too many errors to permit recommendation of the text for use in schools.

Kate Nwankwo offers varied narrative perspectives, in a third person limited narration through the views of Chuka, Ngozi, Ihemma and Ogbonna. The shifts in perspective work quite well, especially the trauma Ogbonna experiences as he recognises his mother (Ngozi) and Chuka are committing adultery in the room he sleeps in. The mixture of science ('Unfortunately, his wife's genotype was A.S.', 56), with traditional beliefs (Atikpa, the 'witch-doctor', 58) and loose echoes of Greek mythology (e.g., the Nessus story, 58) do not form a comfortable, integrated synthesis. Rather, each element displays an aspect of the author's (not the characters') learning and each element is breezily dismissed by Ngozi's final confession (113). The Christian ideology is exemplified in Ihemma's blandly consistent acceptance of her husband's murder, her child being framed, and the attempted murder of her child: 'I have forgiven you, Ngozi.' (114).

Afolayan's *Beyond the Silent Grave* is another morality tale, the story of Shola, a sex addict, who eventually, in a twist on the Oedipus story, takes his daughter, 'oneself's same blood' (250) as wife, interrogatively beseeches God for an explanation, and dies. It, like Kate Nwankwo's *Fatal Greed*, is dedicated to God: 'To / the glory of God / ... the Then / ... the Now / ... the Evermore / and / the benefit of mankind; / the human image / of His divinity.' However, as with Milton's Satan, albeit in a less complexly created character and situation, it is the salacious detail that predominates in this book.

The story is more tightly told than others reviewed here. It offers a colourful evocation of its locale, emphasising street names, eating places, and consumer goods that familiarise the reader with Nigerian life. In the details, then, the book has merit. Afolayan's first novel indicates promise for the future once his obvious talent for realism is exploited fully and his dull echo of the magic-realist-mysterious is curtailed.

Stella Martins has three other books to her credit: *The Hellion*, *Hot Shots* and *The Boomerang* apart from *Our Moment in Time*, in which she presents a narrator-controlled long-winded morality tale about the possibility of male-female platonic friendships. Her book would benefit from severe editing; there is a short story within that has something to say. Ngozi, a university student of biology, meets and has a strong friendship with Obi, a fellow student. She is also courted by Chike, who lives in London. In accordance with Ngozi's desire to maintain her virginity until marriage and a belaboured presentation of her thoughts (23ff) on why she should choose Chike rather than Obi, this soap opera moves into high gear and the reader sees, but does not experience, Ngozi's time in London as a wife, mother of two, medical student and researcher in paediatrics. (All this takes some 12 pages). Obi, meanwhile, has achieved similar success in the United States, marrying there to gain a work permit (2 pages). Inevitably, the two come together again to work at Enugu Teaching Hospital, where Ngozi is Head of Paediatrics Research. Neither has completely 'got over' the other and so an 'anguished' set of narrator-presented interior disquisitions follows, first for Ngozi, then for Obi. These are resolved in a discussion between the two that takes the shape of a thesis, antithesis, synthesis plot development.

There is the odd typographical error and infelicity of style. For example, we encounter 'breaks' for brakes (14), 'saw' for say (21), 'However, in their culture' (22), and 'As the enormity of all of this dawned on her, it got darker as night came' (38). Time shifts are clumsily handled ('Now, it is several years later' 48), and the community represented unrecognisable. (Given that the field of Paediatrics Research (globally and) in Nigeria is fairly select and closed, Obi's arrival strikes a false, manufactured note when we read: 'Nobody seemed to know yet who this doctor was' (49). This is despite the fact that he had, presumably, applied for and been interviewed for the position in Ngozi's department!)

A. A. Nwankwo is a prolific author of poetry, novels and non-fiction, which includes history, and political analyses; he is a significant political figure. His publications include *Before I Die: Olusegun Obasanjo/Arthur Nwankwo Correspondence on the one party state* (1989), and he is the subject of Victor Eke Kalu's *The Nigeria Condition: Arthur Nwankwo's Views & Blueprint* (1987). In other words, he is a persistent voice that warrants attention.

The essence of Nwankwo's *Season of Hurricane* is aptly encapsulated in the odd blurb on its back cover:

> Rich in imagery and poetic use of language, and drawing extensively from both indigenous verbal art forms and the received Western tradition of aesthetics, the story is a poignant evocation of a land caught in the dance of death, and the affirmative principles that come with the destruction of life over death, light over darkness.

In fact, the book is an uneasy fusion of oral and literary, where the orality of the text – the narrator's intrusiveness (see p. 28) raises questions about the narrator's proximity to events and complicity in them. The issue is never resolved satisfactorily. The tale of a coup and military rule, *Season of Hurricane* emphasises the roles of the Christian 'heroes', Mark, Peter, Michael, John and Zachariah, who oppose an unnamed 'Leader'. Neither the named nor the anonymous despot are sufficiently well-realised as characters to induce interest or empathy.

This is the second edition of Nwankwo's novel, but many of the troublesome syntactical convolutions, misplaced punctuation marks (21, etc) and excesses in expression remain, as with the contradictory 'destruction of life over death' in the blurb quoted above. Other problems include redundancy: 'hired hands: hirelings' (4); confused expression: 'trembling with excitement and anxious anticipation of the authority' (5) where the alliterative flow of the line undermines the action described; overcooked oppositions: 'pain and sorrow, death and agony ... life over death ... light over darkness ... realities that became illusions and dreams which turned into nightmares' (15); mixed metaphors: 'My story will thus commence as a whisper, the rattling of melodious flutes that bore Peter's killer to the Palace' (17), and undeveloped cultural summation: 'On the part of the people, there was the unwillingness to make sacrifices steeped, as they were, in the lores and mores of the old ways' (21). It is evident, then, that Nwankwo prefers sound to sense.

The novel closes with a nod to the complicated and heart-wrenching plight of the Igbo people following the Biafran War, when the 'Leader' is publicly humiliated and the nation votes to 'split into five after a unanimous resolution' (257). Neither the 'indigenous verbal art forms [nor] the received Western tradition of aesthetics' have been comfortably deployed here.

Reckoning at Storm End concerns itself with similar material to *Season of Hurricane*: the violent overthrow of a despot. The narrative perspective is third person limited, alternating between the despot, Abraham, leader of the 'resistance' and Keith, an intelligence officer who switches allegiance to become the interim military leader of the resistance. The book has vague echoes of Soyinka's *Season of Anomy* (1980), but without Soyinka's nuanced awareness. Nwankwo is much less complex, hurrying to the execution of his despot, and leaving the people involved 'with joyful hearts and easy minds' (118) about the parts they have played. Even the manifesto for change is presented uncritically: 'There was little debate on the proposals for its [sic] cogency, logic and practicability were unquestionable' (119).

The haste of the resolution of the plot is mirrored in the presentation of this volume. Although the text is written in a clearer, less 'poetic' style than *Season of Hurricane,* errors abound. One could argue that the style is aimed at a lower mean literacy level, but the mistakes suggest otherwise: incorrect diction, 'descent education', 'John gazed at the manger who looked back' (10), 'he would be dead in the next forty-eighth house' (22), 'Planes ... roared down the runways towards their various stopping pints' (29); confused syntax, 'they barely survived and left were drinking' (1), 'you got had a delivery' (10), 'When what has been happening interjected to happen, the dictator interjected' (16), 'occasionally they corrugated iron sheet passed some houses too' (32), omitted conjunctions 'strafing the land with bombs rockets' (6), subject verb agreement 'His shouts ... was drowned' (6), needless repetition 'the edge of the forest edge' (8), 'the car bearing Keith bore out' (30), tense shifts 'The secretary appear ... and stood' (10), and jumps in logic 'Damages and losses were calculated in hundreds, if not billions of dollars' (14), 'everything would be carried out to the least detail' (25). Plot confusions exist, such as the one on page 11, where the members of the resistance are seeking a place 'to bury the money' they have taken from a government bank, but the narrative jumps to them digging up a pipeline to plant dynamite. These mistakes have to be emphasised (and they are but a small sampling of the muddied picture the reader enters on picking up this book) because Nwankwo sets himself up as a man with the blueprint for Nigeria's future. The lack of care in expression directly corresponds to the degree of depth and thought put into the formation of a national blueprint: far from idealistic, characters associated with the resistance, like Jozzy, 'longed for adventure, excitement and intrigue' (34). The narrator, unnamed, but textually aligned with the 'resistance', is a recurring problem in Nwankwo's fiction.

Emeka Aniagolu is an Assistant Professor and the Assistant Director for the Black World Studies of Ohio Wesleyan University, where he teaches African, African-American Studies and Political Science. He has written scholarly studies, works of fiction, short stories and short-plays. His first novel was heralded by writers and critics alike: Chinua Achebe, to whom the book is dedicated, Abiola Irele, Editor of *Research in African Literatures*, and Laura Chrisman, author of *Colonial Discourse and Postcolonial Theory* (1994). The novel lives up to the plaudits it has received, though there are some weaknesses, including the ubiquitous errors in typography, diction and syntax.

The ninety-one chapters of *Black Mustard Seed* are brief; this brevity permits Aniagolu to switch between the two couples (Chike and Bisi, Igbo and Yoruba respectively, though both are Catholic; Mohammed and Ngozi, Hausa and Igbo, Muslim and Catholic respectively) and three sets of tribal customs that dominate his narrative. A reader might begin with a review of the title's import that brings together Matthew 13: 31–2 with the association of black mustard seeds with disturbance and strife. The title offers a potential binary between the good (growth) and the bad (discord). The growth is emphatically endorsed by Aniagolu's gift of reflectiveness and verbal proficiency, especially to the younger generation of Chike, Bisi, Mohammed, Ngozi. Discord arrives in the author's mediation of these young lives in the context of Wazobian (Nigerian) pre-colonial, colonial and post-colonial history. The author reinforces this faith in the younger generation as well as in the cultural hybrid that will resolve tribal issues in the nation's name: Wa (Come, Yoruba), Zo (Come, Hausa), Bia (Come, Igbo). Aniagolu offers two stanzas from Merrell Vories Hitotsuyanagi's 'The Mustard Seed' (1907) to alert readers to the path of planting, death and redemption to 'The Life of the Spirit'. He ends quoting the Gospel of Luke (17.6) to underscore the faith in the future, following the birth of the four protagonists' children. Ali Mazrui's novel *The Trial of Christopher Okigbo* (1971) is an obvious precedent for *Black Mustard Seed* in the irresolution of the endings: Mazrui deploys the third verdict of Scots' Law, 'Not Proven', whereas Aniagolu suggests a better life in the 'dehistoricized', culturally hybrid future. Both works are by political scientists, which may have affected the rhetorical flourishes that dominate the writing.

Aniagolu builds on the title with a Preface, a miscue, I think, as he lays bare his intent: 'I have ... told a story – my own story – the best I can, with a view towards making a positive contribution to Nigeria's self-transformation from modern *state*hood to modern *nation*hood' (6). In one respect, then, the novel is a bildungsroman; in another, an autophylography (*phylum*: tribe: race). The two couples, as microcosm for the nation, are not sufficiently drawn to carry the weight. Aniagolu frequently writes beautifully and precisely about different cultural practices and different locales, including Kano, in Nigeria, but the characters are an uneasy fit – rhetorical chess pieces for the exposition of his thesis. A case in point is Chike's brief affair with Azaku, his dismissal of her during pregnancy and then his bizarre invitation (post abortion) of her to his wedding to Bisi. Presumably the latter invitation is an attempt to draw all potential conflicting forces together, but it is awkward and does not work.

156 *Reviews*

The novel opens with the same promise as Ben Okri's *The Famished Road* (1993):

> Chike met Bisi at the medical school of the renowned University of Ibadan two harmattans ago. He remembers well how all the leaves turned brown and fell off the dry, skeleton-like branches of trees. The dry season in the tropical environs of Africa has a way of rendering unsolicited testimony. Stripped of his vegetational clothing, he stands naked for all to bear witness to his seasonal fragility. (9)

Less mythic than *The Famished Road*, Aniagolu's *Black Mustard Seed* has a mannered, at times attention-seeking, style. There is, unlike the other novels covered in this review, an assuredness with language, plot and characterisation. Achebe's response to Conrad in *Things Fall Apart* is an obvious allusion in Aniagolu's opening: 'One Anglian ex-colonial officer ... in his memoirs ... *Footprints on the Sands of Time: A Personal Account of Anglian Exploits in the Dark Continent*' (13). Aniagolu's hybrid children at the novel's close are an explicit allusion to Armah's 1968 novel, 'Chike thought to himself, perhaps, the beautiful ones have at last been born' (308). Not yet, as Armah presciently observed, but a new talent in Nigerian and Igbo literature has decisively announced his arrival.

Craig McLuckie
Department of English, Okanagan University College, Canada.

Short Notices – Reviews Editor

Kari Dako. *The Baobabs of Tete and Other Stories*
Accra: Sub-Saharan, 2002, 116 pp., $17.95; ISBN 9988-550-29-4

The author, who is known to readers of *African Literature Today* as a critic and as the editor of Ernest Obeng's *Eighteen Pence*, emerges from this volume as versatile and assured creative writer. In fifteen pieces of prose she explores a variety of forms, often combining anger, amusement and irritation with compassion.

Norwegian by birth, Dako is married to a Ghanaian academic and has spent much of her professional career as a university lecturer in the English Department at the University of Ghana. However, many of her stories draw on her experience when on attachment to aid programmes. English provides a supple and expressive instrument, as she 'catches' different voices and explores situations in Liberia, Ghana, Mozambique, Angola, and Kenya. Wherever they are set, her stories/anecdotes/accounts repeatedly expose injustice and exploitation, employing diverse strategies that insist on the reader listening closely for false notes.

Dako turns her observant eye on a wide range of anti-social individuals and compromised institutions. She exposes, for example, selfish men, hypocritical religious leaders, white hunters masquerading as aid workers, aid organisations being used as tour operators, arrogant European tourists, stiff African bureaucrats, and predatory school teachers. She celebrates tenacity, determination and courage, but she is under no illusions about the odds stacked against happiness and fulfilment, particularly against women's happiness and fulfilment.

In Dako's delight in rendering different voices in print, and in the confident centrality of women's experience to her writing, there is much that recalls Ama Ata Aidoo's short stories. This makes it particularly appropriate that Aidoo should have written the Preface. It is also fitting that the volume, which has high production standards, should have been produced by Akoss Ofori-Mensah's Sub-Saharan Publishers.

Kevin J. Wetmore Jr. *The Athenian Sun in an African Sky*
Jefferson: McFarland 2002, 232 pp., $30.40 ISBN 0-7864-1093-0

The sub-title clarifies Wetmore's area of interest: this book is about 'Modern African Adaptations of Classical Greek Tragedy'. In six chapters, an introduction ('The Library Doors of Classical Africa') and a Conclusion ('African Theatre in a Postcultural World'), Wetmore engages with issues of impact and influence that have produced important texts by African authors. He looks, for example at plays by Bekederemo-Clark, Butler, Fugard, Rotimi, Soyinka, Sutherland, Zulu, and brings together a clutch of 'African Antigones' by Brathwaite, Osofisan, Fugard, Kani, Ntshona and Bemba. He provides a definition of 'postcultural' but it doesn't impress.

Links between Ancient Greece and Yorubaland struck Leo Frobenius, and more recently parallels have been insisted on. They informed Geoffrey Axworthy's decision to put on a double bill of plays entitled *Antigone*, one by Sophocles, the other by Anouilh, at Ibadan in the early 1960s, and have been justified by the works considered by Wetmore, and by Soyinka's adaptation of *Oedipus at Colonus* for performance at Delphi (2002). With extra jerks of the arm, Wetmore spreads his net beyond the well-trodden West African catchment area to take in the Republic of the Congo and South Africa. He also takes in a couple of works from the 1990s, including Osofisan's *Tegonni* which he examines as an unpublished manuscript.

On occasions, Wetmore brings to his analysis welcome insights from having directed the text he is discussing. But, like all researchers, he is at the mercy of his raw material. So long as he has invaluable resources of the National English Literary Museum (NELM) in Grahamstown, he can proceed with cautious confidence. Writing about South Africa in this vein he offers the following: 'Most of the scholarly material available indicates that South Africa has had several Aristophanes adaptations, primarily in the 1970s' (50). That's rather unsteady, but I think we get the point. A few lines later we can hear ominous cracking as he steps out onto thin ice. 'Other than these three productions, Aristophanes remains relatively unadapted in South Africa. Furthermore, very few productions of straightforward translations of the

Greek originals appear to have been performed in South Africa in the last half century, as reviews of only a handful of university and community productions indicate. Even less information is available about productions of Aristophanes throughout the rest of the continent. While, as noted above, absence of evidence is not necessarily evidence of absence, it seems fairly safe to conclude that Greek comedy is not nearly as popular as Greek tragedy, in any African nation.' Yes, that is a fairly safe assumption. But the reader wants to know what evidence of productions Wetmore has found. None it would seem. He writes: 'There is very little, if any, adaptation of Aristophanes's works into African contexts. Even performances of translations of the Greek originals seem fairly nonexistent.' (51). 'Very little, if any, ...fairly nonexistent' are classic examples of a researcher hedging his bets. How can something be 'fairly nonexistent'? The formulation shows that Wetmore has simply not been able to find out what has been happening: who has been adapting what, who producing what? One can sympathise with him. In the absence of 'a NELM' for other African countries or a theatre archive for the whole of Africa, an assessment of the situation is impossible. He should have been honest and begun: 'I have not found …'

Wetmore fails to take into account *Akin Mata*, an adaptation of *Lysistrata* by James Simmons and Tony Harrison that was produced as Nigeria drifted into Civil War and subsequently published. Such ventures should not be neglected or forgotten, and it would be sad if the fire that destroyed some of the Theatre Arts Department at the University of Ibadan succeeded in erasing all records of Geoffrey Axworthy's production of Aristophanes on the campus or meant that the input of John Ferguson into the theatrical life of the institution was forgotten.

The involvement of the Ferguson Centre of the Open University (UK) – yes, named after John Ferguson – in organising a conference on the classics in the post-colonial world during May 2004 shows a stirring of academic interest in a range of issues that Wetmore touches on. When more research has been carried out in the area mapped by Wetmore, I suspect it will be apparent that, while he has not been as potent a presence in African theatre as Sophocles, Aristophanes has had at least a walk on part. He has been 'fairly existent'.

Palavers of African Literature, ed. Toyin Falola and Barbara Harlow
Trenton, NJ: Africa World Press, 2002, 383 pp., $89.95; ISBN HB 0-86543-991-5. and $29.95 Vol. 1 ISBN PB 0-86543-992-3

African Writers and Their Readers, ed. Toyin Falola and Barbara Harlow
Trenton, NJ: Africa World Press, 2002, 542 pp., $99.95; ISBN HB 0-86543-859-5 and $34.95 Vol. 2 PB 0-86543-860-9

It is, I think, a mark of the productivity and generosity of Bernth Lindfors that colleagues at the University of Texas (Austin) compiled two volumes of essays in his honour as he moved towards retirement. A paragraph in the 'Acknowledgements' written by Toyin Falola and Barbara Harlow provides a context for the collections:

> At once student and teacher of African literature, Bernth Lindfors has through his own exemplary and unrelentingly wide-ranging work and his unflagging individual example, in turn inspired students to become teachers, and teachers to embark on new studies. Many of those students and teachers, who have been influenced by Ben over the decades, have contributed to the composition and the disposition of these volumes. They represent no less that three generations of scholarship, straddle five continents, and bespeak the diverse and diverged debates that have distinguished the literary critical world of African cultural production – and its reception and review in academic arenas, both African and non-African. The very heterogeneity of the essays included in these two volumes – their discrepant perspectives, their shared recollections, even their competing selectivity – is itself testimony both to the breadth and Ben's interest and investment in the study of African literature and to the generosity of his intellectual acumen and personal commitments.

'Amen' to that, and 'Bravo' to the editors who have initiated efforts to ensure that copies of these volumes reach the shelves of libraries in African universities. This is excellent news, indeed it is the sort of gesture that makes the effort that went into the publication worthwhile. Nowadays there is talk of the 'digital divide' and concern about the obvious discrepancies in access to new technologies, but this should not deafen us to the problems with the old technologies. Attention must be paid in these circumstances to making publications about African literature accessible to students and scholars in Africa. Good, old-fashioned books have a part to play.

I do not intend to comment on particular contributions to the volumes except to say that Lemuel Johnson has a fifty-one page essay on '(En)Countering Traditions of the Erotic in African Narratives' in *African Writers and their Readers*. In scope and detail it represents decades of study, of consideration, note-taking and thought. Within a book celebrating Lindfors' continuing life's work is to be found a message from beyond the grave by a major contributor to the study of African literature. As we read Johnson's essay we recall that, as when we tread on dead leaves, the pages allow the departed speak.

Journals

Humanities Review Journal, ed. Foluke M. Ogunleye
1, 1 (June 2001), 87 pp., 1, 2 (December 2001), 96 pp., 2, 1 (June 2002), 147 pp. Ile-Ife: Humanities Research Forum ISSN 1596 0749, Subscription details Humanities Publishers, P O Box 1417, University Post Office, Ibadan, Oyo State, Nigeria.

As might be expected, the *Humanities Review Journal* covers a wide range of academic disciplines. Each volume contains 11 or 12 articles of, on average, about 3,500 words. Initially dramatists, including Femi Osofisan, Ola Rotimi,

Wole Soyinka and Sam Ukala, came in for examination, but clearly the editorial board welcomes submissions on fiction and poetry. Several papers on language, including linguistic ingenuity and vocabularies in African dance, and ethical issues have recently appeared.

It is a worrying mark of the times that in the call for papers the Editor, indicates that contributors whose papers are accepted for publication will be required to pay a token amount towards the publication of the volume. The editorial address is Humanities Review Journal, P O Box 1904, Department of Dramatic Arts, Obafemi Awolowo University, Ile-Ife, Nigeria. Humanitiesjournal2001@yahoo.com In an ideal world it would not be appropriate to ask for such support, but this is not an ideal world.

No Condition is Permanent: Nigerian Writing and the Struggle for Democracy, ed. Holger Ehling and Claus-Peter Holste-von Mutius, Matatu 23/24 (2001), Amsterdam, New York: Rodopi, 2001, 374 pp.; ISBN 90-420-1496-2

'Many of the articles in this issue of *Matatu* were presented as papers at a conference on "Art and Development of Civil Society in Nigeria: The Role of Literature in the Democratic Process", which was held in Ijebu-Ode from May 13-15, 1996, under the auspices of the Friedrich Ebert Foundation. Following precedent, this double issue of *Matatu* brings together the formal and the relatively informal (articles and 'market place') with creative writing, interviews and book reviews.

The volume is dedicated to Ken Saro-Wiwa and includes two interviews with him. It also includes an essay on 'the Role of the Writer in a Developing Society' by Bola Ige whose assassination raises many questions about the struggle for democracy. The volume includes material on or by (and in some cases both) established authors Okara (born 1921), Segun (b. 1930), Achebe (b. 1930), Soyinka (b. 1934), Sofola (b. 1935), Saro-Wiwa (b. 1941), Vatsa (b. 1944), Osundare (b. 1946), Osofisan (b. 1946), Iyayi (b. 1947), Ojaide (b. 1948) as well as younger writers, Adeniyi, Bandele, Ifowodu, Obiwu, Sanni – whose birthdates are not so easily looked up! Ehling and Mutius have assembled a rich, varied collection that manages to throw new light on successive generations of Nigerian writers.

The coverage indicates that a conscious effort has been made to extend the scope of the publication to take in a 'younger generation' of Nigerian writers. To some extent the Association of Nigerian Authors has provided a framework in which they can establish themselves. Literary pages in the vigorous Nigerian press, particularly *The Guardian*, *Vanguard*, and *The Post Express*, have played their part, and so has the publication that took on the mantles of *Black Orpheus* and *Transition*, *Glendora Review*. Indeed, there may be said to be a Glendora Group, or a Glendora Generation, made up of those who as critics or poets, and guided by Dapo Adeniyi, published in the journal. I'm thinking of writers such as Sesan Ajayi, Martha Modena Vertreace, Kayode Aderinokun, Ogaga Ifowodo, Obi Nwakanma, Chiedu Ezeanah. Inevitably, some of them became more widely known through reviews in the *Glendora*

Book Supplement. More recently and for limited circulation, vigorous debates about literary matters have been held by e-mail newsgroups, and there may come a time when the archives of 'virtual publications' such as 'krazitivity' will be raided by conventional publishers.

Three Playwrights Crossing Borders

1. Ade-Yemi Ajibade

Fingers Only and A Man Named Mokai
Ibadan Y-Book Drama series 2001, 142 pp.; ISBN 978-2659-88-6

Parcel Post and Behind the Mountain
Ibadan Y-Book Drama series 2001, 147 pp.; ISBN 978-2659-89-4

These two volumes bring together plays that made an impact in London with those dating from Yemi Ajibade's period in Ibadan during the late 1970s. The roller-coastering *Parcel Post* was presented at the Royal Court for twenty-nine performances (1976/7), and *Fingers Only*, originally, *Lagos, Yes Lagos,* was seen at the Factory Theatre, Battersea Arts Centre and Albany Empire (1982).

Behind the Mountain is dedicated to members of the Unibadan Masques, recalling Ajibade's involvement with that ambitious attempt to establish a professional, university-linked company. To his work with them, as a writer and director (1976-9), and to his writing, he brought an actor's eye and ear, cultivated from his time as a student at The Actors' Workshop on, and all his experience as a director that included taking Obi Egbuna's *Wind versus Polygamy* to the First Festival of Negro Arts, Dakar (1966).

Perhaps most important of all are the lessons Ajibade learned over a long period from contact with the BBC's radio drama for Africa. A version of *Lagos, Yes Lagos* was broadcast in 1971, and readers have been able to glimpse Ajibade in print since that play was published in *Nine African Plays for Radio* (1973). The two volumes now available permit a fuller assessment of Ajibade's stature as a writer.

2. Pierre Meunier

The Little Kings
Ibadan: Spectrum, 2001, 179 pp., £5.95/$9.95; ISBN 978-0293-00-0

The Coffee Party
Ibadan: Spectrum, 2001, 124 pp., £4.95/$8.95; ISBN 978-0292-85-3

Farin Dutse
Ibadan: Spectrum, 171 pp., £5.95/$9.95; ISBN 978-0293-05-1

All distributed by African Books Collective, Unit 13, King's Meadow, Ferry Hinksey Rd, Oxford OX2 0DP www.africanbookscollective.com

These three volumes contain a total of seven plays. Added to those contained in the other five volumes by Pierre Eugene Meunier that Spectrum has published since 1992 and to those published by Space in Zaria, they contribute to a substantial body of work that occupies a special space in writing in Africa. Meunier, who was born in Eastern France and started working for SCOA in Nigeria in 1948, became a Nigerian citizen in 1978.

He draws on his wide acquaintance with commercial life in Nigeria, and his work has a particular authority when it moves into that territory. Varied and generally vigorous, the oeuvre has been given some attention by Nigerian scholars, but the real test for a play text is always in performance.

3. Femi Osofisan

Recent Outings: Tegonni, an African Antigone and many Colours Make the Thunder King
Ibadan: Opon Ifa Readers. An imprint of Centre STAGE-AFRICA, 1999, 243 pp.; ISBN 978-33259-1-4

Insidious Treason: Drama in Postcolonial State (Essays)
Ibadan: Opon Ifa Publishers, 2001, 256 pp.; ISBN 978-33259-6-5

Literature and the Pressures of Freedom: essays, speeches and songs
Ibadan: Opon Ifa Readers, 198 pp.; ISBN 978-33259-7-3

In *Literature and the Pressures of Freedom*, Osofisan lists the twenty-six plays he had published by 1998, two of which have been translated into Yoruba. If I read the 'Other Works' correctly, he has also had some sixteen other plays performed. The quality of this very, very substantial body of work has established Osofisan (born 1946) as the most important playwright of his generation. Indeed, he was so prominent that he was put in charge of the National Theatre, Igammu, Lagos. His job was an impossible one given, for example, that the hideous building, bought 'off the shelf' from Bulgaria, leaked from the beginning and had been shamefully neglected for many years. After hanging the albatross of this office around his neck, President Olusegun Obasanjo cut the ground from beneath his feet and 'blackspotted' him by announcing that the building was to be sold! There were suggestions that the grounds could be turned into a golf course!

With determination, Osofisan fought on: he brought major productions, such as *King Baabu* (August 2001), to the theatre, and had the National Troupe undertake a series of productions, sometimes directed by Ahmed Yerimah, of Nigerian classics in a style that moved, even in the case of a verse drama such as *Song of a Goat*, towards total African theatre. He even managed to continue with the publishing venture, Opon Ifa, he initiated while teaching at the University of Ibadan. *Recent Outings,* one of the fruits of this, brings together his version of *Antigone* (directed at Emory University, Atlanta, 1994), with a play that had been first published in 1997.

As with so much Nigerian drama Chris Dunton's *Nigerian Theatre in English: A Critical Bibliography* (1998) is inevitably the first stop for anyone curious about such work. In this instance, researchers will not, however, find anything on the first text, and may resort to Wetmore's chapter on African versions of *Antigone* in *The Athenian Sun in an African Sky*. (See above.)

Osofisan is a critic as well as a creative writer, and he has been a trenchant contributor to controversies in the Nigerian press over the years. The ease with which his critical prose breaks into narrative and song is well illustrated in *Literature and the Pressures of Freedom* which, the sub-title informs, is made up of essays, speeches and songs.

Insidious Treason includes eight essays helpfully organised into three sections. Part One is headed 'Departing from Soyinka', Part Two 'Commitment and its Problems', and Part Three: 'The International Dimension'. The volume appeared in 2001 by which time the walls of the National Theatre were closing in on Osofisan. I suspect that his time at Igammu will have spawned several essays and plays to add to the impressive output already in the public domain. Perhaps there will be a section headed 'The National Drama' in a forthcoming volume.

At the end of *Insidious Treasons*, the oral informs the literary in the form of the transcription of an interview conducted by Biodun Jeyifo. It provides abundant insight into *Tegonni*.

Nasidi, Taiwo and Ebewo: Three Nigerian Critics

Yakubu A. Nasidi, *Beyond the Limits of Experience: Theory, Criticism and Power in African Literature*
Ibadan: Caltop, 2001, 132 pp.; ISBN 978 31653 6 4

Oladele Taiwo. *Social Experience in African Literature*
Enugu: Fourth Dimension, 1986, reprinted 2002, 169 pp., £14.95/$24.95; ISBN 978156136X

Patrick Ebewo. *Barbs: A Study of Satire in the Plays of Wole Soyinka*
Kampala: JANyeko, 2002, 221 pp., £18.95/$30.95; ISBN 9970-510-03-X
Last two titles distributed by African Books Collective, Unit 13, King's Meadow, Ferry Hinksey Rd, Oxford OX2 0DP www.africanbookscollective.com

Publishing in Africa and the existence of learned journals in which creative work in the arts is discussed are essential ingredients of cultural autonomy. In this context it is good to be able to report on the developing list of titles being brought out by Caltop and to welcome Yakubu Nasidi's study. The chapter headings and the index reveal that the grasp is somewhat less than the reach implied by the reference to 'African Literature' in the title. Very few African writers are listed in the, admittedly fallible, index and, except for the work of Achebe and Soyinka, African writing is given little attention. Ayi Kwei Armah is mentioned, it seems, on 3 pages, Mphahlele on 4, Senghor on 7, Ngugi on one, Tutuola (in the index at 'Tubuola') on one. In contrast Raymond Williams is mentioned on 11 pages. Surprisingly Williams does not get into the 'Select Bibliography', but then neither does anything Achebe has written since 1980. For Armah the cut-off date is 1985, for Soyinka 1981. The binding of the copy that came into my hands was totally inadequate, and the book deconstructed itself as I turned over the pages. This was unfortunate since Nasidi's arguments are not without a certain musty cogency

The preface to the volume of ten essays by Oladele Taiwo is dated 'January 1982'. The 'historic' nature of this reprint is confirmed by the copyright, 1978, and the date it was first published by Fourth Dimension, 1986. For those librarians anxious to give some depth to their collections, this will be a useful buy. It will fill gaps in shelves with the work of a critic who established himself with his *Introduction to West African Literature* (1967) and *Culture and the Nigerian Novel* (1976), but who has since taken few opportunities to publish critical work. He has, apparently, written an autobiography, *In a Literary Vineyard*, that was reviewed during 2001.

Taiwo's opening chapter, on 'Vital issues in the Criticism of African Literature' (no precise publication date give) begins 'The criticism of African Literature has gone on actively for about twenty years and has passed through several stages'. At which point the reader might interject that the passage of years has added further stages. Taiwo has rarely contributed to these further stages, to the on-going discussion, and the expression 'resting on his laurels' comes to mind. According to recent volumes of Lindfors' invaluable *Black African Literature in English*, Taiwo contributed a chapter on 'Trends in English Literary Studies' to a volume edited by S. O. Unoh (1986). He wrote the Preface to *Introductory Readings in the Humanities and Social Sciences*, edited by Gloria Chukukere (1988), and had an entry on Charity Waciuma in Lillian S. Robinson's reference book *Modern Women Writers* (1996). He delivered an inaugural lecture in 1990 on the Nigerian experience of 'Reading and Writing for National Development', that was published by the University of Lagos, where he held a chair and shouldered numerous administrative responsibilities. For lovers of literature, however, the list of publications appears to be a meagre harvest for the decade covered by the volumes of *BALE* consulted.

The reprinting of *Social Experience in African Literature* confirms the image of Taiwo as a critic who emerged during the first phases of post-independence African writing. He cut his teeth on the work of Amos Tutuola, T.M. Aluko, Tafawa Balewa, Onoura Nzekwu, Nkem Nwankwo, Flora Nwapa, Gabriel Okara, and D.O. Olagoke. His Ola Rotimi is the Rotimi of *Kurumni*; his Soyinka that of *The Strong Breed*. Taiwo's 'hot off the conference podium papers' are from the Commonwealth Literature Conference he attended in Kampala in ... 1974.

The references to the wider discussion of ideas about literature include David Lodge *The Language of Fiction* (1966), Lynn Altenberend and Leslie Lewis's *Handbook for the Study of Fiction* (1969), and Graham Hough's *An Essay on Criticism* (1966). These are not the authorities invoked by the critics currently engaged with the analysis of African literature.

Taiwo is at his best when he reminds us of the ephemeral sources he caught as he was preparing his essay. These include Ola Rotimi's contribution to Artist's Show Case reported in the *Daily Times* (18 September 1980, see Taiwo p. 132). He is also helpful when directing attention to periodicals, such as *Afriscope,* that briefly carried on energetic debates about African writing (see p. 142), and when his special interests in folklore and language inform his criticism. The volume has neither a bibliography nor an index, and this limits its value as an academic resource. The 'Vital Issues in the Criticism of African Literature' that take up the first chapter are not without interest or relevance, but they are not as spry and vigorous as they once were.

The next book for consideration has not been published before, but it reeks of the musty 'bottom drawer' in which it languished for years before being brought out. In 1988, Patrick Ebewo, now a Senior Lecturer at the University of Swaziland, wrote a PhD thesis for the University of Ibadan on *Satire in Select Plays of Wole Soyinka.* In the Preface to *Barbs*, he writes that his book grew out of the doctoral dissertation. One can only say that it has been extended to cover some recent writing, but it has not focused its concern and it has not spread its net wide enough.

Although advertised as an 'in-depth, up-to-date and comprehensive study' with coverage from '*Childe Internationale* to ... *King Baabu*', *Barbs* is neither 'up-to-date' nor comprehensive. There is, for example, no response to *Before the Blowout*, and no first-hand criticism of *King Baabu*. Regarding the latter, Ebewo acknowledges that he has had to cover that play on the basis of a review that appeared in *The Vanguard*! In this instance, he has admitted that he has had no access to a piece of creative writing and has found very little critical comment.

Barbs shows little evidence of purposeful reading about satire in Soyinka since Ebewo completed his doctorate more than fifteen years ago. Indeed though Ebewo sometimes lists recent critical work, he rarely shows close acquaintance with it. For example, Derek Wright's excellent 1993 study of Soyinka is listed in the bibliography, but Ebewo neglects its relevant chapter on 'Shot-Gun Satires: The Revue Plays'. I. Peter Ukpokodu, author of *Socio-Political Theatre in Nigeria*, makes the bibliography but not the index. Furthermore, Ebewo does not list Edde M. Iji's *Understanding Brecht and Soyinka* (1991), even though it devotes considerable space to Soyinka's version of *The Three-Penny Opera* which must be examined from many angles in any comprehensive study of satire in Soyinka's plays. Ebewo does not seem to be acquainted with much of what Soyinka has said about satire over the years, some of which has been reproduced in *Conversations with Wole Soyinka*, edited by Biodun Jeyifo (2001). Understandably not in the bibliography.

Ebewo claims his book is 'user friendly', but this doesn't prevent him referring on several bewildering occasions to 'satire *per se*'. When he finds occasion to quote Chaucer's *Wife of Bath*, he begins with 'unfriendly' authenticity: 'I swoor that al my walkinge ...' The Chaucer comparison is not, in any case, particularly helpful, but this is typical since Ebewo is a poor judge of the relevant reference. Molière, Shaw, and more arcane authors are roughly dragged into his book, while Swift's *Bickerstaff Letters,* a key text in relation to *Requiem for a Futurologist,* is passed over.

A comment on Ebewo's response to one sketch from *Before the Blackout* illustrates some general weaknesses. Perhaps distracted by a desire to include references to Chaucer and to 'The Gospel According to Saint Silver Mark' (predictably the Latin title is included), Ebewo offers a bizarre reading of 'In Carcarem Conicio' in relation to what he calls 'ecclesiastical infidelity' (106). By neglecting to investigate the events, some of them linked with the very University of Ibadan where he was once a student, that are alluded to in the sketch, Ebewo contrives to miss Soyinka's satirical point entirely. Targets might have emerged had Ebewo consulted Soyinka's *Ibadan* (1994), but, sadly, that is among the many relevant works not used, and not even listed in the bibliography.

Chris Dunton has written a 'Foreword' to *Barbs* in which he refers to phrasing that 'is often fresh, sometimes barbed'. I have already indicated my concern about Ebewo's use of cross-references. I am also worried about his vocabulary. It includes, for example, 'bisociation' (64), and 'caricaturishly' (65). I am also concerned about his use of English. A cluster of infelicities ('He abates crime', 'to mellow down' and 'a more sour detail') can be found on p. 71.

Ebewo's thesis supervisor, Dapo Adelugba, has published eloquent and important work on some of Soyinka's satirical writing, notably *Unlimited Liability Company,* a work neglected by Ebewo but relevant – if only because some lyrics were used in a slightly amended form in *The Beatification of Area Boy*. Ebewo knows Adelugba's essay, but neither makes the connection between the record and the play, nor employs the illuminating critical approach Adelugba used. Ebewo has paid insufficient attention to the example of enquiry, curiosity, and clear writing set by his dedicated supervisor over decades of critical appraisal of the Nigerian theatre.

Electronic Publishing

Binyavanga Wainaina. 'Discovering Home'
Special to www.G21.net/Africa31.html, winner of the Caine Prize for African writing, 2002

The Caine Prize is often assumed to be 'a short story prize', but it is actually designated as being simply 'for African Writing'. The carefully formulated terms and conditions of the award include: 'The focus will be on the African story-telling tradition, and the prize may be awarded for a short story, a collection of short stories, a novella or narrative poem. The minimum length requirement is 3,000 words'. The judges thus have considerable latitude, and in 2002 they enjoyed using it in awarding the prize to 'Discovering Home' by Binyavanga Wainaina. Whether travelogue or tale, it is certainly story-telling.

When the establishment of the prize was announced in 1999, there was considerable criticism of the thinking behind it and the *modus operandi* proposed. That it was sponsored by the Sir Michael Caine Foundation in memory of a former chairman of Booker plc and that it had a London base inevitably suggested the continuation of colonial patterns of assessment. The organising committee came in for further criticism over the selection of judges. Ben Okri was the first Chair, and his position as a British or Nigerian, or Nigerian-British writer has been variously assessed. By the time the 2002 announcement was made Egyptian author Ahdaf Soueif chaired the panel of judges, heading a board that included academic/author Abdulrazak Gurnah. Without insisting that literary quality has been sacrificed to 'Pan-African character', it is noteworthy that West, East and Central Africa, black and white, male and female, Anglophone and Francophone were 'represented' on the 2002 shortlist. The $15,000 prize money went to Binyavanga Wainaina, in whose body, as his autobiographical writing makes clear, DNA from several different nations may be found. Furthermore, he was educated partly in Kenya and partly in South Africa. All Africa has gone into the making of him.

The shortlisted candidates are given travel awards and they are 'invited to participate in writers' workshops in Africa and elsewhere as resources permit'. During July 2002, the five candidates were in Oxford for the announcement of the winner, and then moved on to London for symposia at the Africa Centre and at the Senate House, University of London. At both functions, there was some discussion of the short story form and of electronic publishing.

Given Sir Michael's links with the Africa Centre – he was Chairman of the board – there might have been some excuse for the reverential manner in which the occasion was conducted there. Unfortunately inhibitions also marked the discussion by the panel that Mpalive Msiska assembled at the University of London. Robert Fraser led off, providing a succinct response to the work of each of the writers. Shirley Chew, introduced as a Professor of 'Post-Colonial Literature' at Leeds but I think the title should be 'Literatures', had little to add. Indeed, it seemed that the panellists had simply been asked to 'respond' to the shortlisted works and Fraser had taken all the wind from everyone's sails. Chew pointed out that African writing was not her specialist area, and so left the audience wondering why she had been invited and why she had accepted the invitation. Nana Wilson-Tagoe stood somewhat aloof: she drew attention to what she considered a lack of critical writing on African short stories, and hesitated towards dissenting from an assumption that had been frequently made by this time that the short story was a European form. Gurnah passed up the chance of making a significant contribution in the interest of hearing from the floor. At this point, Nick Elam, who administers the Prize, pointed out that it was for 'African writing' not a short story. This point was particularly apposite since Wainaina's writing only makes occasional gestures, not the less interesting for their infrequency, towards the way expectation affects the rendering of experience.

The second session involved Msiska gently asking the astonishingly patient, shortlisted writers about their work. His questions frequently required the answer: 'If I could tell you that I wouldn't have written what I have written.' The authors 'played along' making some revealing autobiographical statements and reading, with admirable brevity and with an unusual awareness of what makes a good extract for public presentation, from their shortlisted work.

The afternoon exchanges revealed the part which virtual contacts and e-journals played in the lives of the writers. It seems that Wainaina and two of the others on the shortlist had 'met on the web' some months before, and that e-journals had become the publishing outlet of preference for Wainaina and others. Wainaina's 'Discovering Home' had appeared on G21.net, and Amanda Ngozi Adichie's 'You in America' on Zoetrope (www.allstory.com). I got the impression that Wainaina had submitted to the site in anticipation of his being entered for the Caine Prize. This impression was reinforced by the 'editor's note' that preceded the text on G21.net in which 'RA' indicated that he had 'felt (the text) would make a suitable nomination for the Cein [sic] Prize in [sic] African Writing'.

I hope that after the award has been appropriately celebrated there will be time for close, critical reading of the shortlist. I would look for the cultivation of a greater distance between author and narrator in the winning entry, an inclusion of an awareness of the limitations of an observer who records 'There is always that point at a party when people are too drunk to be having fun'. This could go together with a closer scrutiny of language that would eliminate such sentences as 'This is the main artery of movement to and from Public Transport Vehicles'. I would also look for consequences so that, for example, we know why the narrator of 'Discovering Home' goes to the kitchen, and for closer observation. What sort of elephants leave 'enormous pancakes of shit'? Or, alternatively, what sort of pancakes tower over plates like robust elephant turds waiting for Chris Ofili? I hope, too, for the development of self-criticism that will eliminate vacuous expressions such as 'basic tenets of Empowerment' and for vigorous debate that will clarify reactions to such sensitive issues as Female Genital Mutilation. In short I hope for a dialogue that will assist the honing of the distinct sensibility that produced 'I switch to Swahili and she pours herself into another person'.

The discussion of e-publication at the Senate House prompted reflection on Manu Herbstein's major work, *Ama,* which was initially published electronically. In some ways this was a liberating development, but, despite winning the Africa Section of the Commonwealth Prize, Herbstein has found it difficult to negotiate a conventional publishing contract. At a meeting of the Bellagio Publishing Network held at Oxford during July 2002, this case was raised by Dirk Koehler who works for the publishing division of the World Bank. From Herbstein's experience, Koehler moved on to examine the possibility of establishing a Print-on-Demand Network in Africa. He indicated that the Perfect Book technology being developed by 3Billion Books might be used, and that the Mellon Foundation might fund the purchase of appropriate machines for Africa. Clearly this development is some way in the future and has many implications. It is one that should be kept in view by all concerned with African literature today and tomorrow.

James Gibbs, School of English and Drama
University of the West of England, Bristol, UK

Index

Abago, Mary 124, 127; *Sour Honey* 124, 127
Aboulela, Leila 96, 103-5; *The Translator* 96, 103-5
Abrahams, Peter 3, 5, 8, 44, 111, 113-17; *Tell Freedom* 44
Achebe, Chinua xi, 1, 3, 5-6, 18, 22, 33, 83-4, 96, 111-18, 121, 125, 137, 142, 155-6, 160, 163-4; *Anthills of the Savannah* 96; *Things Fall Apart* 1, 3, 33, 83-5, 121, 125, 156
Adejare, Oluwole 137; *Language and Style in Soyinka: A Systemic Textlinguistic Study of a Literary Idiolect* 137
Aeneid 2, 50
Afolayan, Sunday 151-2; *Beyond the Silent Grave,* 151-2
African American 26-9, 43, 155
African Childhood 41, 43-4, 47, 50-1, 51n
African culture 24, 26, 30, 77, 133, 149, 150; conflict with Western culture 23
African dream 5
African literature; criticism 1, 5-8, 16, 129, 132, 134, 164, 165; deconstruction 6-7; diaspora 18-9; publishing 2-3, 8, 120-1, 123, 162-3, 166-8
African Literature Today (ALT) xii-xiii, 156
African personality xii, 2-4, 9

African Universities 128-32, 159
African Writers Series 120-1, 131, 148
Aidoo, Ama Ata 67-9, 74-7, 79-80, 83, 91-3, 96, 111-17, 147-8, 157; *Changes: A Love Story* 91-2; *Our Sister Killjoy* 96; *The Girl Who Can and Other Stories* 68-9, 74-5, 80, 147-9
Ajibade, Ade-Yemi 161; *Fingers Only and A Man Named Mokai* 161; *Parcel Post and Behind the Mountain* 161
Akin Mata 158
Algeria 11, 13
ALT, see *African Literature Today*
Amadi, Elechi 111, 116-17, 137
America, see United States of America
American 4, 24, 26-30, 45, 62, 99, 144
American dream 26
ANA, see Association of Nigerian Authors 3
Aniagolu, Emeka 151, 155-6; *Black Mustard Seed* 151, 155-6; *Footprints on the Sands of Time: A Personal Account of Anglian Exploits in the Dark Continent,* 156
Anozie, Sunday 8; *Christopher Ikigbo: Creative Rhetoric* 8
Anyidoho, Kofi 143-5; *Ancestral*

169

Logic and Caribbean Blues 143; *PraiseSong for the Land* 143-5
Arabic language 14, 17
Apparadurai, Arjun 94-5, 98, 100, 102-4, 106-7n; 'Disjuncture and Difference in the Global Cultural Economy' 106n
Archibong, F.M. 124, 126; *Boko* 124, 126
Are, Lekan 120, 123; *The Challenge of the Barons* 120, 123
Armah, Ayi Kwei 2-3, 5, 8, 111-14, 116-17, 121, 128, 131-2, 143, 145-7, 156, 163-4; *KMT: In the House of Life* 143, 145-7; *Osiris Rising* 146-7
Asante, Molefi Kete 12
Asma'u, Nana 14; *One Woman's Jihad,* 14
Association for African Literature 120
Association of Nigerian Authors (ANA) 3, 160
ANA, see Association of Nigerian Authors
Awoonor, Kofi 111, 113-16
Axum 13; *Kebra Negast* 13

Bâ, Mariama 5, 85
Barthes, Roland 6; *Elements of Semiology* 6; *S/Z* 6; *The Pleasure of the Text* 6
Bedford, Simi 45-9, *Yoruba Girl Dancing* 45-9
Ben Jelloun, Tahar 42; *L'enfant de sable* 42
Beowulf 2
Bernal, Martin 12
Beyala, Calixthe 18
Biersteker, Anne 14-15; 'Language, Poetry, and Power: A Reconsideration of "Utendi wa Mwana Kupona"', 14-15
bone-healing 23-5, 31
bride price 78
Brooks, Miguel F. 13; *Kebra Negast* 13

Brutus, Dennis 3, 5, 111-18
Budge, W.A. Wallis 12-13; *The Book of the Dead* 12-13
Burstein, Stanley 13; *Land of Enchanters: Egyptian Short Stories from the Earliest Times to the Present Day* 13

Cary, Joyce 83; *Mister Johnson* 83
Cazenave, Odile 16, 18; *Afrique sur Seine: une nouvelle génération de romanciers africains à Paris* 18
Centre for the Study of the Literatures and the Cultures of the Emerging Areas 133
Chanson de Roland 2
Chinweizu 5
Chrisman, Laura 155; *Colonial Discourse and Postcolonial Theory* 155
Chukwuma, Helen 6
Clark-Bekederemo, John Pepper 110-18, 121, 125, 157; *Song of a Goat* 125, 162
Coe, Richard 51n, *When the Grass Was Taller* 51n
Coetzee, J.M. 46-9; *Boyhood* 46-9
colonial xii 1, 4, 8, 12, 15-18, 55, 57, 66, 69, 80, 83-5, 98, 101, 104-6, 133-4, 136, 167
colonialism 1-2, 26, 32, 54-7, 79, 100-1, 104, 130, 134, 7, 146
Congress of Soviet Writers 3
Conrad, Joseph 4-5, 54, 56, 142; *Heart of Darkness* 4-5, 54, 56, 142
Conteh, J. Sorie 31-40; *The Diamonds* 22, 31-40
Conton, William 42, 51n; *The African* 42, 51n
Crawford, Clinton 12
Culler, Jonathan 6; *Structuralist Poetics* 6

Dako, Kari 156-7; *The Baobabs of Tete and Other Stories* 156-7
Dangarembga, Tsitsi 44, 112, 116-18; *Nervous Conditions* 44

Darko, Amma 67, 68-74, 78-80; *The Housemaid* 68-74, 78-80
de Saussure, children of 6-7
deconstruction 6-7, 9n, 53, 66, 139
Derrida, Jacques 6; *Of Grammatology* 6; *Writing and Difference* 6
Di Maio, Alessandra 132-4; *Tutuola at the University: The Italian Voice of a Yoruba Ancestor* 132-4
Diallo, Nafissatou 44; *De Tilène au plateau: Une enfance Dakaroise* 44
diamonds 32-6, 37-9, 59, 63
Diop, Cheikh Anta 12
Dongala, Emmanuel 48-9, 51n; *Johnny chien méchant* 48-9; *Le feu des origins* 51n; *Les petits garçons naissent aussi des étoiles* 51n
Duh, Samuel 149-50; *One More Time* 149-50

Easmon, Sarif 22
East Africa, language 14, 120; novelists 127-8; regional song 17
East African Publishing House 121
Ebewo, Patrick 163, 165-6; *A Study of Satire in the Plays of Wole Soyinka* 163, 165-6
Ebong, Inih Akpan 8
Egypt 11-14, 101, 145-7, 167
Egyptian literature 12-13
Egyptian scribes 145
Ehling, Holger 160-1; *No Condition is Permanent: Nigerian Writing and the Struggle for Democracy* 160-1
Ekwensi, Cyprian 3, 5, 8, 92, 111-19, 137; *Jagua Nana* 92
El Cid 1
electronic publishing 166-7
Emecheta, Buchi 3, 5, 18, 51n, 67, 85, 86, 111-17, 137; *The Joys of Motherhood* 51n, 67, 86
Emenyonu, Ernest xi-xiv, 5, 8, 82, 86; *African Literature Comes of Age* 82; *Cyprian Ekwensi* 8

Enlightenment 55-8, 66
Equiano, Olaudah 111-12, 116-17
Ethiopia 42
European American 43, 147

Falola, Toyin 158-9; *African Writers and Their Readers* 158-9; *Palavers of African Literature* 158-9
Farah, Nuruddin xii, 3, 6, 9, 42, 43, 111-8; *Maps* 9, 42, 43
feminist accounts, mother-daughter relations 69
feminist cause 6, 105
feminist consciousness 69
feminist perspective 135
feminist theme 38
feminist values 122
Forster, E.M. 4; *A Passage to India* 4
Foster, John L. 13; *Ancient Egyptian Literature: An Anthology* 13; *Echoes of Egyptian Voices: An Anthology of Ancient Egyptian Poetry* 13
Foucauldian 57-8, 62
Foucault, Michel 7, 53-7, 60, 62, 68; *Discipline and Punish* 53-6, 60; *The Archaeology of the Self* 7
Fraser, Robert 8, 167; *The Novels of Ayi Kwei* 8
Fulani 14, 16

Gambia 42
Gatheru, R. Mugo 44; *Child of Two Worlds* 44
Genette, Gerard 7; *Narrative Discourse* 7
Ghana 42, 72, 74, 132, 143-4, 147, 149-50, 156
Gikandi, Simon 57, 97, 103; *Maps of Englishness* 57
globalisation 94-100, 102-3, 105-6
Goody, Jack 16
Gurnah, Abdulrazak 96, 100-3, 167; *By the Sea* 96, 100-3

Haggard, Rider 4

Harlow, Barbara 158-9; *African Writers and Their Readers,* 158-9; *Palavers of African Literature* 158-9
Harrison, Tony 158; *Lysistrata* 158
Hassane, Safi 15; *Epic of Good Brides and Young Women* 15
Hausa 14, 16-17, 140, 155
Head, Bessie 111-17
Heron, George A. 8; *The Poetry of Okot p'Bitek* 8
HIV/Aids 2, 7
Hiyalwa, Kaleni 124, 127-8; *Meekulu's Children* 124, 127-8
Hochschild, Adam 55; *King Leopold's Ghost* 55
Holste-von Mutius, Claus-Peter 160-1; *No Condition is Permanent: Nigerian Writing and the Struggle for Democracy* 160-1
Humanities Review Journal, The 159-60
Huxley, Elspeth 5

Igbo 123, 137-8, 154-6
Igboanusi, Herbert 137-8; *A Dictionary of Nigerian English Usage* 137; *Igbo English in the Nigerian Novel* 137-8; *The Igbo Tradition in the Nigerian Novel* 137; *Language Attitude and Language Conflict in West Africa* 137
Ike, Chukwuemeka 123, 137-8; *Toads for Supper* 123, 138
Iliad 2
intertexuality theory 7, 129
Ìsarà, A Voyage Around 43

James, Henry 4
Jarry, Alfred 138; *Ubu Roi* 138
Jemie, Onwuchekwa 5
Jones, Eldred 7; *The Writings of Wole Soyinka* 8

Kalu, Victor Eke 153; *The Nigeria Condition* 153

Kandakai, Dwaboyea E.S. 120, 123; *The Village Son* 120, 123
Kane, Hamidou 18; *L'Aventure ambiguë* 18
Killam, Douglas 8; *The Novels and Plays of Ngugi wa Thiong'o* 8
King Piankhy 13
Knappert, Jan 15; *Four Centuries of Swahili Verse* 15
Kourouma, Ahmadou 48; *Allah n'est pas obligé* 48
Kposowa, Tibbie 22
Kristeva, Julie 7; intertexuality theory 7
Kunda, Manika 23-4, 26, 28-9
Kupona, Mwana 14-15; 'Utendi we Mwana Kupona' 14-15

La Guma, Alex 3, 5, 111-17
Lacan, Jacques 6; *The Language of the Self* 6
Latin American 19
Laye, Camara 18, 41-2, 47, 50, 51n; *L'enfant noir* 18, 41-2, 47, 51n
Lessing, Doris 44, 47; *Martha Quest* 44, 47
Levi-Strauss, Claude 6; *Structural Anthropology* 6
Lewis, Bernard 13; *Land of Enchanters: Egyptian Short Stories from the Earliest Times to the Present Day* 13
Libya 11, 13-14
Lichtheim, Miriam 13; *Ancient Egyptian Literature* 13
Lifschitz, Mikhail 151; *Marxism and Art* 151
Lindfors, Bernth xiii, 5, 8, 109, 111-12, 116, 118, 158-9, 164; Famous Authors' Reputation Test 109, 111-12, 116, 118
literary analysis 129
literary creativity, African xiii
literary criticism 16, 129, 132, 134
literary diaspora, African 18
literary domain, African, 6
literary scholarship, African 129

literary studies, African 118, 129
literary tradition, African xi
literary vision xii
literary work in English, African 84

Madubuike, Ihechukwu 5
Mahabharata 1
Mali 13-7, 22, 42
Malraux, Andre 3
Mansa Musa 22
Mansaray, Alasan 22-31, 39-40; *A Haunting Heritage* 22-31, 39-40
Maodzwa-Taruvinga, Mandivavarira 134-5; *Sign and Taboo: Perspectives on the Poetic Fiction of Yvonne Vera* 134-5
Maraire, Nozipo 68-70, 77-80; *Zenzele: A Letter for My Daughter* 68-70, 77-80
Marechera, Dambudzo 111-13, 116-18
marriage, forced 78
marriage 16, 36-7, 65, 76, 83, 87, 88, 92, 105, 145, 148, 150, 152
Martins, Stella 151-3; *The Boomerang* 152; *The Hellion* 152; *Hot Shots* 152; *Our Moment in Time* 151-3
Marxist 59, 136, 151
Marxist/Socialist 6
Matabane, Mark 44; *Kaffi Boy: The True Story of a Black Youth's Coming of Age in Apartheid South Africa* 44
Matatu 160
Mauritania 11
Mazrui, Ali xii, 9, 112, 155; *The Trial of Christopher Ikigbo* xii, 9, 112, 155
Mbuli, Mzwakhe 111-13, 116
Mediterranean 11, 13
Mende society 22
Meunier, Pierre 161-2; *The Coffee Party* 161-2; *Farin Dutse* 161-2; *The Little Kings* 161-2
Mezlekia, Nega 44, 48; *Notes from the Hyena's Belly* 44, 48

Middle Eastern 11, 13
modernism 6, 57, 62
Moh, Felicia Okah 128-32; *Ben Okri: An Introduction to his Early Fiction* 128-32
Monénembo, Tierno 44, 48; *L'aîné des orphelins* 44, 48
Morocco 11, 42-3
mother-daughter, relationships xiii, 67-70, 72-5, 78-9
motherhood 67-9, 72-3, 76, 78, 86, 87, 92
Moudileno, Lydie 19; *Littératures africaines francophones des années 1980 et 1990* 19
Mphahlele, Ezekiel 111-16, 118
Muponde, Robert 134-5; *Sign and Taboo: Perspectives on the Poetic Fiction of Yvonne Vera* 134-5
Murphy, David 135-6; *Sembene: imagining alternatives in film and fiction* 135-6
Mwangi, Meja 3
Mwindo Epic 1
Mzamane, Mbulelo 44; *The Children of Soweto* 44

Nasidi, Yakubu A. 163-4; *Beyond the Limits of Experience: Theory, Criticism and Power in African Literature* 163-4
national era 15
National Research Council 132
Ndebele, Njabulo S. 111-13, 116
Ndunguru, S.N. 124, 127-8; *Divine Providence* 124, 127-8
Negritude 2, 4-5
neo-colonialism 69-70, 72, 78, 80
Neo-Tarzanism 5
Ngema, Mbongeni 111-13, 116
Niebelungenslied 2
Niger 13, 15-17, 45
Nigeria, University of 2
Nigeria 3, 14, 43-6, 91, 97-100, 110, 115, 121-3, 124-5, 131-2, 137-9, 141, 151-6, 158-60, 162-7; critics 163-6; fiction 151-6

Nigeria Magazine 121
Nigerian Foreign service 23
Nnolim, Charles xii
North Africa 12, 14
North African influence 19
North African literature 11-12
North American 136
Nubia 12-13
Nubian, texts 15
Nuruddin, Farah xii, 3, 6, 9, 42
Nwankwo, Agwuncha Arthur 137, 151, 153-5; *Before I Die: Olesegun Obasanjo/Arthur Nwankwo Correspondence on the one party state* 153; *Reckoning at Storm End* 151, 154-5; *Season of Hurricane* 151, 153-4
Nwankwo, Kate I. 151-2; *Fatal Greed* 151-2
Nwapa, Flora 5, 67, 83, 85-8, 111-17, 150, 164; *Efuru* 67; *One is Enough* 67; *Two Women in Conversation* 86-7; *Women are Different* 88

Obeng, Ernest 156; *Eighteen Pence* 156
Ocen, Laury Lawrence 124, 126-7; *The Alien Woman* 124, 126-7
O'Connor, David 12; *Ancient Nubia: Egypt's Rival in Africa* 12
Odyssey 2
Ogaden 42
Oguine, Ike 96-100, 107n; *A Squatter's Tale* 96-100
Ogundipe-Leslie, Molara 6
Ogunleye, Foluke M. 159-60; *Humanities Review Journal* 159-60
Ogunyemi, Chikwenye 6
Okara, Gabriel 111, 113-17, 127, 160
Okekwe, Promise 83, 90-1; *Hall of Memories* 90; *Zita-Zita* 90-1
Okigbo, Christopher 5, 111-18
Okoh, Julie 83, 88; *Edewede: The Dawn of a New Day* 88
Okri, Ben 3, 6, 111-13, 116-18, 121, 128, 131-2, 156, 167; *The Famished Road* 132, 156
Olney, James 51n; *Tell Me Africa* 51n
Omotoso, Kole 111, 116, 121
Onwueme, Osonye Tess 89-90; *What Mama Said: An Epic Drama* 89-90
oral epic, see oral tradition
oral tradition, see also verbal art 15-18, 128, 133
Orwell, George 4; *Burmese Days* 4
Osofisan, Femi 111-18, 121, 157, 159-60, 162-3; *Insidious Treason: Drama in Postcolonial State (Essays)* 162-3; *Literature and the Pressures of Freedom: essays, speeches and songs* 162-3; *Recent Outings: Tegonni, an African Antigone and many Colours make the Thunder King* 162-3; *Tegonni* 157, 162-3
Osundare, Niyi 3, 6, 111-13, 116-8, 121, 160
Oyono, Ferdinand 44; *Une vie de boy* 44
Ozidi Saga 1

Pakistan 11
Palmer, Prince Dowu 32; *The Mocking Stones* 32
Parkinson, R. B. 13; *The Tale of Sinuhe and other Ancient Egyptian Poems, 1940-1640 BC* 13
Paton, Alan 1, *Cry the Beloved Country* 1
p'Bitek, Okot 8, 111, 113-18, 121, 128-31; *The Defence of Lawino* 128-32; *Song of Lawino* 128, 130-1
Piaget, Jean *Structuralism* 6
Plaatje, Solomon T. 111-13, 116-17
polygamy 16, 29, 33, 36, 38
postcolonial xiii, 11, 54, 97, 100-1, 103, 106, 155, 162
post-colonial 6-8, 11, 17, 42, 67-8, 72, 94-101, 105, 126, 136, 155, 158, 167; post-colonial literatures 9n

post-modernism 6, 134
post-structuralism 6
pre-colonial 15, 101, 106, 134, 155
publishing, see African literature, publishing

Redford, Donald 12; *From Slave to Pharaoh: The Black Experience of Ancient Egypt* 12
Research in African Literatures 155
Rive, Richard 111, 113, 115-16
Rosenberg, Aaron 17
Rotimi, Ola 110-13, 116-17, 157, 159, 164-5

Salih, Tayeb 104; *Season of Migration to the North* 104
Saro-Wiwa, Ken 111-18, 138, 160; *Sozaboy* 138
science fiction 4-5
Selormey, Francis 44; *The Narrow Path* 44
Sembene, Ousmane 135-6
Serote, Mongane Wally 111, 113, 116
sexual exploitation 78, 80
Shakespeare, William 138; *Macbeth* 138
Sidikou, Aissata 15-16
Sierra Leone 23, 32, 35, 42, 46
Sierra Leonean 22, 24-5, 30-2, 36-7, 40
Simmons, James 158; *Lysistrata* 158
Simpson, William Kelly 13; *The Literature of Ancient Egypt: An Anthology of Stories, Instructions, and Poetry* 13
slave trade, see slavery
slavery 1-2, 8, 26, 55, 101, 133, 136
Socialist, see Marxist/Socialist
Solimane, Alhassan ag 14; *Les Gens de la Parole Disent* 14
Somalia 42
Songhai/Songhay 14, 22, 42
Soundjata 15
Soundjata: l'épopée mandingue 17
South American 133
Soyinka, Wole 3, 5, 8, 23, 43-4, 110-18, 121-3, 137-42, 154, 157, 160, 163-6; *Aké The Years of Childhood* 43; *King Baabu* 138-41, 162, 165; *Samarkand and other Markets I have Known* 138, 140-2; *Season of Anomy* 154; *The Interpreters* 23, 123
Stoler, Ann 54; *Race and the Education of Desire* 54
structuralism 6
structuralist criticism 9n
sub-Saharan Africa 10-13, 121, 132, 136
Sundiata 22
Sundiata epic 1
supernatural 25, 31, 35, 122
Sutherland, Efua 85, 111, 115-16, 145, 157
Swahili 14-15, 168

Taine, Hippolyte 1
Taiwo, Oladele 163-5; *Social Experience in African Literature* 163-5
Tarikh el-Fettâch 14
Taylor, John H. 12; *Egypt and Nubia* 12
Thiong'o, Ngugi wa 1, 3, 5, 8, 18, 44, 120; *The River Between* 44
Tifinar 13-5
Timbuktu 14
Toffler, Alvin 4; *Future Shock* 4
Tuareg, people 14
Tunisia 11
Tutuola, Amos 111-18, 132-4, 164; *The Palm-Wine Drinkard* 132

Ukala, Grace 120, 122-3; *The Broken Bond* 120, 122-3
Ukala, Sam 160
United States of America xii, 3, 5, 9, 22, 24-8, 30, 77, 95, 97-100, 144, 146, 149, 152

Vassa, Gustav 1
Vera, Yvonne 134-5; *Nehanda* 134-5; *The Stone Virgins* 135; *Under the*

Tongue 135
verbal art, see also oral tradition 15-17, 19, 153-4
Verne, Jules 4
Virgil 2, 50; *The Aeneid* 2, 50

Wade, Michael 8; *Peter Abrahams* 8
Wainaina, Binyavanga 166-8; *Discovering Home* 166-8
Walentowitz, Saskia 14; *Les Gens de la Parole Disent* 14
Walker, Alice 26; *The Color Purple* 26; *Possessing the Secret of Joy* 26
Wallace, Edgar 4
Wer pa Lawino, see *Song of Lawino*
West Africa 14, 16, 120, 123
West African 22, 39, 42, 44, 75, 123, 137, 145, 157, 164; Mandinka, 22

Western culture, conflict with African culture 23-4
Western Sahara 11
Wetmore Jr., Kevin J. 157-8, 163; *The Athenian Sun in an African Sky* 157-8, 163
Wheatley, Phyllis 1
white man 2, 130
Wicomb, Zoë 53-4, 58, 60, 62-4, 66; *David's Story* 53-66

xenophobia 27

Yankson, K.E. 128-32; *The Rot of the Land and the Birth of the Beautyful Ones: The World of Ayi Kwei Armah's Novels* 128-32
Yoruba 44-7, 120, 123, 132-3, 155, 162

Printed by Libri Plureos GmbH in Hamburg, Germany